EU Common Foreign and Security Policy After Lisbon

Luigi Lonardo

EU Common Foreign and Security Policy After Lisbon

Between Law and Geopolitics

Springer

Luigi Lonardo
University College Cork
Cork, Ireland

ISBN 978-3-031-19130-5 ISBN 978-3-031-19131-2 (eBook)
https://doi.org/10.1007/978-3-031-19131-2

This Springer imprint is published by the registered company Springer Nature Switzerland AG
The registered company address is: Gewerbestrasse 11, 6330 Cham, Switzerland

The book is dedicated to my teachers and to my students

Foreword

The numerous crises of the past decade have put EU policy-making under unprecedented strain. In the past, crises—of an internal and/or external nature—have often triggered responses by the EU and its member states that have strengthened economic and political integration and widened its scope. However, the sequence of critical events and developments that has hit the EU since the entry into force of the Lisbon Treaty has put to a severe test a 'system' that had not been set up to deal with such contingencies. The financial and euro-zone crisis (first external and then internal), the so-called Arab Spring (external) and its ramifications (also internal, from terrorism to refugees), Russia's annexation of Crimea and destabilisation of Ukraine (mainly external), the COVID-19 pandemic (mainly internal but with external spin-offs) and, now, Russia's invasion of Ukraine—not to mention Brexit (internal) and the Trump presidency (external)—have all contributed to highlighting the inadequacy of a legal and institutional framework that had been built incrementally over the years against the backdrop of the immediate post-Cold War environment and a Union of only 12/15 member states.

Still a predominantly 'fair-weather' set-up—whose core elements date back to the Maastricht Treaty (agreed in late 1991) and were marginally adjusted during the following decade—the European Union has thus found itself painfully exposed and vulnerable to the crises of the last decade, most of which came as a surprise and a shock. Responding to the euro-zone crisis required actions that the treaties did not necessarily envisage or allow for, thus forcing the member states to adopt decisions that, in the end, imposed a limited review of the existing rules but did not fundamentally change the overall architecture. The Arab uprisings put into question the EU collective approach to its southern neighbours, while the Ukrainian crises did the same with its approach to the eastern neighbours. Refugees, illegal migrants, and terrorist attacks affected the internal/external nexus and challenged internal cohesion and solidarity at large—as also did, to some extent, the COVID-19 pandemic. Both the Brexit referendum and the Trump presidency highlighted and aggravated tensions that had been simmering for some time already and contributed to the overall decline of the liberal international order created at the end of the Cold War that the

EU had supported and thrived in. And the return to great power competition—of which Russia's aggressions are also a manifestation—has drastically challenged the Union's own modus operandi, as European integration was launched to overcome precisely that in the first place (at least within Europe).

In this book, Luigi Lonardo addresses in particular how and why EU 'law' (its legal and institutional rules and procedures) seems now to be out of sync with 'geopolitics' and the current unstable and unpredictable international landscape. He focuses primarily on the procedures and policies that fall under the rubric CFSP/CSDP but increasingly encompass (or relate to) other types of EU 'external action', especially since the entry into force of the Lisbon Treaty. He correctly emphasises the initial and structural 'distinctiveness' of CFSP/CSDP—since at least the Single European Act (1987)—and the constant challenge of making it ever more 'consistent' with other forms of collective international action by the EU and its member states. He also pays special attention to the specific internal 'geopolitical' challenge represented by the successive enlargements of the Union, whose 'law' had been first created and then adapted by and for a smaller and essentially western Europe. And he does so by providing comprehensive information and in-depth analysis on the main aspects of both EU 'law' and EU policy as well as delving into the 'geopolitical' issues that have come to test them.

Admittedly, the term 'geopolitics' is charged. It has its historical roots in an intellectual tradition—from Rudolf Kjellen to Halford Mackinder and Karl Haushofer—that often flirted with (or was bent to) imperialistic territorial visions, and was thus widely discredited after WW2. Later on, it flourished in France—through the discipline of historical and political geography promoted by the periodical 'Herodote', from Yves Lacoste to Michel Foucher—where it gained an autonomous space in the academic and public debate. More recently, it has enjoyed some editorial and political success in Italy, mainly through the periodical 'Limes'—but, especially in the latter case, not without some excesses in terms of geographic and ethno-historical determinism and neglect of other sources of international behaviour. In the Anglosphere, it has long remained confined to a few 'realist' scholars of international relations, but the term has now become almost a synonym for great power competition—especially between the West (starting with the US) and rival actors at both global and regional level. This book makes some interesting connections between all these different receptions and perceptions of 'geopolitics' in relation to the European 'space'—and not only in geographic but also in political, institutional, and legal terms.

How and to what extent can the current gap between 'law' and 'geopolitics' be addressed? The author illustrates a number of arguments for change in the EU institutional and legal 'system' and discusses also the feasibility of some of them. In fact, any substantial treaty change would have to overcome the structural difficulty of reaching consensus at 27, including the challenge of overcoming unanimity by unanimity, so to speak. It is a difficulty made even bigger now by the increased political heterogeneity of the member states—with sometimes divergent interests, attitudes, and preferences—and by the persistent threat of national referenda in the ratification phase—a threat that is bigger the more significant the changes will be, as the experience of the past decades has proved.

Moreover, as the discussion around the Conference on the Future of Europe has shown, a significant number of member states—especially small and recent—oppose significant reforms, especially in the domain of CFSP/CSDP, as they fear the potential 'hegemony' of their bigger partners. And the European public itself seems torn between the demand for 'more Europe' when it comes to handling major international crises and the concern for preserving or even regaining some 'control' at the national level.

Nevertheless, some reasonable adjustments to the 'brave new world' we may have to be confronted with in the years to come are worth considering in some detail, as the book does. Herein lies, too, its originality as well as the added value it brings to a discussion that is bound to continue for some time among officials, academics, and the wider public.

Brussels, Belgium
August 2022

Antonio Missiroli

Acknowledgments

I would like to thank Antonio Missiroli, whom I am proud to call my maestro. I had the privilege of teaching with him at the Paris School of International Affairs, where many of the ideas for this book matured. The reader will realise that this book owes much to his volume *L'Europa Come Potenza. Diplomazia, sicurezza e difesa*, published in Italian in 2022, from which I occasionally borrow verbatim. Less obvious to the reader, but more profound for the author, is the influence of the long conversations at Basile in rue St Guillaume.

Thanks are due to my other maestro, Takis Tridimas, who supervised my Ph.D. thesis at King's College London and with whom we had discussed many of the themes on the law of Common Foreign and Security Policy presented in this book.

I was lucky to have the chance to learn from them.

I would also like to thank all the other people who helped me write the book.

At University College Cork, Mark Poustie and Aoife Guinee were helpful in the organisation of a hybrid mini-workshop in July 2022 where colleagues from all over Europe joined me for an in-depth discussion of the entire manuscript.

Stefania Rutigliano, Sara Notario, Stephen Coutts, Massimiliano Trovato, Filiz Dogan, Mark Konstantinidis, Andrea Faraci, and Andrea Chiarello were the lucky participants to that workshop. I am lucky to have them. The way they all spent their time to shake the full draft manuscript to remove the dust, and make something worthy appear, made me rejoice of their friendship. *'Et tanta stultitia mortalium est ut quae minima et vilissima sunt, certe reparabilia, imputari sibi cum impetravere patiantur, nemo se iudicet quicquam debere qui tempus accepit, cum interim hoc unum est quod ne gratus quidem potest reddere'* (Seneca).

Christopher Devenish helped with the research on Chap. 6, his invaluable assistance being funded by the Irish Department of Foreign Affairs and gratefully acknowledged. Archishman Ray Goswami and Baris Çelik also commented very helpfully on Chap. 6. Fulvio Lonardo on Chap. 7. Nico Sauter provided invaluable comments on all the chapters, and Conal O'Gadhra helped me enormously with both the editing and the content of the entire book.

If I managed to convey any sophistication in this book, it is probably the merit of all of them. It goes without saying, as Burke said in his reflections on the Revolution in France, that 'my reputation alone is to answer for any mistakes'.

I am happy to acknowledge that some of the ideas discussed in the book draw on previous publications of mine, either single-authored or co-authored. Section 3.2 draws on Lonardo, Common Foreign and Security Policy and the EU's external action objectives: an analysis of Article 21 of the Treaty on the European Union (2018) European Constitutional Law Review; Section 5.2 on Lonardo and Missiroli, 'From EnCo to PeSCo' (Bruges Research Papers 2019/2); Section 5.4 on Lonardo, Integration in European Defence: Some Legal Considerations (2017) 2(3) European Papers 887–903.

The maps are all publicly available under a creative commons licence, the credits being as follows:

Figure 2.1. 'EU physical map': Alexrk2derivative work: Pethrus, CC BY-SA 3.0 <https://creativecommons.org/licenses/by-sa/3.0>, via Wikimedia Commons

Figure 2.2. 'Main Russian gas pipelines': Samuel Bailey (sam.bailus@gmail.com), CC BY 3.0 <https://creativecommons.org/licenses/by/3.0>, via Wikimedia Commons

Figure 2.3. 'Blue, Gold, and Green bananas': Luan, CC BY-SA 3.0 BR <https://creativecommons.org/licenses/by-sa/3.0/br/deed.en>, via Wikimedia Commons

I first thought of this book when I was in London. It grew up in Paris. It matured in Ireland. The core of it was written in Athens, nourished by Mediterranean light and all that comes with it.

2022

Athens, Greece Luigi Lonardo

Contents

About the Author

Luigi Lonardo is a lecturer in EU law at University College Cork, Ireland, and a visiting lecturer in European Foreign Security and Defence Policy at Sciences Po in Paris, France. Previously, he has been a lecturer and visiting lecturer in EU law at King's College London and at the University of Westminster. He has published articles on EU foreign policy in the European Law Review, the European Constitutional Law Review, European Papers, and the European Foreign Affairs Review.

List of Abbreviations

AA	Association Agreement
AFSJ	Area of Freedom, Security and Justice
CAP	Common Agricultural Policy
CEPA	Comprehensive Enhanced Partnership Agreement
CJEU	Court of Justice of the European Union
COREPER	Committee of Permanent Representatives
DCFTA	Deep and Comprehensive Free Trade Agreement
DOSA	Defence of Space Assets
DRC	Democratic Republic of Congo
EaP	Eastern Partnership
ECHR	European Convention for the Protection of Human Rights
EC	European Community
ECJ	European Court of Justice
EDC	European Defence Community
EEAS	European External Action Service
EMAA	Euro-Mediterranean Agreement establishing an Association
ENP	European Neighbourhood Policy
EP	European Parliament
EU	European Union
CCP	Common Commercial Policy
CFSP	Common Foreign and Security Policy
CSDP	Common Security and Defence Policy
GC	General Court
HARSMSPRO	Harbour and Maritime Surveillance and Protection
HR/VP	High Representative/Vice President of the Commission
IS	Islamic State
MUSAS	Maritime Unmanned Anti-Submarine System
NATO	North Atlantic Treaty Organisation
PCA	Partnership Cooperation Agreement
PeSCo	Permanent Structured Cooperation

PSC	Political and Security Committee
QMV	Qualified Majority Voting
SAA	Stabilisation and Association Agreement
SAP	Stabilisation and Association Process
TEU	Treaty on the European Union
TFEU	Treaty on the Functioning of the European Union
TNC	Transitional National Council
UfM	Union for the Mediterranean
UN	United Nations
UNSC	United Nations Security Council
USSR	Union of Soviet Socialist Republics
V4	Visegrad Four

List of Figures

Chapter 1
Introduction

Contents

The need to study geopolitics and law is manifested on the one hand by the occurrence of the word geopolitics in official EU rhetoric as well as by some major geopolitical 'surprises' in the recent past; and on the other hand by the fact that the EU is a law-based organisation, which, although not a nation-state, has been equipped with a very sophisticated legal system to face security challenges (including aggression, terrorism, and hybrid threats). In November 2019, in her speech as President-elect of the European Commission, Ursula von der Leyen stated that hers would be a 'geopolitical Commission'.[1] The Strategic Compass of March 2022 appears to consider the EU's response to the Russian invasion of Ukraine as the EU's 'geopolitical awakening'.[2] The word is now omnipresent in EU strategic documents. The geopolitical 'surprises' that took place in the EU's neighbourhood are the Arab uprisings, which shook the Southern and Eastern shores of the Mediterranean from 2011; the Russian seizure of Crimea in 2014; and the most shocking of them: the war of aggression waged by Russia against Ukraine in 2022. The fact that, for the EU, they are surprises in the first place suggests that geopolitics should be important in EU activities and thus in EU law:[3] first, with a view to avoid future

[1] von der Leyen (2019).

[2] European Union (2022), p. 4; Van Middelaar describes this geopolitical awakening as a conceptual watershed, van Middelaar (2022).

[3] Strictly speaking, the Russian invasion in February 2022 was largely anticipated by US intelligence in the preceding months.

L. Lonardo, *EU Common Foreign and Security Policy After Lisbon*,
https://doi.org/10.1007/978-3-031-19131-2_1

surprises as much as possible, and second, because all EU action should be based on the rule of law (rather than, for example, on military power), so if the EU needs to react to a geopolitical crisis, this can only be done through law.

Geopolitics and law matter for EU foreign policy: geopolitics matters in so far as it provides a context for EU foreign policy, influencing (but in no way determining) the preferences and political priorities of Member States; and law matters in so far as it provides a structure to give coherence, accountability, and effectiveness to EU action. But how to conceptualise the interaction 'between law and geopolitics', a key theme of this book, is something that we do not know, for the two disciplines (geopolitics and EU law) hardly speak to each other. Yet, it is important for legal scholars to delve deeper into the interaction to seek to improve the legal framework. This need for incorporating geopolitics into EU action is the important challenge from which this book commences, and it will be shown that geopolitics can in fact add a further layer to our understanding of the legal aspects of Common Foreign and Security Policy (CFSP).

It is the key argument of this book that there is a mismatch between the geopolitical reality created by the 2004 enlargement of the EU, and the law of CFSP as crystallised in the Lisbon Treaty in 2009 (this in turn is arguably the continuation a mismatch that was already present between the geopolitical reality created by the collapse of the Soviet Union in 1991 and the law of CFSP crystallised in the 1993 Maastricht Treaty). This engagement with geopolitics constitutes an added value for EU lawyers because it sheds new light on a normative debate that this book identifies, a debate concerning the desirability of the legal 'distinctiveness' of CFSP. As a matter of law, it will be shown, CFSP is a very special policy of the EU, and while some argue that it should remain so, other take the view that it should be 'normalised'. The book suggests that the mismatch with geopolitics is a normative reason to 'normalise' (to reduce to a minimum the constitutional ambiguity of) CFSP.

1.1 Common Foreign and Security Policy

The EU is about collective action, in two senses: people acting collectively at the national level to elect their representatives and organise their political communities; and those representatives acting collectively within the EU. CFSP is a portion of the latter, and concerns, very roughly speaking, the security and defence cooperation between EU Member States. To have an idea of the quantitative weight of CFSP, its funding amounts to 2.4% of the EU budget (and, in addition, there is also a 2.1% allowance for security and defence) in the current multi-annual financial framework. As a different indicator, out of over 10,000 cases decided by the Court of Justice of the European Union since the entry into force of the Lisbon Treaty in December 2009, 619 concern CFSP.

The policy context has two important characteristics: it is highly asymmetrical and highly fragmented. It is highly asymmetrical because the size, capabilities, geography, alliances of the Member States—and therefore their preferences—vary significantly between themselves. It is also highly fragmented because there are 27 of those actors (the Member States), to which a plethora of institutions, bodies, and agencies at EU level should be added.

These two characteristics make it unsurprising that common themes are bound to arise any time the EU tries to act: coherence (both horizontal between policies, and vertical between the EU and the Member States), accountability (the identification of the authority responsible for the design, operationalisation, or implementation of a decision), and effectiveness (in the simplest possible terms: can EU foreign policy be any good?)

1.2 Law: The Constitutional Ambiguity of Common Foreign and Security Policy

The Lisbon Treaty is an agreement between the Member States, negotiated in 2007 and entered into force on 1 December 2009. It established that the EU is based on several Treaties: the Treaty on the European Union (TEU), the Treaty on the Functioning of the European Union (TFEU), the Charter of Fundamental Rights, and the EURATOM Treaty. On the basis of those Treaties (referred to as primary legislation), EU institutions can adopt other acts, such as (among others) regulations, directives, and (of particular relevance for CFSP) decisions (all these acts are secondary legislation). In extreme synthesis, EU law consists of primary and secondary legislation, of some general principles identified by the Court of Justice of the European Union, and of international agreements which become part of the EU legal order.

In the orthodoxy established by the Court of Justice of the European Union, the EU is an autonomous legal order, which interacts with—but is separate from—the legal systems of its Member States or from international law. The focus of this book is primarily on EU law, even though mention will be made, where relevant, of other legal systems with which CFSP interacts.

Within that autonomous legal system, the EU enjoys certain powers to conduct its policies. These powers are known as competences. In technical terms, Common Foreign and Security Policy is a (very special) competence of the EU,[4] whereas national security is a competence of the Member States[5] (meaning that the EU cannot act in that field). Needless to say, the boundaries between EU security and national security are very blurred.

The position of CFSP in EU law is special because it 'is characterized by two threads that are, at times, in conflict. The first thread is about distinctiveness (. . .) The second thread running through the CFSP rules is about integration in the Union's

[4] Article 2(4) TFEU.

[5] Article 4(2) TEU.

overall architecture.'[6] Thus Koutrakos sums up the textual constitutional ambiguity of CFSP.[7]

The ambiguity derives from the fact that on the one hand, CFSP enjoys a distinctive position within EU law, from which specific rules derive. The policy is the only one detailed in the TEU, not in the TFEU.[8] Doctrinally, the 'specific rules and procedure' (Article 24 TEU) concern procedures for decision-making; the effect of CFSP acts and remedies against them (including the absence, in principle, of judicial review[9]); and the non-applicability of certain provisions of general application (Article 48(7) TEU does not apply to decisions with military implications or those in the area of defence; similarly, there are special provisions for military expenses—Article 41(2) TEU). CFSP is distinctive also in another sense, identified by Cremona: in addition to being its 'own' policy, it is also, by virtue of its special institutional arrangements, a policy through which the EU should formulate its overall foreign policy.[10]

On the other hand, the Union is a single legal order with legal personality; the objectives of CFSP and other external actions are merged into a single list (Article 21(2) TEU); the EU's principles and strategies are unitary (Article 3(5) TEU and 22 TEU); and general provisions (environmental protection (Article 11 TFEU), transparency (Article 15 TFEU), and protection of general data (Article 16 TFEU)) may be considered to apply to all of the Union's actions, including CFSP.[11] The interface between CFSP law and the rest of EU law is managed by Article 23 TEU (containing provisions of general applications), by Article 215 TFEU (providing the procedure for the adoption of restrictive measures when a CFSP decision says so), and by Article 40 TEU (establishing that CFSP and other competences shall not affect each other).

The above is a description of EU 'primary law'. There is also 'secondary law', which is the one adopted pursuant to primary law. That primary and secondary law is the 'law' with which this book is concerned—even though the discussion will often be broadened to consider other areas of EU law.[12] Occasionally, such as in Chap. 6, it shall become clear that 'law' is used simply as shorthand for EU behaviour. This is an acceptable shortcut, because the EU is based on the rule of law and its behaviour is regulated to a very large extent by legal documents (in our case: the Decisions

[6] Koutrakos (2018), p. 3.

[7] Pugliese (2013) identified the same threads, without developing on their implications, as far CFSP budgetary discipline is concerned.

[8] Something whose significance ought to be null or perhaps symbolic, since the two Treaties have equal value (Article 1 TEU). This was also the opinion of Professor Peers in the evidence given to the House of Lords, see (House of Lords, 2008, pp. 18–19).

[9] The lack of the Court's jurisdiction is 'the most significant of these specific rules' (according to Cremona, 2018, p. 10).

[10] Ibid.

[11] Ibid.

[12] Due to the technical reasons that shall become clear in Chap. 3, the Legal Context: there is a 'split' in EU external relations law, giving rise to a perennial issue of coherence.

adopted pursuant to the Common Foreign and Security Policy). This does not mean that the sum of all EU foreign policy is equivalent to its CFSP Decisions. Law is, so to speak, a portion of EU foreign policy, which is carried out also through informal instruments (official speeches, declarations, even Tweets or Instagram stories) with no formal regulation under EU law, nor with any intended legal consequences.

1.3 Geopolitics

There is no canonical definition but broadly speaking geopolitics is the study of how geography influences the history of states and their policies, in particular their foreign policy.[13] The term itself was coined in the late 1890s by the Swedish Rudolf Kjellén. In an influential 1904 article, often quoted in the Anglosphere as the founding text of contemporary geopolitics, British geographer Mackinder (1861–1947) believed it possible to find 'a formula which shall express certain aspects, at any rate, of geographical causation in history'.[14] In this sense, it is essentially a synonym of political geography and geostrategy,[15] which includes a study of both the physical features of a space,[16] and of its historical developments[17] (but, at least for the purposes of this book, not law). It is a descriptive academic discipline, a small niche of human geography.[18] This is the meaning of geopolitics used throughout this book—and not what appears to be its use in common, non-technical discourse, where it is used as a synonym of international relations.[19]

In a narrow sense, geopolitics is also the name used to describe the work of the Munich School. From the 1920s through to the 1940s, the Munich School—and its main figure, Haushofer (1869–1946)—studied the influence of space on politics, and developed doctrines justifying the expansionist political project of the Third Reich. It

[13] It studies 'the interaction between politically acting (wo)men and their surrounding territoriality (in its three dimensions; physical geography, human geography and the spatial dimension)' (Criekemans, 2022, p. 4).

[14] Mackinder (1904), p. 422. For a different definition, Fondation pour les Études de Défense Nationale, "Stratégique", 1991, 88: 'Geopolitics studies spheres of influence, while geostrategy has as main object the study of the buffer zones that protect the spheres of influence', author's translation.

[15] Agnew et al. (2015), p. 23.

[16] Or of a place, or area, including in the conceptual, non-literal senses of these words. Consider the various meanings of the German word Raum.

[17] The label 'political geography' was first used by French economist and politician Turgot in 1750 (Turgot & Gordon, 2011, p. 512) and established by German geographer Friedrich Ratzel with his book *Politische Geographie* (1897).

[18] Mamadouh (2015).

[19] As I was finishing the research for this book, I entered one of the biggest bookstores in Europe (it shall remain nameless, but it is next to the red line of the underground in the capital of a former Member State). When I asked if they had a section on geopolitics, the shop assistant explained that 'we [in this shop?] call it international relations'.

originated, in turn, from the biologist turned geographer Ratzel (1844–1904). German *Geopolitik* (as it will be called herein) was a normative discipline, but one which departed nonetheless from traditional geopolitics, which they defined as the 'science studying political facts in relation to their dependence from geographical environment'.[20]

Geopolitics in the broad sense posits that geography matters, and scholars of the discipline range from ultra-determinism (geography determines history) to more sophisticated, rational choice theory-oriented explanation of the influence of geography on people's choices.[21] Further, critical[22] or feminist geopolitics 'are primarily aimed at deconstructing geopolitical discourses and [...] at disclosing the relations between geopolitics and everyday life'.[23] In addition, the discipline has several national 'ramifications' and traditions, reference to which is made throughout the book.

What many geopolitical approaches have in common is that they seek to uncover regular 'laws' of geopolitics. For example, with regard to Europe, an important geopolitical theory[24] which has had momentous policy repercussions is the 'Heartland theory': developed by Mackinder and later by the Dutch-born Harvard professor Spykman (1893–1943), it posits that control of the mainland (central Asia, Eastern Europe) is what ultimately enables control of most of the world.[25] It is not only a 'Western' idea: some Russian ideologues of Eurasian imperialism share it, such as Savitsky (1895–1968) and Dugin,[26] by many considered one of Putin's *maîtres à penser*.[27] The Heartland theory stresses the importance of land (over sea), of centre (over coast) and, in the case of Europe, of the region corresponding roughly to contemporary Germany, Poland, Belarus, and Russia, control of which is considered not only desirable, but vital. Such strategic vision inspired not only Russian thinkers, but also, by contrast, American diplomats: countering the Russian geopolitical assumptions was at the origin of the US Cold War strategy of containment.[28]

This notion of explanation as covering law is perhaps too ambitious, and not supported empirically. For this reason, this book refers to 'mechanisms'[29] or 'patterns' of geopolitics:[30] there are some frequently occurring instances in which geography influences political behaviour, but these are not law-like occurrences. It is possible to identify them in various works of geopolitics and history, the

[20] This is the definition provided by Haushofer's journal, Zeitschrift für Geopolitik, author's translation.

[21] Criekemans (2020) is an excellent introduction.

[22] Ó Tuathail (1996).

[23] Mamadouh (2015).

[24] A 'covering law' that I do not share.

[25] See further Chap. 2, the Geopolitical context.

[26] Dugin (1997, 2015).

[27] On the antecedents of Putin's geopolitical ideology see Lonardo (2023).

[28] Or, more correctly of what Harper (1996) calls 'protocontainment'.

[29] For the notion of 'covering law' and 'mechanism', see Tilly (2001).

[30] For a more detailed methodological discussion see Lonardo (2022).

frequentation of which enables to build a 'tool-box' of ways in which geography may affect foreign policy and economics. Some of the most significant patterns are discussed already in this introduction (below), then appear scattered throughout the book, and form the structure of Chap. 7; other patterns are simply mentioned throughout the book. While these patterns are presented as causal explanations, they have no predictive value.

The reader may be surprised by the amount of attention this book dedicates to the geopolitics of Europe, rather than to the rest of the world. The choice to focus on Europe is because, despite globalisation, the drivers of EU foreign policy are geographically proximate.[31] Even in the era of the internet, logistics matter because goods must move from one place to another. Even in an era of intercontinental ballistic missiles, geography and infrastructures are crucial because people (including the military) must have the capacity to move quickly. Technological developments, which stimulated a rush toward rare raw materials, and the political will to reduce EU energy dependence from Russia, are further reminders of the enduring importance of natural resources.

1.4 The Argument of This Book

The key argument of this book is that the rules on CFSP contained in the Lisbon Treaty did not reflect the geopolitical reality that had been created by the 2004 enlargement, a major re-ordering of political space on the continent.[32] A similar point could be made to say that the Maastricht Treaty did not reflect the geopolitical reality created by the collapse of the Soviet Union. And since the Commission's rhetoric is about being 'geopolitical', it is the case that a 'capabilities-expectations gap'[33] still endures. It is suggested that the reason for this mismatch is that CFSP has always—both in the Maastricht Treaty and the in the Lisbon—retained its legal 'distinctiveness' deriving from the informal developments of the European Political Cooperation in the 70s, despite formal (Maastricht) or structural (Lisbon) adjustment to integrate it into the EU unitary legal order: CFSP belongs to the Cold War. For the law of CFSP, it is as if the Berlin wall had never fallen. Nor has the law changed after Lisbon. The only significant development in the law of CFSP is an increased role for the Court in judicial review, which in fact may amount to implicit Treaty amendment, but even that is not predicated on geopolitical needs.

Geopolitics entails that there is a sensitive space in central and Eastern Europe.[34] In turn, the EU reacted by reordering that political space, through the 2004

[31] For Europe in global history, Motadel (2021).

[32] Scott (2011).

[33] To use the fortunate formula of Hill (1993).

[34] This is an important contribution of classic works of geopolitics, Mackinder (1904); Kaplan (2013); Spykman (2007).

enlargement and the ENP,[35] and later through sanctions, CSDP missions and operations, and association agreements. The crucial difference after the 2004 enlargement is that the acquisition of new territories and populations in the East and the Mediterranean entailed much more heterogeneity in the system of alliances of its Member States, in their patterns of energy dependence, and in their trade partnership and diplomatic styles. This results in increased difficulty in achieving coherence and unanimity. Albeit not a direct consequence of the 2004 enlargement (but perhaps a consequence of the post-Cold War environment), EU action through CFSP increased and it affected more individuals or third states, as well as EU institutions, bodies, agencies or Member States.

The reason why this book identifies a mismatch is that the EU (still) requires unanimity for most CFSP decisions, including for the most used and most important tool: restrictive measures. There is also a mismatch because EU diplomatic action is still split between CFSP and other external relations competence, and these shall not affect each other (Article 40 TEU). Finally, the Lisbon Treaty foresaw limited judicial review by EU courts, even in a context in which the EU is very active and the rights of natural and legal persons are affected by CFSP measures. The Court has only partially remedied the shortcomings in judicial protection. This mismatch between law and political reality is not exclusive to foreign policy. Geopolitical surprises are not the only ones which have put a strain on EU law. The economic and financial crisis (exogenous) and the rule of law crisis (endogenous) have also stressed the legal system, which reacted through constitutional ingenuity (implicit Treaty amendments, hybrid action by EU and Member States, collective action by Member States outside the Treaties)—and it is now the turn of CFSP to act as laboratory for constitutional experimentation.[36] In sum, the EU legal system is still trying to ‘catch up’ with the choice of Maastricht to unite (but keeping somewhat distinct) economic and political integration. Fundamentally, in fact, the requirement of unanimity in CFSP envisage a system in which there cannot be a political minority: reality has shown otherwise. The phrase ‘catching up’ is always used in inverted commas because there is nothing unidirectional or inevitable in the direction in which law ‘evolves’, but it will be argued that, if it is to be functional,[37] the law of CFSP will need to better adapt to geopolitics.

What is the added value, for EU lawyers, of considering geopolitics and detecting this mismatch? In short, geopolitical considerations weight in on a normative debate within EU legal scholarship. EU lawyers are not comfortable with the constitutional ambiguity of CFSP. The particularity of the law of CFSP within the EU legal order is a well-studied phenomenon, and a geopolitical reading confirms what (some) EU

---

[35] This is an important contribution of the literature on EU geopolitics and border studies, Scott (2011); Bialasiewicz (2011a); Bialasiewicz et al. (2009).

[36] Consider the Council’s request to extend EU competence in criminal law in order to enforce CFSP sanctions. This would enable adoption of legislation by QMV to extend the ‘Eurocrimes’ (those with a cross-border dimension in particularly serious areas) of Article 83(1) TFEU. On the point of constitutional experimentation in relation to hybrid threats and Article 83 TFEU (Lonardo, 2021, p. 1090).

[37] Isiksel (2016).

lawyers have long suspected: the legal eccentricity is dysfunctional. Even though it is not phrased as such, it is possible to identify a tension between two normative commitments:[38] those in favour of a 'normalisation' of the CFSP (meaning that the ambiguity should be reduced or eliminated altogether);[39] and other in favour of maintaining a 'hard core' of distinctiveness of CFSP, as the drafters of the Treaties intended it, protecting this policy from the application of general principles of EU law, as last sanctuary, as it were, of Member States' sovereignty.[40] This book presents an argument that strengthens the first position, even though, doctrinally, I am more cautious about the extent to which a process of 'normalisation' is occurring, and normatively, about its desirability.[41] In any case, both sides usually argue by reference to 'doctrinal' legal benchmarks (compliance with international law,[42] systematic interpretation,[43] intentions of the drafters of the Treaties[44]), whereas 'external' non-legal benchmarks (geopolitics, political desirability, historical necessity, aesthetics...) are next to absent.[45] This book is an attempt at providing such external benchmarks, in the hope that someone (inside or outside the legal community) will consider them relevant.

1.5 Method

The book seeks to advance the field of EU law by considering what one may call 'extra-legal' factors.[46] To build the argument, this book in fact draws from various strands of literature, including geopolitics, foreign policy studies[47] and EU studies,[48] and occasionally history.

---

[38] Sometimes it happens that in academic debates (on EU constitutionalism) 'Normative commitments [...] are never made explicit and justified' (Kumm, 2006, pp. 505–506). The debate identified here is not so much between individuals, but between normative commitments indeed.

[39] I read in this sense, for example (Butler, 2017; Hillion & Wessel, 2018; Poli, 2022, p. 1077).

[40] I read in this sense, for example (Dashwood, 2011, p. 55: 'I am very clear that there's no room for any principle that is not fully consistent with the particular character of the CFSP'; Koutrakos, 2018, p. 25: 'The choice of integration should come from the drafters of the Treaties, rather than the Courts').

[41] For the purposes of this debate, an engagement with theories of European integration might usefully complement the one with geopolitics. So far, European integration theory appears unable to determine what CFSP *should* look like.

[42] Wessel (2016), p. 464.

[43] Craig (2013), p. 182; Verellen (2021), p. 24; Koutrakos (2018), p. 24; Van Elsuwege (2021), p. 1733; Poli (2022), p. 1054.

[44] Cremona (2018).

[45] Occasionally, mention is made to EU policy documents (Wessel, 2016, p. 466).

[46] What is legal and what is extra-legal is a matter of definition.

[47] Irondelle et al. (2017) is a terrific concise overview of the evolution of security and defence studies.

[48] Jørgensen (2015) is an excellent starting point for a review of the contributions of foreign policy studies and EU studies to the understanding EU foreign policy.

The result is a book that sits perhaps uncomfortably within one single disciplines, but brings together insights from post-colonial studies (legacies of empire and coloniality[49] not only shape the preferences of some Member States,[50] but also constitute an implicit model for the EU's geopolitical outlook on Europe;[51] geography itself as a discipline is deeply implicated in colonial categories[52]); critical and feminist geography (bodies are a terrain of struggle[53]); the de-centring agenda[54] (there exists indigenous geopolitics, for example, in the Arctic region;[55] consultation of local sources, paints a different picture for the Mediterranean than do studies in English[56]); theories of legal reasoning and especially legal realism (it is plausible that some 'extra-legal' factors influence judicial reasoning[57]); and rational choice theory (for insights from game theory: the geopolitical border of Europe creates a game of mixed cooperation and conflict between the EU and Russia). On some occasions, I have not resisted the temptation to mention classic works of European cultural history or of historical linguistics which I thought would help in illustrating a point.

1.6 The Key Theme: Between Law and Geopolitics

Geopolitics led the genesis and design of CFSP, in the sense that the creation of (the predecessor of) this policy in the 70s, and the formalisation of CFSP in the Maastricht Treaty owes much to the geopolitical context: to the boundaries of the European Union as they then were, to the (changing) systems of alliances, and the evolving political priorities of Member States. But the geopolitical context changed

[49] Weldeab Sebhatu (2021), p. 19; Zielonka (2010).

[50] Haastrup (2021), p. 511; Snyder (1987), p. 170 'The European Community is often considered to be inherently neo-colonial. Acting for the rich and north in its manifold relations with the poor and south, it represents at best an unfortunate if inevitable legacy of the past, at worst a new form of foreign, capitalist domination'.

[51] Behr (2007); Foster (2013).

[52] Noxolo (2017), p. 318.

[53] Gökarıksel et al. (2021), p. 10.

[54] Keuleers et al. (2016); Onar and Nicolaïdis (2013) The impact of EU action in third country is obviously part of the analysis: still, the book is about Europe as seen from the inside, not from outside.

[55] Dodds and Nuttall (2019), p. 73.

[56] Among others: the Spanish Revista de Estudios Mediterraneos established in 1941 and Revista de Estudios Internacionales Mediterráneos (2007); the French Méditerranée (1960), Revue des mondes musulmans et de la Méditerranée (since 1966), Cahiers de la Méditerranée (1968), Confluences Méditerranées (since 2001); the Italian Bollettino di Studi Mediterranei and the Mediterranean Journal of Social Sciences (since 2010. English); the Portuguese Mediterrâneo; the Maltese Journal of Mediterranean Studies (since 1991. English); the Greek Athens Journal of Mediterranean Studies (since 2015. English).

[57] Llewellyn (1960); Rasmussen (1986); Bengoetxea (1993); Beck (2013); Cotter (2022).

profoundly with the 2004 enlargement. The EU acquired significant territory Eastward, a new border with Russia, and englobed countries which had been on the other side of the Iron Curtain during the Cold War. From economics to energy supply, from labour mobility to welfare, the enlargement did nothing short of revolutionising EU governance—but (and this is crucial) it did not revolutionise EU law. In particular, it did not revolutionise CFSP, which was translated with only minor changes from Maastricht to Lisbon.[58] Add to this the massive shock of the Russian war against Ukraine in 2022 and the crumbling security architecture in Europe: geopolitics now leads the implementation, the operation, and the day-to-day functioning of a CFSP whose legal machinery appears increasingly out of date.

Some frequently occurring patterns in the interaction between law and geopolitics may be spelt out, and the most relevant of these (encountered throughout the book) form the basic structure of Chap. 7. Firstly there is the quest for autonomy: to survive, a community needs territory, resources, and possibly technology. This pattern is usually presented as a 'covering law' by neo-realist theorists of international relations. It is no such a thing, of course. Communities can survive also without one or more of those elements. But it is a frequently occurring pattern. The quest for autonomy leads the EU to pursue geopolitical considerations (energy independence, acquisition of raw material) both through the CFSP and other competences (trade, energy policy). But striving for autonomy—with a cumbersome and increasingly outdated legal system—results in a plethora of legal issues: horizontal coherence, vertical coherence, accountability, and indeed effectiveness. More broadly, it even raises the question of the desirability for a sophisticated, multilayered, binding legal system to pursue geopolitical games in which the other participants are unprejudiced, cynical, or downright lawless.

Secondly, the most consequential of these 'geopolitical' patterns, for EU foreign policy, is spelt out by an American journalist: 'a man-made border that does not match a natural frontier zone is particularly vulnerable'.[59] For the EU, this applies to Ireland and Cyprus, but also to the area roughly comprised between the Rhine River and the Volga River. This is a region made up by vast plains without a significant physical border. This area is particularly crucial, so EU action here will be exceptionally important. Readers will have already recognised that area as key to European history: the outer borders of the Roman Empire, the Carolingian Kingdom, and now the project of European integration. *Das Rheingold*. Indeed, the EU, by uniting the two sides of the Rhine, is in itself 'an antidote to European history'.[60] The notion of border is key:[61] a border is studied not for where it lies, but for *ce qui*

---

[58] This process is spelt out in some detail in Chap. 3.

[59] Kaplan (2013), p. xix. Rome's founding myth entails a vulnerable, very sensitive, indeed holy border, that cost Remus his life.

[60] Dashwood (2011), p. 55.

[61] For a survey of 'border studies' discussing the changes in nature, function, and location of EU borders see Mamadouh (2015); For the etymology of the words border, frontière, and Grenze see Amilhat Szary (2015).

s'agite au dedans (what is restless within it).[62] A sensitive border conjures 'feelings of urgency, pain, and danger without defining them. Evoked in political contexts, it summons concerns over security without specifying the nature of the threats'.[63] The EU's action since the end of the Cold War (since it has had a fully-fledged CFSP), has had the objective consequence (if not intended consequence) of securing a political border where there is no geographical one. By extending membership to Poland, the Czech Republic, Slovakia, and Hungary, by sanctioning Belarus and Russia, the EU creates a border. There, it engages with the physical and conceptual 'space' for encountering and creating the other and the self.[64] Geopolitics—and geopolitical thought—are inextricably linked to foreign policy identity.[65] Even though not done through CFSP, enlargement was effectively foreign policy by other means,[66] aimed at protecting what was considered the continent's spinal cord. The European Neighbourhood Policy and its very mixed success can also be read in the same light of creating an Eastern border. Conceptually, it is interesting to note that the notion of 'bordered political space' is a legacy of the Roman Empire, mediated through modern empires:[67] the EU, a very spatialised endeavour, is instrumental to the creation of new borders.[68]

Another mechanism of geopolitics concerns the trade-off between land and sea power. The EU's focus on the East has also come at a price for other regions: the Atlantic and the Mediterranean. To be sure, the decline in the geopolitical importance of Atlanticism (with emphasis on maritime power, i.e., in European context, on the US security guarantee post WW2[69]) and of the Mediterranean is not primarily due to the EU. It is the result of profound mutations of the *longue durée*. As Bloch wrote in 1935, Europe was born when the Roman Empire fell, referring to the shift from a Mediterranean-based world to a Rhine-oriented one (with Charlemagne). But the EU has indulged—or taken advantage of—those trends: it has never shied away from mounting anti-American feelings to concentrate on continental integration (in fact, significant developments such as the Permanent Structured Cooperation may be explained also by a desire to distance Europe from the Trump presidency); through a one-size-fit-all neighbourhood policy, it has further crystallised the shattering of the Mediterranean into two, and indeed the 'othering' of Eastern Mediterranean (even though, unlike what the use of the Said-inspired vocabulary might suggest,[70] one would need to prove that the 'othering' was deliberate; I could not). This reorganisation of Europe away from the sea and deep into the land would

[62] Ancel (1938), p. 3.
[63] Cons (2016), p. 7.
[64] Bialasiewicz (2011b), pp. 1–2.
[65] Guzzini (2012), p. 3.
[66] Missiroli et al. (2015), p. 9.
[67] Armitage (2013), p. 52.
[68] Sometimes literally so, for example in the Western Balkans, as evidenced in Chap. 2.
[69] On the geopolitical origins of which see again Harper (1996).
[70] Said (2003).

seem to provide some empirical support to the Heartland theory, but this author prefers the more sober connection to intellectual history rather than to an all-encompassing explanation: 'The histories of oceans and empires [. . .] rest upon an old and deep opposition between empires of the land and empires of the sea whose roots can be found in Judaic and Greek, as well as Roman and neo-Roman, traditions.'[71] The EU is a land entity more than a maritime one, because so are France (albeit paradoxically) and Germany—the UK having been unable to impose its Atlantic vocation. In the simplest possible terms, geopolitically, the EU and Russia now share the same assumption: it is necessary to exercise political control over eastern Europe. It was not always like that. The US doctrine of containment was predicated upon the simple assumption that 'the Soviet Union's self-generated problems would frustrate its ambitions if the West was patient enough to wait for this to happen and firm enough to resist making concessions'.[72] Post-Cold War, enlargement (of NATO, of the Council of Europe, of the EU) started instead.[73]

1.7 The Plan of This Book

The book is divided in three parts.

Part 1 introduces the context. Chapter 2 presents the geopolitical context of CFSP: how geographical features may help understanding the history and size, system of alliances, and bureaucratic organisation of the Member States and their main neighbours. Chapter 3 sets out the legal context, by recalling the history of the constitutional ambiguity of CFSP, and then outlining the current institutional and legal features of the policy: institutional involvement, decision-making, objectives and scope, and judicial protection.

Part 2 systematises the salient actions (or inactions) of CFSP after Lisbon, grouped in three chapters: sanctions (Chap. 4), CSDP in action (Chap. 5), and instances of inaction (Chap. 6). This part is rather illustrative—even though it contains also original analysis, especially in the rather theoretical Chap. 6.

Part 3 draws the threads together, presenting in Chap. 7 reflections of the interaction between law and geopolitics, and their mismatch, wrapped around the three common themes of coherence, accountability and effectiveness.

Some disclaimers about what the book is not: it is not a systematic or in-depth analysis of the legal and political aspects, even though it is hoped that the choice to do away with many legal technicalities does not result in a loss of nuance. And the exposition is not primarily concerned with the many disciplines, fields, and frameworks through which it is possible to analyse CFSP, so the engagement with these is deliberately limited to focus on law and geopolitics. As shown earlier, this does not

---

[71] Armitage (2013), p. 47.

[72] Gaddis (2011), p. 196.

[73] Sarotte (2021).

mean that the book ignores the insights provided by those frameworks, but rather that there is no systematic reference or presentation of those. This book considers EU—as opposed to Member States—foreign policy.[74] It was mentioned, and will become even clearer, that the distinction between the two is deliberately blurred in the constitutional framework of the EU, but this book does not engage specifically with the foreign policy of individual Member States, except when these are directly relevant to the picture of *EU* foreign policy.

References

Agnew, J. A., Mamadouh, V., Secor, A. J., & Sharp, J. P. (Eds.). (2015). *The Wiley Blackwell companion to political geography* (2nd ed.). John Wiley & Sons.

Amilhat Szary, A.-L. (2015). In J. A. Agnew, V. Mamadouh, A. J. Secor, & J. P. Sharp (Eds.), *The Wiley Blackwell companion to political geography* (2nd ed.). John Wiley & Sons.

Ancel, J. (1938). *Géographie Des Frontières*. Gallimard.

Armitage, D. (2013). *Foundations of modern international thought*. Cambridge University Press.

Beck, G. (2013). *The legal reasoning of the Court of Justice of the EU*. Hart Publishing Ltd.

Behr, H. (2007). The European Union in the legacies of imperial rule? EU accession politics viewed from a historical comparative perspective. *European Journal of International Relations, 13*(2), 239–262.

Bengoetxea, J. (1993). *The legal reasoning of the European Court of Justice: Towards a European Jurisprudence*. Clarendon Press; Oxford University Press.

Bialasiewicz, L. (Ed.). (2011a). *Europe in the World: EU geopolitics and the making of European space*. Ashgate.

Bialasiewicz, L. (Ed.), (2011b). Introduction: Europe in the world? In *Europe in the world: EU geopolitics and the making of European space* (pp. 1–16). Ashgate.

Bialasiewicz, L., Dahlman, C., Apuzzo, G. M., Ciută, F., Jones, A., Rumford, C., Wodak, R., Anderson, J., & Ingram, A. (2009). Interventions in the new political geographies of the European "Neighborhood". *Political Geography, 28*(2), 79–89.

Butler, G. (2017). The coming of age of the Court's Jurisdiction in the common foreign and security policy. *European Constitutional Law Review, 13*(04), 673–703.

Cons, J. (2016). *Sensitive space: Fragmented territory at the India-Bangladesh border*. University of Washington Press.

Cotter, J. (2022). *Legal certainty in the preliminary reference procedure: The role of extra-legal steadying factors*. Edward Elgar Publishing.

Craig, P. P. (2013). *The Lisbon Treaty: Law, politics, and treaty reform*, First paperback edn. Oxford University Press.

Cremona, M. (2018). The position of CFSP/CSDP in the EU's constitutional architecture. *Research Handbook on the EU's Common Foreign and Security Policy*.

Criekemans, D. (2020) 'Geopolitical schools of thought: A concise overview from 1890 till 2020, and beyond'. In *Geopolitical traditions: A century of geopolitical thought* (pp. 97–155). Routledge.

Criekemans, D. (2022). Introduction. The need for a renewed "Grounding" of international relations. In D. Criekemans (Ed.), *Geopolitics and international relations: Grounding world politics anew*. Brill | Nijhoff.

[74] For the interplay between them, see the literature review in Jørgensen (2015).

Dashwood, A. (2011). Years an EU lawyer— *Apologia Pro Vita Sua* Or EU law—A 40-year journey and still motoring. *Cambridge Yearbook of European Legal Studies, 13*, 47–64.
Dodds, K., & Nuttall, M. (2019). *The Arctic: What everyone needs to know*. Oxford University Press.
Dugin, A. G. (1997). *Osnovy geopolitiki: geopolitičeskoe buduščee Rossii*. Arktogeja.
Dugin, A. G. (2015). *Last war of the World-Island: The geopolitics of contemporary Russia*. Arktos.
European Union. (2022). *A Strategic Compass for Security and Defence*.
Foster, R. (2013). *Tabula Imperii Europae*: A cartographic approach to the current debate on the European Union as Empire. *Geopolitics, 18*(2), 371–402.
Gaddis, J. L. (2011). *George F. Kennan: An American Life*. Penguin Press.
Gökarıksel, B., Hawkins, M., Neubert, C., & Smith, S. (Eds.). (2021). *Feminist geography unbound: Discomfort, bodies, and prefigured futures* (1st ed.). West Virginia University Press.
Guzzini, S. (2012). The argument:: Geopolitics for fixing the coordinates of foreign policy identity. In S. Guzzini (Ed.), *The Return of Geopolitics in Europe?* (1st ed., pp. 1–6). Cambridge University Press.
Haastrup, T. (2021). Critical perspectives on Africa's relationship with the European Union. In D. Bigo, T. Diez, E. Fanoulis, B. Rosamond, & Y. A. Stivachtis (Eds.), *The Routledge handbook of critical European studies*. Routledge, Taylor & Francis Group.
Harper, J. L. (1996) *American visions of Europe: Franklin D. Roosevelt, George F. Kennan, and Dean G. Acheson*, 1. paperback edn. Cambridge University Press.
Hill, C. (1993). The capability-expectations gap, or conceptualizing Europe's international role. *Journal of Common Market Studies, 31*, 305.
Hillion, C., & Wessel, R. A. (2018). "The Good, the Bad and the Ugly": Three levels of judicial control over the CFSP. In *Research handbook on the EU's common foreign and security policy* (pp. 65–87). Edward Elgar Publishing.
House of Lords. (2008). *The treaty of Lisbon: An impact assessment*. House of Lords.
Irondelle, B., Joana, J., & Mérand, F. (2017). *Defense and security policy*. Oxford University Press.
Isiksel, T. (2016). *Europe's functional constitution: A theory of constitutionalism beyond the state*. Oxford University Press.
Jørgensen, K. (2015). The Study of European Foreign Policy: Trends and advances. In *The SAGE Handbook of European Foreign Policy: Two Volume Set* (pp. 14–27). SAGE Publications Ltd.
Kaplan, R. D. (2013). *The revenge of geography: What the map tells us about coming conflicts and the battle against fate*. Random House Trade Paperbacks.
Keuleers, F., Fonck, D., & Keukeleire, S. (2016). Beyond EU navel-gazing: Taking stock of EU-centrism in the analysis of EU foreign policy. *Cooperation and Conflict, 51*(3), 345–364.
Koutrakos, P. (2018). Judicial review in the EU's common foreign and security policy. *International and Comparative Law Quarterly, 67*(1), 1–35.
Kumm, M. (2006). Beyond golf clubs and the judicialization of politics: Why Europe has a constitution properly so called. *The American Journal of Comparative Law, 54*(1), 505–530.
Llewellyn, K. (1960). *The common law tradition: Deciding appeals*. QUID PRO, LLC.
Lonardo, L. (2021). EU law against hybrid threats: A first assessment. *European Papers - A Journal on Law and Integration, 6*, 10751096.
Lonardo, L. (2022). The contribution of geopolitics to the study of EU foreign policy illustrated through the example of empire and colonialism. *European Foreign Affairs Review, 27*(4), 1–18.
Lonardo, L. (2023) *Russia's 2022 war against Ukraine and EU foreign policy*. Palgrave Macmillan.
Mackinder, H. (1904). The geographical pivot of history. *Royal Geographical Society, IV*, 298–321.
Mamadouh, V. (2015). The geopolitics of EU external relations. In *The SAGE handbook of European foreign policy: Two volume set* (pp. 53–72). SAGE Publications Ltd.
Missiroli, A., Mogherini, F., & Institute for Security Studies Paris, F. (2015). *Towards an EU global strategy: Background, Process, References*.
Motadel, D. (2021). Globaliser l'Europe. *Annales. Histoire, Sciences Sociales, 76*(4), 645–667.

Noxolo, P. (2017). Introduction: Decolonising geographical knowledge in a colonised and re-colonising postcolonial world. *Area, 49*(3), 317–319.
Ó Tuathail, G. (1996). *Critical geopolitics: The politics of writing global space*. Routledge.
Onar, N. F., & Nicolaïdis, K. (2013). The decentring Agenda: Europe as a post-colonial power. *Cooperation and Conflict, 48*(2), 283–303.
Poli, S. (2022). The right to effective judicial protection with respect to acts imposing restrictive measures and its ransformative force for the common foreign and security policy. *Common Market Law Review*, 1045–1080.
Pugliese, S. (2013). Il Finanziamento Della PESC Tra Tendenze All'Integrazione e Istanze Centrifughe. *Il Diritto dell'Unione Europea, 2*, 363–379.
Rasmussen, H. (1986). *On law and policy in the European Court of Justice: A comparative study in judicial policymaking*. M. Nijhoff.
Said, E. W. (2003). *Orientalism*, Facsimile edn. Penguin.
Sarotte, M. E. (2021). *Not one inch: America, Russia, and the making of post-cold war stalemate*. Yale University Press.
Scott, J. W. (2011). Reflections on EU geopolitics: Consolidation, neighbourhood and civil society in the reordering of European space. *Geopolitics, 16*(1), 146–175.
Snyder, F. (1987). New directions in European community law. *Journal of Law and Society, 14*(1), 167.
Spykman, N. J. (2007). *America's strategy in world politics: The United States and the balance of power*. Transaction Publishers.
Tilly, C. (2001). Mechanisms in political processes. *Annual Review of Political Science, 4*(1), 21–41.
Turgot, A.-R., & Gordon, D. (2011). *The Turgot collection writings, speeches, and letters*. Ludwig von Mises Institute.
Van Elsuwege, P. (2021). Judicial review and the common foreign and security policy: Limits to the gap-filling role of the Court of Justice. *Common Market Law Review*, 1731–1760.
van Middelaar, L. (2022). *Le réveil géopolitique de l'Europe*. Collège de France Editions.
Verellen, T. (2021). In the name of the rule of law? CJEU further extends Jurisdiction in CFSP (Bank Refah Kargaran). *European Papers - A Journal on Law and Integration, 6*, 1724.
von der Leyen, U. (2019). *Speech by President-elect von der Leyen in the EP*.
Weldeab Sebhatu, R. (2021). Applying postcolonial approaches to studies of Africa-EU relations. In T. Haastrup, L. Mah, & N. Duggan (Eds.), *The Routledge handbook of EU-Africa relations*. Routledge.
Wessel, R. A. (2016). Lex Imperfecta: Law and integration in European foreign and security policy. *European Papers - A Journal on Law and Integration, 1*, 439468.
Zielonka, J. (2010). *Europe as empire: The nature of the enlarged European Union, Reprint*. Oxford University Press.

Part I
The Context

Chapter 2
The Geopolitical Context

Contents

It is a key theme of this book that the legal distinctiveness—and therefore the concrete functioning of EU security and defence policy—ought to be studied in synergy with the *geopolitical* context of Europe: the European Union, its Member States, and their neighbourhood. Geography (Sect. 2.1) provides an interesting lens for reading the history (Sect. 2.2), systems of alliances (Sect. 2.3), and bureaucratic organisation (Sect. 2.4) of the Member States and (Sect. 2.5) their neighbourhood. This chapter will provide some brief introductory remarks on the geopolitical contexts of these countries, and will provide some key bibliographic suggestions for further readings.

2.1 Europe's Geography

2.1.1 A Continent with No Eastern Frontier

Europe does not have a *frontière naturelle*, for, in the words of Lucien Febvre, 'there are no Eastern limits to Europe, no impassable river, no insurmountable mountain chains, no arm of the sea, no great lake, no desert of burning sands or glacial

L. Lonardo, *EU Common Foreign and Security Policy After Lisbon*,
https://doi.org/10.1007/978-3-031-19131-2_2

Fig 2.1 Physical map of the EU. *Source* Wikipedia

stones'.[1] The continent of Europe, extending traditionally from Portugal (including Madeira and the Azores)[2] to the Urals in Russia, from Norway (including the Arctic islands Jan Mayen, Svalbard) to the southernmost islands in the Mediterranean is, geographically, an appendix of the most vast mass of land of Eurasia.[3] Within the borders drawn by the Artic Ocean in the north, the Atlantic Ocean in the west, and the Mediterranean in the south, the territory of Europe is characterised by few physical barriers: 'wide and fertile plains, an indented coastline that allowed for many good natural harbours, navigable rivers flowing northward across these plains'.[4] And it is a continent without a clear geographical border. Traditionally, the Ural Mountains have been considered such a border, but the Urals do not really mark any physical, economic or cultural discontinuity, and south of the Ural Mountains there is no natural border between Europe and Asia anyways (Fig. 2.1).[5]

[1] Febvre et al. (1999), p. 132.

[2] Another island in the Atlantic Ocean, Iceland, is usually considered part of Europe.

[3] Diamond (1999) considers some implications of the geography of Eurasia for world history.

[4] Kaplan (2013), p. 44.

[5] Strictly speaking, even the straits of Gibraltar, the Channel of Sicily, and the Turkish straits do not constitute a significant discontinuity between the shores they separate. More generally, a border is 'peut-etrê preparée, mais jamais determinée par la nature' (Ancel, 1938, p. 4).

As a result, the geopolitical borders of Europe (especially the Eastern ones) are far from straightforward: Europe is a conceptual as much as a physical space.[6] Europe is almost an ideal, to which Padgen recently dedicated a very detailed historical study.[7] This ideal formed the basis for a sense of community between states and people on the continent, but it also served as purported justification for racist projects predicated on the alleged superiority of European culture. Thus, to take but one example of the blurred 'conceptual' borders of Europe, the region of Eastern Mediterranean—going from the shores of modern day Lebanon (from which Europa, daughter of the king of Tyrus, was kidnapped by Zeus according to the myth) and Israel to the Western coast of Greece—includes and EU and NATO member (Greece), an EU non-NATO member (Cyprus), a NATO non-EU member (Turkey), and a series of states who are not members of either, but who have very close cultural or political ties with the EU (Israel participates in the EU budget and, for what it matters, in the Eurovision Song Contest; Jordan seconds personnel to EU CSDP missions,[8] etc). Turkey herself is usually thought of as having a European and an Asian aspect.

Unsurprisingly, classic works of geopolitics have concentrated on the significance of the region between the Rhine and the Volga—roughly equivalent to present day Germany-Poland-Belarus-Ukraine-Russia. Even though they do not say it explicitly, their speculation is probably due to the operation of the general pattern identified (not for this region) by Kaplan: 'a man-made border that does not match a natural frontier zone is particularly vulnerable'.[9] In his 1904 article on 'the geographical pivot of history', British geographer Mackinder read world's history as a function of the cyclical migrations from the steppes of Eurasia to the periphery (from Asia to Central and Eastern Europe and the Eastern Mediterranean), the 'remarkable succession of Turanian nomadic peoples—Huns, Avars, Bulgarians, Magyars, Khazars, Patzinaks, Cumans, Mongols, Kamuks'[10]. In Kaplan's words, Mackinder's reading meant that Europe had its 'destiny shaped by the influx of Asian hordes'.[11] Spykman's Heartland theory, published during WW2, also posited that whoever controls the heartland of Eurasia (from the steppe of Siberia to the planes of Europe) will control, essentially, the rest of the world. Some, such as Cohen, have gone so far as to see the Elbe River as the border between maritime Europe and the Heartland: 'the boundary zone that divides the East from West Germany. . .is one of the oldest in history';[12] and Mackinder 'the line through Germany. . .is the very line which we have on other grounds taken as demarking the Heartland in a strategical sense from

[6]As intuited by Cacciari (2003) who wrote a 'geophilosophy' of Europe.

[7]Pagden (2021), p. 11.

[8]Agreement between the European Union and the Hashemite Kingdom of Jordan establishing a framework for the participation of the Hashemite Kingdom of Jordan in European Union crisis management operations of 2019.

[9]Kaplan (2013), p. xix.

[10]Mackinder (1904), p. 426.

[11]Kaplan (2013), p. 136.

[12]Cohen (1973), p. 79.

the Coastland'[13] (but this is reading too much into geography: there is no evidence that the river being there actually caused anything, let alone determine the maritime orientation of the countries to its West). The importance of the Rhine for European history, however, cannot be overstated.[14]

It is a key contention of this book that the lack of a geographical Eastern border is a lens through which developments in the law of CFSP—thus, in EU foreign policy—can be read, as detailed in Chap. 7.

2.1.2 Geopolitics of Energy and Raw Materials

The enlargement of the EU meant the inclusion of new Member States 'with specific patterns of energy supply and demand, based on their former orientation towards the Soviet Union'.[15] Security of energy supply is at the core of any energy policy, and for the EU this is complicated by the different patterns of dependence of the Western and Easter parts of the continent.

For oil, security of supply is still an issue, even after the watershed oil crisis of the 70s. Ever since then, political movements advocated for a significant reduction in reliance on this source of energy. Recently, the EU is moving to an 'energy transition' also through the European Green Deal (with the target of bringing renewable sources in the EU's energy mix to 40%). Being the world's most traded commodity, its price influences the world economy. It is characterised by great asymmetry: few countries provide oil to the rest of the world.[16] This makes the EU particularly dependent, as it imports 90% of its crude oil (until 2022, one quarter from Russia, around half from Iraq, Nigeria, Saudi Arabia, Kazakhstan and Libya, and the remaining quarter from other countries).[17] The pipelines importing crude oil from West Siberia into the EU have two main arteries: the Baltic one (arriving at the ports of Latvia and Lithuania) and the Druzhba one (northern Druzhba arrives at the German port of Rostock and in Leipzig; southern Druzhba to Central Europe and to the Adriatic Sea in Croatia).

It is therefore unsurprising that the sanctions against the Russian oil industry in 2014 proved particularly delicate from a legal perspective, and the challenge brought by the Russian oil company resulted in one of the landmark judgments in CFSP: the *Rosneft* case (and further cases as well).[18] These sanctions are riven with legal issues. When, after the heavy 2022 sanctions targeting the Russian central bank, Putin decided to accept payment for gas and oil only in roubles, the question arose as to the

[13] Mackinder (2015), p. 90.

[14] It is discussed below in Sect. 2.1.4.

[15] Correljé and van der Linde (2006), p. 532.

[16] Overland (2015).

[17] Rangel Hernandez (2022), p. 15.

[18] On which see also Chaps. 4 and 7.

compatibility of such payment with the EU's restrictive measures. When, following re-election in April 2022, the Hungarian President Orban decided to halt or delay the adoption of sanctions against Russian gas and oil, other Member States looked for options to bypass the unanimity requirement and thus create, de facto, a political majority.

For gas, a similar pattern holds: the EU imports 70% of its natural gas. Russia is the main supplier (over 40%), especially to Germany, Italy, and Eastern Europe; followed by Algeria (16%) and Norway (7.6%).[19] There are two main pipelines (Yamal and Brotherhood-Soyuz) from Russia into the EU. From Yamal (through Belarus and Poland to Frankfurt an der Oder; and through Slovakia to Vienna) Nord Stream detaches and reaches Germany through the Baltic Sea. Brotherhood-Soyuz, in the south, goes through Ukraine to Italy. As part of the efforts to reduce dependence on Russian gas, in 2008 the EU proposed the creation of the Southern Gas Corridor: from the Caspian Sea (Azerbaijan) through Turkey, gas is now imported to Greece, the Balkans, and Italy. From Hassi R'Mel in Algeria (which is also planned to receive gas from Nigeria through the desert), three streams detach: Maghreb-Europe (Morocco-Andalusia, not operational since Morocco and Algeria broke diplomatic relations in 2021), Medgaz (Algeria-Andalusia) and Trans-Mediterranean (Tunisia-Sicily). From Norway, pipelines flow into ports in the north (such as Dunkerque in France and Rotterdam in the Netherlands) (Fig. 2.2).

The EU is set to replace 50% of gas imports from Russia within a year, through pipelines from Norway, Algeria, and Azerbaijan—but the remaining 50% must come from alternative sources. Thus, the choice to halt the operation of the new and highly controversial gas pipeline Nordstream-2 (set to bring gas directly from Russia to Germany, 'bypassing' Eastern Europe) carried significant symbolic weight.

Other "critical"[20] raw materials such as tungsten (used for armour-piercing ammunition and electrodes), rubber (used for many common use items, from gloves to pacifiers), lithium (for batteries), magnesium (the third most used metal after iron and aluminium)[21] are becoming indispensable to ensure technological independence—but are to be found outside the EU (except for Hafnium and Strontium, found respectively in France and Spain and used for nuclear reactors, microprocessors, and medicine). They tend to be concentrated in few (often extremely poor and politically unstable[22]) countries giving rise again to the geopolitical

[19] Rangel Hernandez (2022), p. 15.

[20] To use the terminology of EU institutions, see e.g. European Green Deal [COM(2019) 640] and (European Commission. Directorate General for Internal Market, Industry, Entrepreneurship and SMEs, 2020).

[21] Currently, the number critical raw materials range from 30 to 60 depending on how economic importance and supply risk are weighted and assessed. Bauxite, Lithium and Titanium, for example, were not considered critical 2017, rubber was not critical in 2014 etc.

[22] The relationship between energy resources and political instability is sometimes referred to as 'the curse of raw materials' (OECD, 2008).

Fig 2.2 Main Russian gas pipelines to Europe. *Source* Wikipedia

asymmetry between exporter and importer. Here, China is 'the new Russia',[23] in so far as it supplies over 40% of EU's raw materials. Other important players are the USA (Beryllium—used for computer and missile components), South Africa (Iridium and Platinum—for semiconductors), and Turkey.

[23] Rangel Hernandez (2022), p. 19.

2.1.3 Geopolitics of Demography

Europe (excluding Russia) has around 600 million inhabitants, less than 10% of the world's population. Of these, around 450 million live in the EU.[24] Demographics matter in world politics, and the European Commission is aware of it.[25] Europeans have fewer children than they did before, the population is ageing (the proportion of people over 65 years being projected to rise from one fifth in 2019 to one third in 2070), and the workforce (people aged 20–64) is steadily declining.

In a context in which the EU's population size is shrinking (in absolute terms and relative to the opposite trend in China and India[26]), migration is key. Net migration in the EU increased considerably from the mid-1980s onwards and was the main determinant of population growth since the 1990s—even though not even net migration could offset the number of deaths in 2020 and 2021, resulting in a decrease in population in the past 2 years.

It also means that the markets which are burgeoning are a geopolitical reality impossible to ignore. Interdependence is a feature of the world in which the EU finds itself.

2.1.4 Geopolitics of Water

The importance of oceans and seas is immediate not only because they separate but also because they join: roughly 80% of international trade takes place through maritime or fluvial transport.

Europe has many natural harbours by virtue of its naturally indented coastline. The EU alone has a coastline that is 68,000 km long—more than three times longer than that of the United States and almost twice that of Russia. Almost half of the EU population lives less than 50 km from the sea.[27] Classic geopolitics may insist on the importance of the heartland, but it is beyond doubt that Europe is—or at least was—a sea-oriented continent.[28] It would be impossible to talk about modern-day Europe without dedicating space to the Mediterranean.[29] It is through the sea that 'civilisation' arrived in modern day Europe. It is through the same sea that the Phoenicians

---

[24] EUROSTAT (2022).

[25] Borrell (2020).

[26] European Parliament. Directorate General for Parliamentary Research Services (2021), p. 1.

[27] European Environment Agency (2020).

[28] From the Odissey to the Portuguese national poem Lusiades, which begins: 'As armas e os barões assinalados,/Que da ocidental praia Lusitana,/Por mares nunca de antes navegados...' (in an English translation: 'Arms and the Heroes, who from Lisbon's shore, Thro' seas where sail was never spread before...').

[29] The standard is the three-volume work Braudel (2017a, 2017b, 2017c); A recent history is Abulafia (2011); an account of definitions according to other sciences is Daget (1984).

first, the city states of Hellas and the Romans then, united the Mediterranean world (later the Arab conquest united only the southern shores, a unity maintained until the demise of the Ottoman Empire).[30]

Now, of course, that geopolitical world has been profoundly shaken—and modern day Greece or Lebanon cannot have any pretence over Western Mediterranean (in fact, Greece's geopolitics is, to a very significant extent, predicated on controlling the Aegean), nor can Italy on the East (as it did until the 30s, when it invaded Albania). Yet, the important harbours of the Mediterranean still play a crucial role in the EU, albeit far less than what they used to in antiquity: that distinctive Mediterranean culture[31] is not central anymore (and this profound geopolitical transformation is analysed in Chap. 7). Now, the EU has three harbours in the top 20 in the world by volume of goods in transit (Rotterdam, Antwerp, Hamburg, part of the so-called Northern range with Bremen and Le Havre). To be sure, the Mediterranean ports have improved the volume of their activities thanks to the doubling of the Suez Canal in 2015: 5 of the top 10 harbours in Europe are Mediterranean (Valencia, Piraeus, Algeciras, Barcelona and Tangier).

Technology has not made geography obsolete either. In the era of cyberoperations, flows of information and people rely, instead, on physical objects. Some of these objects are on the seabed (cables),[32] with landing sites in the in Marseille for the Mediterranean or northern ports for the Atlantic.[33] Ensuring the maintenance and security of these communication cables has become extremely relevant for islands (Malta and Ireland in particular, as they are fully dependent on subsea cable, but also the Canaries, Madeira, and French overseas colonies).[34] Spain and Portugal are crucial for the connectivity to South America and Africa; France and Italy for connectivity to Asia; Denmark and the Netherlands for North America. A PeSCo project,[35] HARMSPRO (coordinated by Italy), is dedicated to the surveillance of sea line of communications and choke points, and another, MUSAS (coordinated by Portugal) to develop a command, control and communication service for anti-submarine warfare.

When it comes to freshwater (that is, the water found in glaciers, lakes, reservoirs, ponds, rivers and underground), one may note that rivers, albeit much shorter by

[30]Hesperia (the land of the sunset) was one of the names of the Italian (then Spanish) peninsula. That same concept, in Arabic, now designates the area of Algeria, Tunisia, and indeed the Western Kingdom (Morocco).

[31]Among the infinite examples one could make of the unity of the Mediterranean until recent: one of the major Italian poets of the twentieth century, Ungaretti (1888–1970), and possibly the most famous modern Greek poet, Kavafis (1863–1933), were born in Alexandria of Egypt, then metropolis of the Mediterranean.

[32]Guilfoyle et al. (2022).

[33]Bueger et al. (2022), p. 19.

[34]Bueger et al. (2022), p. 25.

[35]For PeSCo, see Chap. 5.

comparison to the main rivers of neighbouring Russia[36] and Africa,[37] played an important role in European history (consider the importance of the Rhine as the limit of the Roman Empire; or of the Douro river for the Reconquista; or of the Danube for the 'flow' of culture in the region).[38] Navigable rivers in fact have cross-continent routes (Rhine, Elbe, Danube, Rhone; and in the East the Dnepr and Volga). Add to this the lowland creating horizontal corridors from the Western to the Eastern part of the continent, and here is the recipe for a territory that allows (neither necessitates, nor dictates, nor is perfect for), with the right technology and means of communication, the flourishing of trade. EU water diplomacy will be key to its foreign policy, as the Council stated in its conclusion on Water Diplomacy of November 2018.

2.1.5 Geopolitics of Transports

Even though Europe is characterised by relatively short distances between heartland and sea shores, some important physical barriers are the mountain chains (the Alps separating the Italian peninsula; the Sierra Morena separating Andalusia; the Carpathian mountains and the Balkans); the rivers; and the Channel isolating the continent, as the joke goes, from the UK and Ireland.[39] The short distances and the fact that physical barriers are relatively few has facilitated exchanges and perhaps even economic prosperity[40] between countries in Western and Central or Eastern Europe in the modern era.[41]

At present, significant infrastructure and international hubs in Europe are located on the "blue banana"—that part of territory going roughly from Liverpool in the UK to Milan in Italy, so densely populated that its banana-shape is visible from space at

---

[36] 'Geography determined the paths of Russian expansion. Rivers created corridors of expansion that channeled Russia's advance along clear paths and determined its political, strategic, and commercial objectives; before the construction of railroads there was hardly any substitute for a river-bank for soldiers or merchants.' (LeDonne, 1997, p. xiv).

[37] Meyer et al. (2021).

[38] River basins interesting more than one Member States, or a Member State and a third country, are regulated by Article 13 of the Water Framework Directive. Directive (Directive 2000/60/EC of the European Parliament and of the Council establishing a framework for the Community action in the field of water policy.

[39] Another exception is constituted by the lakes in what geographers call Fennoscandia (Sweden and Finland), which, especially in Finland, have made it historically difficult to move people or resources within the country (Kirby, 2006).

[40] More precisely, one should say that the political organisation of a community influences the use of geography—and consequently economic prosperity. The classic study is Acemoglu and Robinson (2012).

[41] This is a point also implicitly made by Marx in the *Eighteenth Brumaire of Louis Bonaparte* (1852), when he writes that the French peasants could hardly develop class consciousness due to the poor means communication of France.

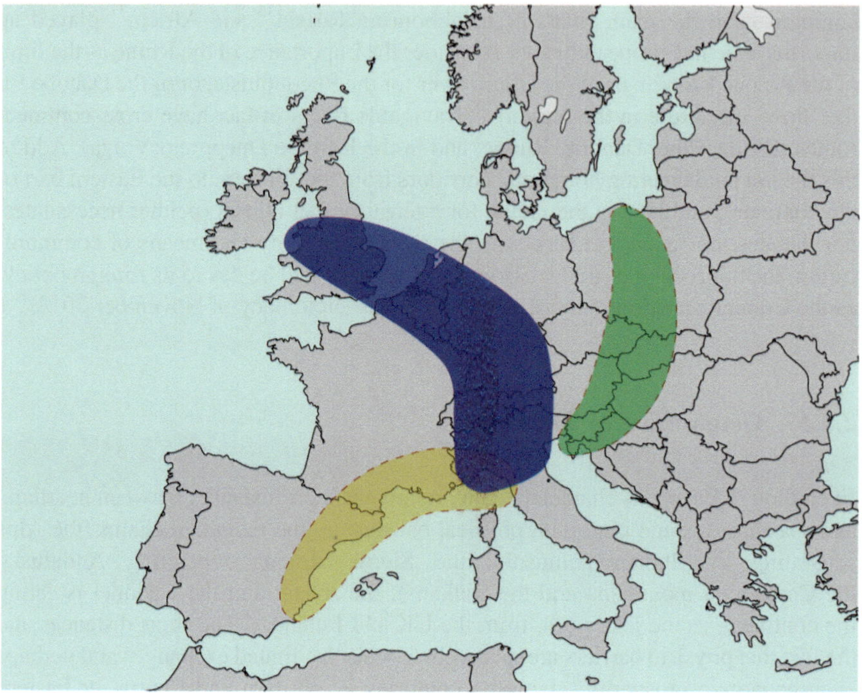

Fig 2.3 Blue, Gold, and Green banana. *Source* Wikipedia

night.[42] In terms of rail network density, the first four countries are the Czech Republic, Belgium, Germany and Luxembourg; in terms of motorway network density, apart from the great capitals, the highest density is in the Randstad region in the West of the Netherlands, as well as around the major northern ports: Rotterdam, Bremen/Bremerhaven, Hamburg.[43] In a study carried out for the European Commission, the author shows that the accessibility of passenger flights (that is, the amount available passenger flights in the nearest airport) is highest in the areas of London, Paris, Ramstad-Brussels, Frankfurt and Zurich region (once again, the blue banana)—and, more interestingly, that only in Eastern Europe (Bulgaria, some regions of Romania, Eastern Poland and rural Latvia and Lithuania) there are areas in which the road trip to the nearest airport takes more than 90 min;[44] but this situation changes significantly for intercontinental flights, of which, outside the blue banana, there are virtually none available within a 90 min car ride.

Bananas started multiplying when geographers started referring to the region on the Mediterranean coast from Valencia to Genoa as "the Golden Banana" (or the European Sunbelt); and there is even the Green Banana—stretching from the coast of Croatia to Gdansk (including Zagreb, Vienna, Krakow, Warsaw, as well as the arrival ports of the Druzhba oil pipelines from Russia) (Fig. 2.3).

---

[42] The expression was coined in 1989 by the researchers led by geographer Roger Brunet.

[43] EUROSTAT (2022).

[44] Poelman (2013). These tend to be less densely populated areas.

In geopolitical terms, a distinction is drawn between those who control the means of transports (the geopolitical Subjects) and those who use them (mobility Subjects).[45] Naturally, the conditions of accessibility of the transport networks are constrained by geographical features but controlled to a large extent by the geopolitical subject: this control being largely a political issue—as opposed to a legal one. What sociological studies of mobility in Europe illuminate that some of us (what Favell calls "Eurostars"[46]) exercise free-movement routinely, especially among the North-Western cities (where some chase dreams and promises, in whose anonymity some find refuge, while others simply are attracted by prosperity). This is not the experience of most Europeans, who are born and bred (and live and work) within the territory of their nation State. The latest intra-EU labour mobility report, published in 2021 by the European Commission, found that 'without looking at data for the UK as a country of residence, the total amount of working-age EU-28 movers [EU citizens who live in an EU Member State other than their country of citizenship] in 2019 was 10.4 million'. This is a mere 2% of the EU's population.

2.2 History and Size of Member States

The intricacies of EU foreign policy originate also in the vast differences and asymmetries between the Member States with regards to their history and size, system of alliances, priorities, hard power, and bureaucratic organisation[47]—all factors influenced, in ways that are impossible to quantify, by geography. It may be possible that reaching common decisions on foreign policy proves harder than on other matters (hence, it is more difficult to have a common foreign policy than a common commercial policy): this is partly due to the characteristics of Member States (outlined below), and because of the characteristics of foreign policy itself, which encompasses an existential requirement (security). Most importantly, asymmetry is a key feature in the distribution of assets between MSs:[48] the United Kingdom until it was a member, and France were key players and, in fact, game changers. Why? Because in collective decision making, if one of the agents is 'too big', it has selfish reasons both to cooperate and not cooperate[49] which can determine the outcome of the 'game'.[50]

The history of European nations saw the birth of modern diplomacy.[51] For the purposes of this book, it will suffice to recall that traditionally, the capacity to enter

45 Ampleman (2021).

46 Favell (2008).

47 Angelucci and Isernia (2019), p. 2.

48 Dashwood (2014), p. 10.

49 As Schelling put it, 'with enough military force a country may not need to bargain.' (Schelling, 2008, p. 1). No EU country is in such a position.

50 Elster (2015), p. 385.

51 The classic study is Mattingly (2008).

relations with other states is the essential hallmark of sovereignty—and indeed the need to manage these relations coincided, during the establishment and ascension of the nation state in Europe, with the birth of professional diplomacy.

The UK (which was an EU member until 1 February 2020) and France, among the oldest nation-states in the world, harboured the birth of modern political and administrative systems in Europe such as parliamentary democracy, the democratic republic, and centralised administration. Arguably, the Kingdom of England did it even before France, at least in so far as it asserted that positive law was superior even to the authority of the King:[52] this is, in essence, the rule of law. Some, such as the great historian Toynbee, consider this precocity of Britain to be due to geography: by virtue of being an island, Great Britain had fewer security threats and this helped its economic and political development (why this would lead to the rule of law, however, is not explained).[53] Be that as it may, those were models to which all other European states aspired to—and often adopted.[54] Echoes of empires are still felt pervasively in Europe's geography[55] and EU foreign policy.[56] France and the UK have been heads of global empires and have topped the might of military power for decades before the twentieth century.[57] EU law applies to 'overseas countries and territories' (effectively, colonies) worldwide.[58] Algeria was part of metropolitan France when the Treaty of Rome was signed. France and the UK still have the full spectrum of nuclear capabilities and sit as permanent Members in the UN Security Council, making France the only current Member State with these characteristics. In terms of traditional forces, the UK and France have respectively the 7th and 5th biggest defence budget in the world (in absolute terms), while within the EU France has the highest defence budget and the second biggest army by size (after Finland).[59] Their colonial legacy also means that they have a powerful and widespread diplomatic network: embassies and consulates in virtually every capital of the world. At the same time, it shall be noted that the UK has contributed little, in relative terms, to

[52] Reference is usually made to the work of a most influential British judge, Sir Edward Coke (1552–1634), who 'argued for a single set of laws, common throughout the realm, according to which liberty and property would be reliably regulated, without the recurrent loss of liberty that accompanied courts held as special privileges by local lords, crown administrators, and church officials. The law, as Coke articulated it, protected the individual from tyrannical abuse'. Coke and Sheppard (2003), p. xxvi.

[53] Toynbee and Somervell (1987), p. 237.

[54] Consider how, during the Enlightenment attempts at centralisation took place in many European countries (Spain, Austria-Hungary, and later with the objective of unification also in Italy and Germany). In Russia, the attempt of Ivan the Terrible in the same direction was brutally violent (*opritchina*) and largely unsuccessful.

[55] Noxolo (2017), p. 318.

[56] Weldeab Sebhatu (2021); Onar and Nicolaïdis (2013).

[57] The best historical study of empires in the early stages of European integration is Garavini and Nybakken (2012); Hansen and Jonsson (2014) is useful for the influence of empires on the negotiations of the Rome Treaty.

[58] These are French and Dutch overseas territories, and Greenland.

[59] Tian et al. (2018).

CSDP mission personnel,[60] and this is perfectly in line with the reticence shown by that Member State concerning further integration in defence commitments,[61] whereas the financial contributions are more difficult to assess but appear to be substantial.[62]

Germany is a special case: it has the biggest diplomatic service in the EU, but its military power is not nearly comparable to the French or British one. This is so for the peculiar history of the country, which, after the political, economic, and moral devastation of the two World Wars, had been divided into two halves for a long period of the twentieth century and has a constitutional adversity to employing the military. By reason of its geographic location at the heart of Europe, Germany's destiny is inextricably linked to the political destiny of the continent. In geopolitical terms, the Rhine is crucial. It acts as a means of transportation, a resource, and for millennia acted as a 'natural border'. First, between the Roman Empire and the 'Barbarians'; then as the (highly contested) border of the French Kingdom:[63] now, the European Parliament's plenary seat is there, in Strasbourg—the heart of contested Europe. Once more, legacies of empires are relevant: the Carolingian Kingdom—and later the Holy Roman Empire—had their core in regions that comprise modern-day Germany, on the Rhine axis linking the Nordic ports to the rich hinterland, and heralded the 'turn' of Europe away from the Mediterranean and toward the European heartland.

Middle players are Italy, Spain, and Poland, both in terms of size and population and of foreign policy weight. The hard power,[64] that is, the military and economic might of the countries mentioned up to this point is significantly greater than that of the remaining countries. While Polish security interests are mostly oriented towards the EU's eastern neighbours, Spain and Italy concentrate their interests in the Mediterranean region (and, due to colonial legacy, Spain is particularly close to central and South America). While Spain achieved unity early despite being a multi-

---

[60] Figures on the participation of UK's military and civilian personnel were 'modest in comparative terms compared to France, Germany, Italy and even Austria. They are comparable with Greece in terms of overall contributions since 2003'. Written evidence from Dr Simon Duke to the House of Lords European Union Committee, 'Brexit: Common Security and Defence Policy missions and operations' (2018) HL Papers/132 36.

[61] In addition to avoid duplication with NATO tasks and opportunity cost of deploying personnel, the UK's limited participation may be due to the fact that the UK's troops are 'operationally oriented towards higher-intensity missions than those offered by the CSDP portfolio of engagements' (ibid 37).

[62] Ibid 38.

[63] It was a project of revolutionary France to regain that territorial extension, and the 1795 Treaty of Basle, which ended the war of the first coalition against revolutionary France, gave to France precisely that: all territory west of the Rhine (this also prompted Kant to write its articles for a Perpetual Peace (Pagden, 2021, p. 13)). After the 1871 defeat of the Second Empire in Verdun, Germany acquired Alsace-Lorraine; which were lost against with the Treaty of Versailles after the First World War.

[64] Nye (2004).

lingual state,[65] Italy and Poland have been nations split for much of their modern history. Poland was formerly split partly under Prussia, partly under the Kingdom of Poland and the Grand Duchy of Lithuania, and partly under Austria-Hungary. In this crucial region of Central and Eastern Europe, multi-ethnic empires gave way to nation states only in the nineteenth and twentieth centuries.[66] And it was possibly only after the collapse of the Soviet Union that Poland re-acquired geopolitical consciousness, once its Western neighbour (the German Democratic Republic) had been absorbed into the EC and NATO, and the country found itself as a giant in the post-Soviet space that was witnessing the re-birth of Central and Eastern Europe as separate from both Russia and the EU.[67]

Spanish foreign policy is sometimes described as a triangle, at one vertex of which there is Europe (and the EU), and at the two bottom vertexes there are Latin America and the Mediterranean.[68] From the 80s, the new democracy turned increasingly toward Europe (with a process of internationalisation whereby it joined the EC and NATO), while during the dictatorship Spain had developed a national, Mediterranean-based foreign policy.[69] In the 90s, Spain was instrumental in establishing the Barcelona process (the Euro-Mediterranean dialogue that would form the precedent for the Union for Mediterranean).[70]

Italy's security and defence policy since WW2 is best described as Atlanticist, for what the country contributed to (and got from) the NATO alliance, which gave a strong sense of identity to Italy's foreign policy. Italy, like Greece and Turkey, conceived of itself as a 'bridge' between West and East (Italy had the biggest and, in electoral terms, most successful non-governing communist party in Europe) for its geographical location.[71] Italy's commitments in the Mediterranean have increased, if not without hesitation, since the Arab uprisings, which have also significantly affected the country due to the high influx of immigrants.

The borders of those three countries present geopolitical tensions. For example, the Suwałki gap (or corridor), is the narrowest point (about 100 km) between Belarus and the Russian exclave of Kaliningrad.[72] This is a 'choke point',[73] and acquires crucial geopolitical importance since Kaliningrad is a very militarised area and Belarus has

---

[65] The Basques being an indigenous ethno-linguistic group. Basque is one of the few non-Indo-- European languages spoken in the EU.

[66] Thus Pan Tadeusz (1834), the epic of Poland's national poet Adam Mickewicz, who was born in modern-day Belarus, begins with the line 'O Lithuania, my homeland!'.

[67] Kuzniar (2008).

[68] Izuel et al. (2007).

[69] Arteaga (2020).

[70] On which see below, Sect. 2.5.

[71] Del Pero (2015), p. 685 'One needs, however, to seriously stretch the meaning of geography to render Italy "North Atlantic".' (On Italian geopolitical thought, Brighi and Petito, 2012 is strongly recommended.)

[72] Eichler (2021), p. 116.

[73] In military strategy, a choke point is a strait with a narrow width, where only a limited number of ships can pass at a time.

permitted the transit of Russian troops in its territory during the 2022 war in Ukraine. If Russia closed the Suwałki gap, it would surround the Baltic states. For another example, Spain has two land enclaves in Morocco: Ceuta and Melilla. The border, often under the spotlight due to the securitisation it undergoes to prevent illegal crossing from Morocco into EU territory, has complex geopolitical and symbolic functions.[74] This is because there is significant geographical continuity between the two countries (which also have two important harbours (Alcesiras and Tangier) competing for the benefits of the trade through the strait), whereas Spain is neatly separated by the Pyrenees from France and the mountainous reliefs of central Europe. Not surprisingly, during Franco's 'Mediterranean foreign policy',[75] Spanish intellectuals stressed the historical and cultural proximity between Morocco and Spain.[76]

The Be-Ne-Lux countries have reached an outstanding degree of integration between themselves—and have set up a special union within the Union, for fiscal purposes. Their weight in foreign policy matters is greatly enhanced by their EU membership, and their positions tends to be, broadly speaking, aligned.

The so-called Nordic Club (Denmark, Sweden, and Finland) have traditionally had a distinctive approach to security. This changed with the Russian invasion of Ukraine of 2022. Under EU law, Denmark was not bound by decisions with security implications,[77] until a popular referendum in 2022 changed it. Sweden and Finland had remained faithful to their traditional Cold War strategy of non-alignment and were not NATO members until they decided to join in the spring of the same year. The Sami people, living in the Arctic region, are a significant minority living in the Sápmi, spanning the territory of modern-day Norway, Sweden, Finland and Russia. Their geopolitical significance lies in the contribution they can give to challenges in the Arctic,[78] and in the way they represent themselves and are represented.[79] First, they inhabit a cross-border territory, a fact which resulted in a schism when Sami in Russia sided with Putin after the 2022 invasion of Ukraine.[80] Second, as a matter of EU law, the region they inhabit is subject to important derogations (like mount Athos in Greece),[81] calling into question the unitary concept of territory of the EU.[82] Third, Sami's fight for 'indigenous' rights shows the often-neglected existence of

[74] Ferrer-Gallardo (2008).

[75] Huguet Santos (1996).

[76] Thus the Andalusian nationalist Gil Benumeya (Gil Benumeya, 1960).

[77] Protocol 22 on the Position of Denmark attached to the TFEU (OJ C 326/1).

[78] Arctic challenges and EU policy are presented in Chap. 6.

[79] Needless to say, the issue of (self-representation) does not arise only for the Sami people. It is especially critical for any 'subaltern': (Morris & Spivak, 2010).

[80] Last (2022).

[81] Protocol 3 on the Sami people of the Act concerning the conditions of accession of the Kingdom of Norway, the Republic of Austria, the Republic of Finland and the Kingdom of Sweden and the adjustments to the Treaties on which the EU is founded [1994] OJ C241/352.

[82] Article 52 TEU. See (Kellerbauer et al., 2019, p. 355).

indigenous geopolitics in Europe.[83] Finland, Estonia, and Hungary are the only countries in Europe where Finno-Ugric languages are spoken (several millions Finno-Ugric speakers live, instead, in the Russian steppes). Some linguists link Finno-Ugric languages to the Altaic ones (Turco-Mongolic and Tungusic),[84] the languages spoken by the nomadic tribes of the central Asian steppes: precisely those populations who, according to influential geographers, shaped the destiny of Europe.

In terms of size and population, Portugal, Greece, the Czech Republic, Austria and Hungary are roughly comparable: but the past duration of their membership in the EU, their security concerns, and their stances towards European integration differ greatly. Portugal's membership (since the creation of the alliance) in NATO was necessary to hold strategic bases (in the Azores in the Atlantic). Greece's NATO membership, starting in 1952 like Turkey's, had the rationale to foreclose a Soviet access to the Mediterranean: between the end of World War Two and the early 50s, many states in central and eastern Europe, including the Balkans, were in the hands of Communist parties, turning the buffer zones of Italy, Greece, and Turkey into key geopolitical battlegrounds between liberal democracies and communism, West and East, US and Soviet Union. By the time Portugal and Greece joined in the 80s, transitioning to democracy after dictatorships, the security and military situation was less dramatic, but after the breakup of Yugoslavia, Greece has had a tense relationship with North Macedonia (accused of appropriating names and symbols in a way that betrays expansionistic aims), and still has a conflictual relationship with Turkey.[85] The name dispute with North Macedonia was solved thanks to UN mediation in 2018. Even though Hungary and the Czech Republic share some similarities (both formerly part of the Austro-Hungarian Empire, then of the Warsaw Pact, which in fact invaded in 1956 and 1968 respectively, and both joined NATO in 1999 and the EU in 2004), the Czech Republic perceives its geopolitical destiny firmly towards the Euro-Atlantic area, whereas Hungary, has been much more ambiguous, and has close ties with Russia and China which have resulted in awkwardness in EU security and defence.[86]

Bulgaria and Romania are somewhat special cases: members since 2007, their nationals initially enjoyed limited free movement. Romania and Bulgaria host a great part of Europe's most significant ethnic minority, the Roma,[87] who have long been subject to racism and seclusion in the continent and are now, arguably, Europe's most stigmatised internal 'other'.[88] Bulgaria is the only southern Slavic nation not to

[83] The word indigenous is in itself a contested notion (Purcell, 1998).

[84] Schott (1836).

[85] Necessary reading on Greek security and defence is Dokos (2020).

[86] At least since the current president, Orbán, has taken on an identity battle against the values of the EU, as best exemplified by his 2014 speech: https://budapestbeacon.com/full-text-of-viktor-orbans-speech-at-baile-tusnad-tusnadfurdo-of-26-july-2014/.

[87] Encompassing under this umbrella terms as diverse groups as Roma, Sinti, Kale, Romanichels, Boyash/Rudari, Ashkali, Egyptians, Yenish, Dom, Lom, Rom and Abdal.

[88] Hansson (2022).

be part of the former Yugoslavia; it was a close ally of the Soviet Union instead.[89] Its Western part is in the Balkans, the East is a plain on the Black Sea. Romania is, roughly speaking, split into two by the arc of the Carpathians Mountains (the Western part being, geographically, a continuation of the Hungarian plaines).

Finally, there are small and very small states. Slovenia and Croatia are southern Slavic nations, part of former Yugoslavia (and in fact the first to be recognised as independent countries upon declaring independence). Slovenia's independence was (almost) without loss of life; Croatia, instead, fought a war (1991–1995). Slovenia joined the EU in 2004, Croatia in 2013. Still significant border disputes exist between them (see the *Slovenia v Croatia*[90] case). The Baltic states, which joined in 2004, are the only area of the EU with a significant Russophone minority (especially Latvia).[91] Together with Finland, they were part of the empire until 1917, thus sharing an important part of their history with Russia (the three Baltic countries were also annexed to the Soviet Union in 1940 pursuant to the Molotov-Ribbentrop Pact, even though they never recognised their incorporation into the USSR). The three of them gained independence from it in 1991, and they joined the EU in 2004, always together. They border with the most important neighbour of the EU, Russia, but they have differences between them in terms of ethnicity and language. In addition, Estonia and Latvia were conquered by the Teutonic Knights (Prussia's name deriving from another Baltic nation, extinct by the Teutons) and are largely Protestant (bar a Russian minority), whereas Lithuania was part of the (Catholic) *Respublica* of Poland-Lithuania. Malta and Cyprus, Mediterranean islands and former British colonies (Cyprus being part of the Commonwealth), are at the core of the geopolitical tensions in the area.[92] Malta, being the closest (with the Italian Pantelleria, Lampedusa and Linosa) EU territory to Tunisia and Libya, receives a constant flow of immigrants from the southern shore of the sea. Cyprus is split into two, since in 1974 Turkey established a de facto presence in the north (Northern Cyprus has a majority of Cypriot Turks, the Republic of Cyprus of Greek Cypriots). Officially, EU law applies to the entirety of the island. Despite the talks, mediated by the UN and resulting in a referendum (2004) in which the north was overwhelmingly in favour, and the south equally overwhelmingly against reunification, the status quo continues. It creates awkward situations, affecting the EU's and NATO credibility, as the tensions between Greece, Cyprus, and Turkey spill over to other issues both within the EU (where Cyprus and Greece are members) and within NATO (where Turkey and Greece are members).

[89] Bulgarian was at the basis of old ecclesiastic Slavic, the language used by Byzantium in the process of Christianisation of the Rus of Kiev.

[90] Case C-457/18 *Republic of Slovenia v Republic of Croatia* ECLI:EU:C:2020:65.

[91] Indeed, the Russians in the Baltic countries tend to be 'ethnic Russians' (*russkie*), as opposed to mere citizens of Russia (*rossiyane*).

[92] For the communication connection of these islands, see Bueger et al. (2022), pp. 25–26.

2.3 System of Alliances

European history is rich in alliances between MSs and between some MSs and non-EU countries. For our purposes, the most important instance of the latter is the North Atlantic Treaty Organisation, which has a significant overlapping membership with the EU (22 MSs in common),[93] and instead includes European non-EU countries such as Norway or Turkey. The weight of NATO over CFSP's genesis and functioning cannot be overstated: for example, the mutual defence clause of Article 42(7) specifies that it shall not encroach on the defence commitments of some MSs, thus implying some form of superiority of NATO commitments over CFSP duties.[94] Due to the Cyprus issue, and the only partially overlapping membership, the relationship between the EU and NATO has often not worked as smoothly as the common interests would have led to believe. The Organization for Security and Co-operation in Europe (OSCE) is a product of the Cold War (originating with 1975 Helsinki Conference) in which all European countries participated, as well as the US, Canada and Central Asian states). Another alliance was the Western European Union—which was officially dissolved from the entry into force of the Lisbon Treaty. Formal and informal alliances all contribute to a European foreign policy as well as to the formation of the EU's foreign policy. Negotiations with Iran to end the country's nuclear programme, for example, were conducted by the EU3+3 formation, that is, UK, France, and Germany, together with USA, Russia, and China, under the auspices of the High Representative of the EU's Common Foreign and Security Policy (this format was also known as the 5+1). The 2013–2014 crises in Ukraine often reached important milestones, such as the 2015 ceasefire with the 'Minsk II' agreement,[95] through the Normandy format (foreign ministers of France and Germany + Russia and Ukraine). Within the EU, MSs organise themselves in what in International Relations scholarship are defined as 'contact groups', that is, temporary alliances of states with common interests and priorities, mostly to solve crises: Big Three (Germany, France, Italy), Weimar Triangle (Poland, Germany, and France), Visegrad Four (the Czech Republic, Hungary, Poland and Slovakia),

---

[93] Ireland, Cyprus, Malta, and Austria are the EU non-NATO Members (Sweden and Finland having signed accession protocols by June 2022 and only needing ratification).

[94] It appears in fact that, in technical terms, measures adopted on the basis of CSDP can be pre-empted by Member States' action, and especially by NATO commitments: this is the wording of Article 42(2), and the concept is re-stated in Protocols 10 and 11 and Declarations 13 and 14 on CFSP. CFSP in general, and CSDP in particular, is not supreme over 'actual or potential' acts or agreements entered into by Member States, before or after membership, either with third countries (as it is in any case made clear by Article 351 TFEU) or even *inter se*. This would also necessitate the conclusion that, contrary to the case law on other areas of EU law, Article 351 TFEU can also be invoked in the relations between the Member State parties to an agreement with foreign security and defence implications and of which third countries are also contracting parties.

[95] The first Minsk agreement was a ceasefire signed in September 2014 by Ukraine, Russia, the People's Republic of Lugansk and the People's Republic of Donetsk—under the auspices of the OSCE.

Quartet (UK, USA, Russia, and UN Secretary General), etc. The picture of European foreign policy is fluid and volatile: and far more complex than the sum of EU foreign policy or MSs foreign policy. Moreover, all EU MSs are members of the United Nations and the European Convention for Human Rights (ECHR) among others, and obligations of MSs under the UN Charter are heavily relied upon in the fundamental Treaties. Indeed it is evident, even at a cursory glance, that international law plays a significant role in CFSP, albeit what exactly this role is has not been conclusively defined. Here, it must be recalled that while the EU has a constitutional commitment to join the ECHR (Article 6 TEU), the ECJ has found that accession cannot take place due to its curtailed jurisdiction over the provisions of CFSP.[96] Accession would create a situation in which an international court (the European Court for Human Rights) would have the power to hear cases and solve controversies over matters (the CFSP) in which the ECJ itself does not have jurisdiction. This, the ECJ held, would be liable to negatively affect the principle of autonomy of EU law. The legal distinctiveness of CFSP, thus, prevents, at present, accession.

2.4 The Bureaucratic Organisation

The bureaucratic dimension is also significant in shaping EU foreign policy. Traditionally, matters of security and defence, signature of treaties, and trade relations with other states were the competence of the foreign ministers. Today, foreign ministries no longer possess the lion's share of diplomacy. Some might argue that what we have experienced in recent years has been an increasing 'presidentialisation' of foreign policy.[97] Originally, this took place in the discussion on economic matters, to solve the crisis that hit the EU in 2007–2008. A highly diplomatically sensitive issue, it was not confined to diplomats: instead, it was the ministers of economics who have played a more prominent role, as standard narratives of the EU response to the crisis shows. Then, the discussion took place not at ministerial level, but at the top of the decision-making hierarchy, at presidential level: for example in the discussions in the European Council on the migration crisis.

While the increased involvement of the top-executive in diplomacy enhances legitimacy, visibility, and accountability, it may have the downside of neglecting a long-term view. But the 'presidentialisation' of foreign policy may hardly be

[96]Opinion 2/13 [EU accession to ECHR] ECLI:EU:C:2014:2454.

[97]An example of this is the Normandy format for dealing with the crisis in Ukraine.(de Galbert, 2015); some political scientists traced back the phenomenon to the 'personalisation' of politics that would have taken place in the 80s, when, emptied of ideologies, parties would have come to be identified with their leaders (Cotta & Verzichelli, 2016).

established by anything more than anecdotal evidence. The phenomenon cannot be sufficiently circumscribed so as to establish a trend.[98]

Be that as it may, Ministries of Foreign Affairs within the EU vary significantly in size, and so does the diplomatic presence and outreach of each MS, also for the historical reasons outlined above. Similarly, career patterns of diplomats are different in different MSs, and across generations.[99] Finally, diplomatic culture is not uniform throughout the EU, and the 2004 enlargement posed the most significant challenge in that respect, only partially met, as the book shows, by the creation of the EEAS.

2.5 The Neighbourhood and Possible Future Enlargements

After the accession of 10 new Member States became official in 2002, UK and Sweden proposed an initiative aimed at rethinking the EU's relationship with its new and old neighbours. This initiative was translated, by the Commission, into a new policy, the European Neighbourhood Policy (ENP). Following pressure from southern states, it would also include Mediterranean neighbours (already involved, since 1995, in the so-called Barcelona process of Euro-Mediterranean dialogue). In this century, it is mostly outside the EU that Member States acted in the Mediterranean.[100] In 2007, French President Nicolas Sarkozy launched the idea of a Union for the Mediterranean between the countries bordering the sea. The vision was to bring France to the fore in the Mediterranean Basin through this Union, but the declared objective was to promote stability, commerce, development and a friendly neighbourhood. The UfM originally envisaged by Sarkozy was not entirely outside EU structures: it would have drawn from EU resources as well as expertise and existing programmes. But this made it a politically difficult project, as it could end up needlessly duplicating the ENP, and non-Mediterranean EU members felt they would be excluded. The end result of a compromise agreed between Sarkozy and its EU partners was to have an intergovernmental UfM completely separate from the EU, with its own budget and secretariat (in Barcelona). As of today, EU Member States and 15 other Mediterranean countries are members to it. But what is interesting to remark is that those political developments triggered a process focusing on the

[98]Virtually all MSs could lay claim to presidentialisation of foreign policy any time after WW2. For the debate on presidentialisation of foreign policy in Finland before the 2000 Constitution, see e.g. (Anckar, 1984; Huru, 1993).

[99]For how career patterns of Member States' diplomats shape the composition and quality of the EEAS, see (Morgenstern-Pomorski, 2018).

[100]Written before the Arab uprisings, but still necessary read is Cardwell (2011). The EU's engagement in the Mediterranean sea is fairly limited, and the Union for the Mediterranean descibed below is not only outside the EU, but in fact it triggered a political reaction of focusing on the East instead. In addition to the ENP, the EU engaged in the Mediterranean sea with the Frontex-led operation Triton and the CSDP naval operations (Sophia and Irini) on which see Chap. 5.

East instead: as Missiroli notes, 'the tension or geographic polarisation between East and South that the ENP had tried to cancel resurfaced inevitably under the pressure of interests and preferences of national governments'.[101]

The ENP is thus the result of a compromise between attention 'to the East' and 'to the South' that merges as different countries as Morocco and Belarus, Ukraine and Israel, and since 2004, after the so-called Rose Revolution in Georgia, also countries of Southern Caucasus. Russia decided not to be part of this new 'neighbourhood', an EU policy which guarantees significant financial benefits for the participating non-EU countries (Morocco being the recipient of the largest sum in absolute terms). The one-size-fit-all approach of the policy was in fact predicated on the same rationale of enlargement, but without this perspective: the EU establishes conditionality with a view to bring closer those countries economic, political, and administrative systems, but without any promise of membership (except for the Western Balkans[102]). This changed little until the 2022 Russian war against Ukraine, which was revolutionary also in this respect: Ukraine, Moldova, and Georgia presented a formal request to join the EU. After the June 2022 European Council, there are seven recognised candidates for membership of the European Union: Turkey (applied in 1987), North Macedonia (2004), Montenegro (2008), Albania (2009), Serbia (2009), Ukraine (2022), and Moldova (2022). Bosnia and Herzegovina is a 'potential candidate'. This means that the Commission is in bilateral negotiations to finalise accession: the process is largely political (it is not inconceivable that the negotiations be swift, and the adjustment of the country's legal and administrative system take place after membership), usually takes several years, and requires approval by all Member States. Bosnia and Herzegovina, Georgia and Kosovo (whose independence is not recognised by five EU member states) are considered potential candidates for membership.

Relations with the neighbours are not governed through the CFSP but through a mixture of bilateral agreements (usually, Association Agreements, AA) and the ENP. The Commission's Directorate General for External Relations is chiefly responsible for those, even though there is an increasingly large proportion of matters related to CFSP, whose presence creates issues of coherence and uncertainty with the procedure for the conclusions of the agreement discussed in the next chapters.[103] There are many variations of an AA, depending on the depth of the economic, social, and political ties the parties want to establish. In addition, Declaration 3, concerning Article 8 TEU on the relations with the neighbourhood, specifically provides that 'The Union will take into account the particular situation of small-sized countries which maintain specific relations of proximity with it.'

Russia is inevitably a complex neighbour: it has always been close yet exotic, it occupies part of the geographical space in which there is no geographical border of Europe. Due to a particularly aggressive foreign policy, at the time of writing there is

---

[101] Missiroli (2022), p. 102.

[102] Juncos (2018).

[103] See Chapter further 3 and 7.

virtually no security threat to the EU or its Member States that does not significantly involve Russia, from subsurface sea operations to disinformation campaign, from border issues to the threat of military invasion.[104] The complexity also derives from the fact that it was a multi-ethnic empire (religiously, ethnically, linguistically), and it remains a multi-ethnic federation, with a bureaucratic and administrative system of bewildering complexity. Feminist insights that see the body as a site of (political) contestation[105] also help making sense of the (political) diversity of the country,[106] the Pussy Riot movement—a feminist protest and performance group—and Femen—a Ukrainian feminist activist group—being a case in point. Despite its diversity, the last decades have seen the country pursue a mono-ethnic, imperialistic policy inside and outside its borders. Friendly relationship with the EU—on the rise after the collapse of the Soviet Union—came to an abrupt halt with the war in Georgia in 2008, which put Russia and the EU on a trajectory of conflict. The 2014 seizure of Crimea was the first territorial grab by military means in the living memory of many Europeans.[107] The 2022 invasion of Ukraine acted as a shocking reminder, for many, that war in Europe is possible (something that was never in doubt for people who grew up in the Balkans). EU-Russia relations are governed mainly by a PCA signed in 1997, as well through a number of other bilateral agreements.

Belarus is, one could say, a country in quest for an identity. For centuries part of various states (the Polish-Lithuanian Commonwealth, the Russian Empire, the Soviet Union), the country is now a very close—albeit not unambiguously—ally with Russia, with which it has a Union State and in fact it is party of the Collective Security Organisation (sometimes referred to as the NATO of Central Asia), together with Russia and other Central Asian countries. Before sanctions took effect, the EU was Belarus' second main trade partner, representing 19.9% of the country's overall trade in goods. Russia was Belarus' first trading partner, with 49.0% of Belarus' international trade.[108] EU relations with Belarus are governed by a 1989 TCA.

A similar quest exists for a county at the fringe of geopolitical Europe: Ukraine. The 'Rus' of Kiev was the first state of Eastern Slavs, founded around the year 880 AD. Kiev being on the river Dniepr, which originates in a region not far from where the Volga does, facilitated exchanges between the communities living on the two rivers (it is precisely the cross-peninsula navigation facilitated by the Dniepr that the Varangians Vikings could reach the Black Sea from Scandinavia, giving birth to what would evolve into the Kievan Rus). The centre of power later moved to another

[104] The best introduction to Russian geopolitical thought is by Putin's ideologue Dugin (1997) 'foundations of geopolitics', which can be found in a poor quality English translatin online; Dugin (2015), which is a history of Russia's watershed moments through the lens of geopolitics, is among those available in English; Astrov and Morozova (2012) is an excellent synthesis.

[105] Gökarıksel et al. (2021), p. 10.

[106] Fedorova (2019).

[107] Bossuyt and Elsuwege (2021).

[108] *EU Trade Relations with Belarus* (2022).

Rus, the one of Moscow: a fact at the origin of delicate historiographical debates over the genesis and mutual relationships of present-day Ukraine and present-day Russia. The relationship is further complicated by the fact that the Eastern part of Ukraine was part of the Russian Empire; the western part was in the Polish-Lithuanian Commonwealth, then Austria-Hungary, then again Poland during the two wars. Crimea was Ottoman, and today it is inhabited by a significant majority of Tatars (who had arrived there much before the formation of the Ottoman Empire), and even a small number of Greek-speakers (Greek-speaking sailors colonised the norther part of the Black Sea, the 'pontus euxinus' (hospitable sea) millennia ago). The EU and Ukraine signed a DCFTA in 2014.[109] The 2022 invasion by Russia triggered the immediate reaction to push Ukraine to the West: while it is too early to know how the geopolitics of Europe will mutate as a result, the fact that Ukraine, Moldova and Georgia applied to join the EU, Sweden and Finland to join NATO, signal the direction in which those countries intend to go.

The geographically mountainous region of Caucasus is divided by political borders. Nothern Caucasus is part of the Russian Federation and comprises ethnically, linguistically, and religiously varied Chechnya, North Ossetia, known in Western Europe for incidents with Moscow, and Dagestan among others. Southern Caucasus consists instead of three independent countries. Two are traditionally Christian countries Georgia[110] and Armenia,[111] which tends to be close to Russia; and Azerbaijan, which is a country with a Muslim, Turkic-speaking population (and many ethnic minorities[112]). The Nagorno-Karabakh region (in Azerbaijan but governed by an Armenia-backed, internationally unrecognised government) has been theatre of conflict since the 90s. A war broke out in 2020, ended only with a ceasefire brokered by Russia. With Georgia, the EU has a DCFTA (in force since 2016),[113] with Armenia, it has a CEPA (in force since 2018), and with Azerbaijan it has a PCA (1999).

Turkey is a country that prides itself on being partly in Asia, partly in Europe.[114] Its strategic location lies in fact also in the control over one of the three access points by water to the Mediterranean: the straits of Bosphorus[115] and of the Dardanelles[116]

---

[109] On which see Chap. 6.

[110] Georgia was Christian before Constantin, i.e. even before the Roman empire converted. The Georgian language is quite unique, being one of the few languages of the Kartvelian family.

[111] Coptic-Monophysite. The Amernian language is the only one in the Armenian branch of Indo-European languages.

[112] One of the greatest Persian poets, Nizami Ganjavi (1141–1209), was born in modern-day Azerbaijan.

[113] An evaluation of which is available at Akhvlediani et al. (2022).

[114] Bilgin (2012) explores geopolitical thought in Turkey.

[115] Where the emperor Constantine moved the capital of the Roman empire.

[116] The one that Xerses, the Persian king, tried to travers during the second Persian war of 480 bc, and, failing that, he whipped the sea as punishment—and episode at the basis of Aeschylus tragedy The Persians (472 bc).

(the other two chokepoints being Gibraltar[117] and Suez[118]). In 2020, Turkey was the EU's 6th biggest trade partner (3.6% of the EU's total trade in goods with the world), and the EU was by far Turkey's largest import and export partner.[119] With Turkey, the EU has one of the very first association agreements, dating back to 1963 (with a custom union since 1995).

The Balkans have traditionally been a frontier of Europe.[120] To cut a very long story short, in the nineteenth century, the region was the object of Great Power rivalry and resurgent nationalism, as Britain, Russia and Austria-Hungary sought to exploit the political vacuum that was being caused by the fall of the Ottoman Empire. Nationalism, and international rivalries, exacerbated local tensions and resulted in the incident that constituted the *casus belli* for the outbreak of World War 1. After World War 2, Yugoslavia had the only communist party in Europe who was not in the Cominform, the union of communist parties in Europe. In practice, Yugoslavia was a communist anti-Soviet country. In the post–Cold War period, the Balkans have again emerged as a source of instability, with the break-up of Yugoslavia resulting in bloody wars (for the first time in Europe since WW2). With countries in the Western Balkans, the EU has a special programme, the Stabilisation and Association Process (SAP), within which it concluded agreements (SAAs).

Western Mediterranean countries, on the southern shore, are Morocco, Algeria, and Tunisia, whereas Libya now unites two regions that used to be divided—one looking to the West (Tripolitania, with modern day Tripoli) and one to the East (Cyrenaica, with modern day Benghazi): Syrte, right in the middle, being the ideal watershed between the West and East of the Mediterranean, as well as the frontier of the Byzantine Empire. The remaining three countries are, each, very unequally divided in two by the Atlas Mountains. This is more obvious in the case of Morocco. The north, where the main cities lie, is Mediterranean, Muslim, Arabic (or French/ Spanish) speaking. The Atlas is Berber, and it has sturdily resisted Arabisation (like the Rif mountains in the north) and even Islam; the south is climatically Saharan. So Algeria, on the narrow coastal plain, is Mediterranean—south of the Atlas is desert. In Tunisia, the coast is in the ast (where Carthage, and now Tunis, rise, as well as important ports such as Sfax).

The Eastern Mediterranean traditionally enjoyed a relatively high level of cultural (Hellenistic), linguistic (Greek) and then, through Christianity,[121] also religious

[117] The promontories at the eastern entrance of the strait, 'the pillars of Hercules' were considered the boundary of the ancient world ('dov'Ercule segnò li suoi riguardi, acciò che l'uom più oltre non si metta' Dante, Inferno XXVI, 107).

[118] The opera Aida was commissioned for the occasion of the opening of the Suez Canal.

[119] *EU Trade Relations with Turkey* (2022).

[120] Ancel (1938) remains an astonishingly good read on the physical and political geography of Europe's frontiers.

[121] The orthodox churches recognised by the 451 Council of Chalcedony were the Church of Antiochia (modern day Turkey), of Constantinople (modern day Turkey), of Rome (Italy), of Alexandira (Egypt), of Jerusalem and of Cyprus.

closeness;[122] later, the Arab and Ottoman conquests spread, respectively, the Islamic faith[123] and the Turkic language spoken nowadays in Turkey, but for centuries that could not destroy the Mediterranean *koiné* (common culture). Only much later, romantic notions of nationalism in the north, as well as Arab nationalism in the South-East,[124] are seemingly doing precisely that. Since late 2010, many of the countries in the South Mediterranean were shaken by mass protest movements that go under the collective name of Arab Spring (a slogan to which this book prefers the phrase Arab uprisings).[125] The movements had probably colonial, social and demographic remote causes, and strong emotions as proximate ones. It resulted in further instability in the region, with consequences for EU action addressed throughout the book. Mediterranean countries are also covered by the ENP and have a 'Euro-Mediterranean Agreement establishing an Association' (EMAA) with the EU in force, while Palestine has an interim EMAA in force, whereas Syria and Libya do not.

References

Abulafia, D. (2011). *The great sea: A human history of the Mediterranean*. Oxford University Press.

Acemoglu, D., & Robinson, J. A. (2012). *Why nations fail: The origins of power, prosperity, and poverty* (1st ed.). Crown Business.

Akhvlediani, T., Blockmans, S., Bryhn, J., Gogoberidze, L., Gros, D., Hu, W., Iribarren, D., Kovziridze, T., Kustova, I., Rusu, I., & Shamsfakhr, F. (2022). *Ex-Post Evaluation of the Implementation of the Deep and Comprehensive Free Trade Area between the EU and Its Member States and Georgia* (CEPS).

Ampleman, L. (2021). *Transport geopolitics: Decoding and understanding transport as a source of conflicts*. Springer.

Ancel, J. (1938). *Géographie Des Frontières*. Gallimard.

Anckar, D. (1984). *Folket Och Presidenten: En Författningspolitisk Studie*. Societas Scientiarum Fennica.

Angelucci, D., & Isernia, P. (2019). Politicization and security policy: Parties, voters and the European common security and defense policy. *European Union Politics*, p 146511651985119.

Arteaga, F. (2020). Security and defence policy. In D. Muro & I. Lago (Eds.), *The Oxford handbook of Spanish politics* (pp. 667–682). Oxford University Press.

Astrov, A., & Morozova, N. (2012). Russia: Geopolitics from the Heartland. In S. Guzzini (Ed.), *The return of geopolitics in Europe?* (1st ed., pp. 192–216). Cambridge University Press.

Bilgin, P. (2012). Turkey's "Geopolitics Dogma". In S. Guzzini (Ed.), *The return of geopolitics in Europe?* (1st ed., pp. 151–173). Cambridge University Press.

[122] Obviously, with important exceptions such as the language and religion of the Jewish people.

[123] Except on the mountainous area, where camels had difficulty arriving (see the Christian communities in Armenia, Anatolia, Lebanon, and Greece; Jewish presence in modern day Israel; and in the West, the Atlas mountains in Morocco and the Cordillera Central in Spain were the final frontiers of Arab expansions). Silverstein (2010), p. 6.

[124] Gerges (2018).

[125] Gelvin (2015).

Borrell, J. (2020). *Demography and Europe in the World | EEAS Website.*

Bossuyt, F., & Elsuwege, P. V. (Eds.). (2021). *Principled pragmatism in practice: The EU's policy towards Russia after Crimea.* Brill | Nijhoff.

Braudel, F. (2017a). *La Méditerranée et le monde méditerranéen à l'époque de Philippe II. 1: La part du milieu/Fernand Braudel, Dixième édition.* Armand Colin.

Braudel, F. (2017b). *La Méditerranée et le monde méditerranéen à l'époque de Philippe II. 2: Destins collectifs et mouvements d'ensemble/Fernand Braudel, Dixième édition.* Armand Colin.

Braudel, F. (2017c). *La Méditerranée et le monde méditerranéen à l'époque de Philippe II. 3: Les événements, la politique et les hommes/Fernand Braudel, Dixième édition.* Armand Colin.

Brighi, E., & Petito, F. (2012). Geopolitics "in the Land of the Prince":: A *Passe-Partout* to (global) power politics? In S. Guzzini (Ed.), *The return of geopolitics in Europe?* (1st ed., pp. 127–150). Cambridge University Press.

Bueger, C., Liebetrau, T., & Franken, J. (2022). *Security threats to Undersea Communications Cables and Infrastructure–Consequences for the EU.*

Cacciari, M. (2003). *Geofilosofia Dell'Europa*, Nuova ed. riv. e ampliata, 4. edn. Adelphi.

Cardwell, P. J. (2011). EuroMed, European neighbourhood policy and the Union for the Mediterranean: Overlapping policy frames in the EU's Governance of the Mediterranean*. *JCMS: Journal of Common Market Studies, 49*(2), 219–241.

Cohen, S. B. (1973). *Geography and politics in a world divided* (2d ed.). Oxford University Press.

Coke, E., & Sheppard, S. (2003). *The selected writings and speeches of sir Edward Coke.* Liberty Fund.

Correljé, A., & van der Linde, C. (2006). Energy supply security and geopolitics: A European perspective. *Energy Policy, 34*(5), 532–543.

Cotta, M., & Verzichelli, L. (2016). *Il sistema politico italiano.* Il Mulino.

Daget, P. (1984). Introduction à une théorie générale de la méditerranéité. *Bulletin de la Société Botanique de France. Actualités Botaniques, 131*(2–4), 31–36.

Dashwood, A. (2014). The continuing bipolarity of EU external action. In I. Govaere, E. Lannon, P. van Elsuwege, & S. Adam (Eds.), *The European Union in the World.* Brill | Nijhoff.

de Galbert, S. (2015). *The Impact of the Normandy Format on the Conflict in Ukraine: Four Leaders, Three Cease-Fires, and Two Summits.* Available at "https://www.csis.org/analysis/impact-normandy-format-conflict-ukraine-four-leaders-three-cease-fires-and-two-summits".

Del Pero, M. (2015). Italy and the Atlantic alliance. In E. Jones & G. Pasquino (Eds.), *The Oxford handbook of Italian politics* (1st ed.). Oxford University Press.

Diamond, J. M. (1999). *Guns, germs, and steel: The fates of human societies.* Norton.

Dokos, T. (2020). Defence and security policy. In K. Featherstone & D. A. Sotiropoulos (Eds.), *The Oxford handbook of modern Greek politics* (pp. 567–583). Oxford University Press.

Dugin, A. G. (1997). *Osnovy geopolitiki: geopolitičeskoe buduščee Rossii.* Arktogeja.

Dugin, A. G. (2015). *Last war of the World-Island: The geopolitics of contemporary Russia.* Arktos.

Eichler, J. (2021). *NATO's expansion after the cold war: Geopolitics and impacts for international security.* Springer International Publishing.

Elster, J. (2015). *Explaining social behavior: More nuts and bolts for the social sciences* (2nd ed.). Cambridge University Press.

EU Trade Relations with Belarus (2022). Available at "https://policy.trade.ec.europa.eu/eu-trade-relationships-country-and-region/countries-and-regions/belarus_en".

EU Trade Relations with Turkey (2022). Available at "https://policy.trade.ec.europa.eu/eu-trade-relationships-country-and-region/countries-and-regions/turkey_en".

European Commission. Directorate General for Internal Market, Industry, Entrepreneurship and SMEs. (2020). *Study on the EU's List of Critical Raw Materials (2020): Final Report.* Publications Office.

European Environment Agency (2020) *Europe's Seas and Coasts.* Available at "https://www.eea.europa.eu/themes/water/europes-seas-and-coasts".

European Parliament. Directorate General for Parliamentary Research Services. (2021). *Demographic Outlook for the European Union 2021*. Publications Office.
EUROSTAT. (2022). *Population and Population Change Statistics*. Available at "https://ec.europa.eu/eurostat/statistics-explained/index.php?title=Population_and_population_change_statistics".
Favell, A. (2008). *Eurostars and eurocities: Free movement and mobility in an integrating Europe*. Blackwell Pub.
Febvre, L., Charmasson, T., Mazon, B., & Lüdemann, S. (1999). *L'Europe: Genèse d'une Civilisation: Cours Professé Au Collège de France En 1944-1945*. Perrin.
Fedorova, A. (2019). These Portraits Demonstrate the True Diversity of Russian Society, and the Challenges Still Faced by Minorities. *The Calvert Journal*. Available at "https://www.calvertjournal.com/features/show/11333/st-petersburg-diversity-race".
Ferrer-Gallardo, X. (2008). The Spanish–Moroccan border complex: Processes of geopolitical, functional and symbolic rebordering. *Political Geography, 27*(3), 301–321.
Garavini, G., & Nybakken, R. R. (2012). *After empires: European integration, decolonization, and the challenge from the global south 1957-1986*. Oxford University Press.
Gelvin, J. L. (2015). *The Arab uprisings: What everyone needs to know* (2nd ed.). Oxford University Press).
Gerges, F. A. (2018). *Making the arab world: Nasser, Qutb, and the clash that shaped the middle east*. Princeton University Press.
Gil Benumeya, R. (1960). España, Enlace Entre Europa y Africa. *Revista de Política Internacional, 50–51*, 183–190.
Gökarıksel, B., Hawkins, M., Neubert, C., & Smith, S. (Eds.). (2021). *Feminist geography unbound: Discomfort, bodies, and prefigured futures* (1st ed.). West Virginia University Press.
Guilfoyle, D., Paige, T. P., & McLaughlin, R. (2022). The final frontier of cyberspace: The seabed beyond national jurisdiction and the protection of submarine cables. *International and Comparative Law Quarterly, 71*(3), 657–696.
Hansen, P., & Jonsson, S. (2014). *Eurafrica: The untold history of European integration and colonialism*. Bloomsbury Academic.
Hansson, E. (2022). Subjects supposed to know, believe, and enjoy: The geopolitics of ideological transference in the Swedish begging question. *Political Geography, 98*, 102706.
Huguet Santos, M. (1996). El Mediterráneo En La Teoría Sobre La Política Exterior Del Franquismo. *Studia historica. Historia contemporánea, 13–14*, 215–230.
Huru, J. (Ed.). (1993). *Uuden Ulkopolitiikan Haasteet: Kekkosen Ajasta Koiviston Kautta 2000-Luvulle*. Rauhan ja konfliktintutkimuslaitos.
Izuel, E. B., Mestres i Camps, L., & Soler i Lecha, E. (2007). La Política Mediterránea de España: Entre El Proceso de Barcelona y La Política Europea de Vecindad. *Revista CIDOB d'Afers Internacionals, 79/80*, 35–51.
Juncos, A. (2018). The European Union and the Western Balkans. Enlargement as a security strategy. In S. Economides & J. Sperling (Eds.), *EU security strategies: Extending the EU system of security governance*. Routledge.
Kaplan, R. D. (2013). *The revenge of geography: What the map tells us about coming conflicts and the battle against fate*. Random House Trade Paperbacks.
Kellerbauer, M., Klamert, M., & Tomkin, J. (Eds.). (2019). *The EU treaties and the charter of fundamental rights: A commentary*. Oxford University Press.
Kirby, D. G. (2006). *A concise history of Finland*. Cambridge University Press.
Kuzniar, R. (2008). Geopolitics and Poland's security policy. *Polish Quarterly of International Affairs, 17*(1), 55.
Last, J. (2022). The Ukraine war is dividing Europe's Arctic Indigenous People. *Foreign Policy*.
LeDonne, J. P. (1997). *The Russian Empire and the World, 1700-1917: The geopolitics of expansion and containment*. Oxford University Press.
Mackinder, H. (1904). The geographical pivot of history. *Royal Geographical Society, IV*, 298–321.

Mackinder, H. J. (2015). *Democratic Ideals and Reality: A Study in the Politics of Reconstruction.*
Mattingly, G. (2008). *Renaissance diplomacy.* Cosimo.
Meyer, C., Vantaggiato, F., & Youngs, R. (2021). Preparing the CSDP for the new security environment created by climate change. European Parliament In-Depth Analysis.
Missiroli, A. (2022). *L'Europa Come Potenza. Diplomazia, Sicurezza, Difesa.* Il Mulino.
Morgenstern-Pomorski, J.-H. (2018). *The contested diplomacy of the European external action service: Inception, establishment and consolidation.* Routledge, Taylor & Francis Group.
Morris, R. C., & Spivak, G. C. (Eds.). (2010). *Can the Subaltern Speak? Reflections on the history of an idea.* Columbia University Press.
Noxolo, P. (2017). Introduction: Decolonising geographical knowledge in a colonised and re-colonising postcolonial world. *Area, 49*(3), 317–319.
Nye, J. S. (2004). *Soft power: The means to success in world politics* (1st ed.). Public Affairs.
OECD. (2008). *The Curse of Raw Materials?* OECD Development Centre Policy Insights.
Onar, N. F., & Nicolaïdis, K. (2013). The decentring Agenda: Europe as a post-colonial power. *Cooperation and Conflict, 48*(2), 283–303.
Overland, I. (2015). Future petroleum geopolitics: Consequences of climate policy and unconventional oil and gas. In J. Yan (Ed.), *Handbook of clean energy systems* (pp. 1–29). John Wiley & Sons, Ltd.
Pagden, A. (2021). *The pursuit of Europe: A history* (1st ed.). Oxford University Press.
Poelman, H. (2013). *Measuring accessibility to passenger flights in Europe: Towards harmonised indicators at the regional level.* p 16
Purcell, T. (1998). Indigenous knowledge and applied anthropology: Questions of definition and direction. *Human Organization, 57*(3), 258–272.
Rangel Hernandez, A. (2022). Geopolitics of the Energy Transition: Energy Security, New Dependencies and Critical Raw Materials. Old Wine in New Bottles for the EU? *Bruges Political Research Papers/Cahiers de recherche politique de Bruges*, No. 87.
Schelling, T. C. (2008). *Arms and influence.* Yale University Press.
Schott, W. (1836) *Versuch über die Tatarischen Sprachen.* Veit & Comp.
Silverstein, A. J. (2010). *Islamic history: A very short introduction.* Oxford University Press.
Tian, N., Fleurant, A., Kuimova, A., Wezeman, P., & Wezeman, S. (2018). *Trends in World Military Expenditure, 2018.* p 12.
Toynbee, A., & Somervell, D. C. (1987). *A study of history, Facsimile.* Oxford University Press.
Weldeab Sebhatu, R. (2021). Applying postcolonial approaches to studies of Africa-EU relations. In T. Haastrup, L. Mah, & N. Duggan (Eds.), *The Routledge handbook of EU-Africa relations.* Routledge.

Chapter 3
The Legal Context

Contents

3.1 Introduction

In a state, competences to conduct foreign policy typically go by rules that are different from those that regulate internal competences. Broadly speaking, the 'special characteristics' of constitutional rules in foreign affairs are the prominence of the executive (not of the parliament) as decision-maker, and the limited power of the judiciary.[1] This is true of both European Member States (such as Germany) and of third countries (such as India and the United States).[2] CFSP is no exception. The informal and at times troubled development of the EU's foreign policy competence

[1] Martinez (2019).

[2] Larik (2016), p. 54.

L. Lonardo, *EU Common Foreign and Security Policy After Lisbon*,
https://doi.org/10.1007/978-3-031-19131-2_3

recalled below, and which resulted in the rules on CFSP, contributed to some idiosyncratic traits of this policy. The 'distinctiveness' of CFSP was deliberately formalised in the Lisbon Treaty. Hence, the law of EU foreign policy is not unitary. Entering into alliances, concluding trade deals, and nominating ambassadors are examples of activities traditionally seen as part of the undivided craft of diplomacy. Not so for the EU, whose external relations law draws a peculiar distinction. On one hand there is the general Union competence to engage in 'external action' (these include policy fields such as trade, development cooperation, energy, environment, etc);[3] on the other, there is the distinctive competence to conduct a CFSP, which is 'subject to specific rules and procedures' (Article 24 TEU). The differences in objectives, scope, and nature between the external relation competences is not specified in the Treaties and defies easy categorisation. There is only an unhelpful definition of CFSP: it shall cover '*all areas of foreign policy* and all questions relating to the Union's security'.[4] The other competences are never defined as a whole.[5] Article 2 TFEU classifies the Union's competence as exclusive (2 (1) TFEU), shared (2(2) TFEU), coordinated (2(3) TFEU) or, as a special category in its own right, CFSP (2(4) TFEU).

3.2 Legal-Institutional History of EU Security and Defence

There is a growing interest in the history of the European Union, but there is no historiography of EU foreign policy (nor of its law). Contributions on the legal evolution of EU cooperation in foreign policy are few and far between, and even histories of EU foreign policy as such are only beginning to emerge,[6] despite the fact that 'the striving for a common foreign and security policy was one of the driving forces behind the establishment of the European Community.'[7]

It is a key argument of this chapter that the evolution of EU foreign policy law is necessary to frame the current legal context. This is because the reasons for the 'distinctive' legal-constitutional architecture of CFSP are due to a large extent to path-dependency. The peculiar institutional and legal machinery of CFSP outlined in

---

[3]Mostly regulated in Part Five of the Treaty on the Functioning of the European Union (TFEU). This encompasses a number of competences but will be referred to, collectively, in the rest of this book as the 'TFEU competences' or 'other external competences'.

[4]Article 24 TEU. Emphasis added.

[5]They are defined *singulatim*. The phrase 'external action' is used in Chapter 1 of Title V TEU and in Part V of the TFEU to list all external relations competences including CFSP. Article 2 TFEU divides all EU competences into five categories: exclusive, shared, coordinating and supporting, coordinating and supplementing, and CFSP.

[6]Loth (2020), p. 146 is a useful guide to historical writings on the origins of security and defence cooperation in the context of the European Community. see also (Bindi, 2012) for a more general overview of the history of EU foreign policy.

[7]Loth (2020), p. 145. On the role of security in European constitutionalism see (Tuori, 2015).

the introduction and presented in detail in the second part of this chapter derives largely from the complex history of the *legal foundations* of cooperation in Western Europe first—and Central and Eastern Europe after the end of the Cold War—in foreign security and defence.

3.2.1 The European Defence Community

Defining it as a 'complex history' may be an understatement. Strictly speaking, in fact, for decades there was no hard law, and certainly no European Community law, to govern the efforts of Member States to create a common security and defence policy. Such cooperation emerged as a matter of custom, instead. The current rules are, therefore, the formalisation of those political and informal developments dating back to the European Political Cooperation (EPC), originating with the Davignon Report approved in October 1970 by the foreign ministers of the European Community. This chapter will briefly recall those early developments, and presents an overview of the legal evolution of what is today known as CFSP.

Admittedly, an early attempt at formalising in legal terms—through an international treaty between the six founding members of the Community—rose, shined, and prematurely set within a couple of years in the early 50s. It was the European Defence Community, an ambitious project of defence integration with a decisively federal element. It went so far as to foresee a common European army (40 divisions of 13,000 men made available by the Member States, but wearing a common 'European' uniform), placed under the control of a high commander (the Supreme Allied Commander Europe, that is, the NATO military commander); and while the EDC had an intergovernmental mechanism for decision making (the Council of Ministers), the federal element was in Article 38, foreseeing the future election of an Assembly (essentially, a Parliament elected by universal direct suffrage) which would modify the EDC Treaty with a view to 'substitute the present temporary' institutional structure with 'elements of a federal structure, based on the principles of the separation of powers and including, in particular, a bicameral representative system'. The project was presented by the French defence minister Pleven as a way of uniting Western Europe—including West Germany, but without the UK, which was reluctant to join the initiative: the plan was a way to ensure that West Germany's rearmament, inevitable by 1950 as the country had joined NATO, would be acceptable to France. The EDC treaty was never ratified by the French Assemblé Nationale, and with a vote of August 1954 to remove the project from the agenda, that assembly essentially archived the EDC.

The later Treaty of Rome, therefore, gave the newly established EEC limited competences for external trade relations and assisting development in former colonial territories.[8] It was in fact French Gaullists who 'insisted on a clear distinction

[8] Woolcock (2017).

between ‘high’ and ‘low’ politics: the EEC was to be confined to the low politics of commercial diplomacy, leaving the high politics of foreign policy and defence to sovereign states’,[9] a distinction that remains to these days. Federalisation—especially of core state attribution such as security and defence—proved unachievable. Other arrangements, intergovernmental or ‘communitarian’ had to be envisaged instead.[10] A mix between these two would be at the basis of the European Economic Community few months later, established with the Treaty of Rome of 1957, and an intergovernmental and less ambitious alliance, the Western European Union, was formalised in 1954 (with the UK), and ‘nested’ into NATO.

3.2.2 *The European Political Cooperation*

The failure of the EDC meant that the dream of a federalised Europe was politically unfeasible, but it did not mean the end of political cooperation in Western European security and defence—although it did set back ambitions of formalising it in Treaty form. In the 60s, De Gaulle attempted, through the Fouché Plans, of revitalising a form of political cooperation. But the plans were largely perceived as French-dominated, and were never approved by the other five members of the Community. In 1970, once political conditions became again favourable (to this contributed the succession of Pompidou to De Gaulle, the imminent accession of the UK, Ireland and Denmark to the Community, the beginning of détente in Europe, the EC ministers approved the Davignon report—a political document with no legally binding value but setting out a vision for a political union, which would require, in the first place, Member States to find means to harmonise their views on matters of international politics.

It was only several years later, with the Single European Act of 1986, that the common foreign policy entered the Community *legal* structures.

3.2.3 *The Single European Act*

The Single European Act is a treaty modifying the Treaty of Rome instituting the European Economic Community, and it created a link between the EPC and the Community’s institutions,[11] hence connecting the political and economic sides of

[9]Giegerich (2017), p. 439.

[10]Parsons (2017).

[11]The European Council entered into the EC framework; the Commission and the European Parliament were given powers related to the EPC; the SEA established a Presidency of EPC (coincident with the Presidency of the Council), which had the right to take initiatives and to coordinate national positions; a Political Committee made out of national Political Directors, whose tasks were to give “impetus and continuity” to the action; and a Secretariat, to assist the Presidency.

the EC's external action.[12] However, the rules on political international relations were put in a newly created Title III, thus formalising for the first time the 'distinctiveness' of foreign and security policy. Within the Council, the old bureaucratic body of the EPC (the Political Committee) was put on par with COREPER.

The duties imposed by Art 30(2) SEA on the Member States were merely to take intoaccount other Member States' interests before acting individually and were only politically binding.[13]

The SEA excluded the jurisdiction of the Court (Art 31 SEA) over issues of political and security relevance in foreign policy. It introduced jurisdiction only to monitor that EPC did not affect Community law (Art 32).[14] It is the so-called non-affectation clause.

3.2.4 *The Maastricht Treaty*

A plethora of new institutions, projects, and Treaty revisions began at the end of the Cold War.[15] Further to a Belgian proposal for a Political Union backed enthusiastically by the president of the Commission Delors and by a Franco-German initiative, an intergovernmental conference (IGC) was convened in parallel with a conference on a proposed Economic and Monetary Union. Approved in December 1990, the conferences were held in 1991 and the negotiations were concluded in December of that year in the Netherlands.

The Treaty of Maastricht (entered into force in 1993) introduced the 'pillar structure'. It distributed the competences of the Community as follows: the first pillar contained broadly speaking, economic and monetary governance, internal market and 'low foreign policy' external relations (such as trade and development); the second pillar was foreign policy, under the new name Common Foreign and Security Policy; the third pillar was dedicated to Justice and Home Affairs.

The contingent reasons for the introduction of a Common Foreign and Security Policy and Justice and Home Affairs as distinctive pillars are not only path-dependent (such pillars came late to the Community's legal order and foreign policy, as seen above, had always been treated separately), but were also due to the preference of some Member States (France, the UK, Portugal, and Denmark) to retain the final say for their own foreign security and defence policies. Significantly, it was Mitterrand and Kohl who suggested framing a common security and defence,

---

In particular, the Presidency and the Commission were responsible for ensuring consistency between the external policies of the European Communities and the policies agreed in the European Political Cooperation (Art 30(5) of the SEA). (Gosalbo Bono, 2006, p. 340).

[12] Duquette (2001), p. 179.

[13] Gosalbo Bono (2006), p. 340.

[14] Ibid 440.

[15] Wallace (2017) offers a (critical) overview of the developments in the substance of the policy.

implemented through the Western European Union, that shall not affect obligations with regard to NATO and the specific character of each member state's security and defence policy (a wording similar to the one of the current Article 42 TEU, as will be shown).[16]

Given the Union's structure, consistency was a major concern of the drafters of the Maastricht Treaty.[17] Enshrined in Article 3 CFSP was so particular (distinct) in respect to the other competences that some authors did not consider Community Law to apply.[18] Gosalbo Bono instead considered CFSP a shared or concurrent competence,[19] and the Court found it had jurisdiction on a TEU measure that affected EC competences in the *Airport Transit Visa* case,[20] which hinted at the unity of the legal system.

Decision-making in CFSP matters was mainly by unanimity. The only exceptions were the execution of joint actions,[21] procedural questions,[22] and the implementation of economic sanctions.[23] The Treaty also brought the Political Committee under the Council, creating issues of overlapping competences between that Committee and COREPER.[24] Formally, the PC had a subordinate role to COREPER,[25] but the relationship developed, in practice,[26] as a form of non-affectation. The PC would consider political and security issues, whereas the COREPER would deal with legal and other matters.

The Treaty of Maastricht introduced specific CFSP instruments. The European Council was entitled to adopt general CFSP guidelines.[27] The Council could 'define common positions'[28] and adopt 'joint actions'.[29] These instruments committed MSs as far as their positions and actions were concerned.[30] It also introduced CFSP-specific objectives.

---

[16] Message commun de M. François Mitterrand, président de la République et du chancelier allemand, M. Helmut Kohl, à M. Giulo Andreotti, président du Conseil italien et président en exercice du Conseil des Communautés sur l'Union politique (Paris et Bonn, le 6 décembre 1990).

[17] Eeckhout (2013), p. 186.

[18] Koskenniemi (1998), p. 27.

[19] Gosalbo Bono (2006), p. 364.

[20] Case C-170/96 *Commission v Council* [1998] ECR I-2763.

[21] Art. J.3(2).

[22] Art.J.8(2) *in fine*.

[23] Art 228A EC.

[24] Kiso (1997), p. 146.

[25] Hofmann and Türk (2006), p. 373.

[26] Wessels (2013), p. 81.

[27] Art. J.3(1) TEU).

[28] Art. J.2 TEU. Gosalbo Bono writes that these positions were mostly used to ensure compliance with UN Security Council resolutions and coordinate the Union's actions in international organisations, (Gosalbo Bono, 2006, p. 340).

[29] These were used by Member States to share the resources needed to carry out an operational action (e.g. the administration of the town of Mostar by the EU or the conferral of humanitarian aid in Bosnia-Herzegovina).

[30] Art. J.3(4) TEU (Gosalbo Bono, 2006, p. 341).

The Maastricht Treaty excluded the ECJ jurisdiction and maintained the non-affectation clause (Article 47 TEU). Article 47 was a 'legal battleground'[31] because of the difficult interface between the pillars and especially within the external competences.[32] The court clarified the meaning of Article 47 in the landmark decision ECOWAS,[33] about technical and financial assistance for stopping the arms trade in Africa. The Court had to ascertain whether it was about development (a 'Community' competence) or about 'security' (CFSP competence). The Court found that there was a presumption in favour of Community competences.

The so-called Petersberg Tasks were codified on 19 June 1992, as in that town the ministers signed the declaration which included the main objectives of what would become European security and defence. The Petersberg Tasks include humanitarian and rescue tasks, as well as peacekeeping, crisis management and peacemaking responsibilities.

3.2.5 The Amsterdam Treaty

The Treaty of Amsterdam (1999), with the aim of fostering the external representation of CFSP, introduced the High Representative for Common Foreign and Security Policy, a post held by Javier Solana; and special representatives who were chosen by the Council for particular mandates (old Art. 18 TEU).[34]

The St Malo Declaration of 1998 is of pivotal importance for the purposes of the distinctiveness of CFSP because it shows the conflicting interests in the creation of the European Security and Defence Initiative. This Franco-British summit resulted in a declaration that called for the Union to have 'the capacity for autonomous action',[35] within the newly created Amsterdam Treaty. The formulation of the St Malo Declaration, however, is the result of a compromise: while France would have wanted 'independent' action (i.e., independent from the US), the UK was interested in using much more cautious language ('complementary'), in consideration of their 'special relationship' with the US. Given the persistent opposition of previous UK governments to integration in security and defence, the St Malo Declaration was indeed quite an opening from Tony Blair.[36] It is significant that the US Secretary of

---

[31] Eeckhout (2013), p. 165.

[32] The first and second pillar were described in joined cases C-402/05P and C-415/05 P *Kadi* ECLI: EU:C:2008:461 para 202 as 'integrated but separate legal orders'.

[33] Case C-91/05 *Commission v Council (ECOWAS)* [2008] *ECR* I-3651.

[34] Gosalbo Bono (2006), p. 450.

[35] Joint Declaration on European Defence Joint Declaration issued at the British-French Summit (Saint-Malo, 4 December 1998), https://www.cvce.eu/obj/franco_british_st_malo_declaration_4_december_1998-en-f3cd16fb-fc37-4d52-936f-c8e9bc80f24f.html.

[36] Consider that the UK also backed the establishment of Europol—in the other distinct pillar of JHA. For Tony Blair's case on the role of UK in CFSP and JHA see the speech at the London Business School, 27 July 1999.

State, Madeleine Albright, immediately reacted to the St Malo Declaration: 'Any initiative must avoid pre-empting [NATO] Alliance decision-making by de-linking ESDI from NATO, avoid duplicating existing efforts, and avoid discriminating against non-EU members'.[37]

On that impetus, the EU conceived the European Security and Defence Policy (which, with Lisbon, acquired the name of Common Security and Defence Policy) at the Cologne Summit in June 1999. Shortly thereafter, the ambition to make ESDP a reality became apparent, when the Helsinki Council of December 1999 adopted the 'Helsinki Goals', to provide 'teeth' to the ESDP. The Helsinki Goals had the ambition to provide 60,000 EU soldiers, to be mobilised within 60 days.

3.2.6 The Nice Treaty

The Helsinki Council also created the Political and Security Committee, formalised with the Nice Treaty. This 'downgraded version' of the pre-Maastricht Political Committee—no longer on par with COREPER but subordinated to it—was entrusted with the task of directing crisis management operations.

3.2.7 The Lisbon Treaty

The Lisbon Treaty, entered into force on 1 December 2009, is an important milestone in the history of EU integration, as it reflects the constitutional bargain between MSs and Union following the enlargement of 2004 and the failure of the adoption of a Constitutional Treaty. The process that led to the adoption of the Treaty, through an intergovernmental conference held between July and October 2007, was one of cosmetic adjustments to the Constitutional Treaty, a projected 'constitution' for Europe which never entered into force because the French and Dutch public voted against ratification, thus making the project no longer politically viable. The Lisbon Treaty was a less ambitious version, as detailed below, and for this reason some Member States decided that a popular referendum would not be necessary for ratification.[38] The Lisbon Treaty modified the Maastricht Treaty (now renamed

---

[37] Secretary Albright's remarks to the North Atlantic Council ministerial meeting, Brussels, December 8, 1998.

[38] In Ireland, where a referendum on the new Treaty was mandated by the national constitution, the 'no' initially won. This was also due to a geopolitical concern (in addition to other issues of political contention): Irish neutrality, which the public thought might be affected by the new Treaty. After obtaining political reassurance from the European Council, the Irish government put the Lisbon Treaty to a new referendum in 2008, which was carried easily. Other Member States simply ratified the Treaty in Parliament (Italy, France). Other Member States also required the seal of approval

Treaty on the European Union), as well as the European Community Treaty (now renamed Treaty on the Functioning of the European Union).

Formally, the changes made by the Lisbon Treaty to CFSP were deep and pervasive.[39] These concerned a 'normalisation' of CFSP. The Treaty of Lisbon abolished the 'second pillar', integrating instead CFSP within a unitary legal order. The Union acquired a single legal personality, which results in provisions of general application being in principle applicable to CFSP.[40] Other changes expanded the tasks of the EU in the domain of defence, beyond the so-called Petersberg Tasks: in addition to humanitarian, peacekeeping, and crisis management, the TEU allowed the Union to carry out missions providing military advice or post-conflict stabilisation (Article 43(1) TEU).[41] Since some Member States had already bilateral agreements in some defence areas, and with a view to strengthen EU's efficiency and coherence, following a Franco-German proposal the Working Group on Defence at the Convention for the Future of Europe recommended an increase to the role of the HR, that those Member States wishing to undertake firmer commitments than others should be enabled to do so with the Union's framework, and that a CFSP emergency budget should be set up.[42] The second of these items—later to become the permanent structured cooperation—was conceived also with the view to allow Member States to transfer their obligations under the Western European Union (WEU) Treaty into EU law.[43] The UK government's initial reaction was very cautious. As it reminded at a hearing in the UK Parliament, 'none of these structures pretends to provide an operational EU military command structure either at the strategic or the tactical levels. There are no standing EU headquarters (just as there is no EU standing force). Any such EU operational command structure would duplicate existing NATO and national assets'[44]. In particular, the UK government made clear its intention to resist the inclusion of any security guarantee in the new treaty which could rival or come to replace the security guarantee established through NATO.[45] At the Convention for the Future of Europe, negotiating the Constitutional Treaty, the Defence Working Group recommended that Member States should commit to mobilising all instruments to prevent or respond to a terrorist attack or natural disaster within the EU.[46] The recommendation, phrased in those broad terms,

---

from their constitutional court (resulting in landmark judgments such as the *Lissabon-Urteil* of the German Constitutional Court (2 BvE 2/08)).

[39]The Lisbon Treaty changed 'the institutional structure, the functioning and the substance of CFSP'; (Cremona, 2018, p. 5): 'the constitutional architecture of the Treaties has been substantially altered'.

[40]See discussion in the introduction.

[41]Italian Parliament (2007), p. 7.

[42]Working Group VIII 'Defence', 'Franco-German comments on the preliminary draft final report of Working Group VIII "Defence"' 4 December 2002.

[43]This happened with the Lisbon Treaty, and the WEU officially came to an end in 2010.

[44]Response to the Committee's 11th Report, Session 2001–02 on ESDP, paragraph 20.

[45]*A Constitutional Treaty for the EU – The British approach to the EU IGC* Cm 5934 (1 September 2003) para 95.

[46]House of Lords (2003), p. 46.

proved unacceptable for the UK and other Member States that wanted to preserve the status quo. The mutual defence clause that was eventually included in Article 42(7) TEU was instead phrased so as to provide obligation to assist a Member State victim of an 'armed aggression', and it was meant to accommodate three groups of states:[47] those seeking a mutual defence commitment which could be satisfied with the part of the article stating that 'the other Member States shall have (...) an obligation of aid and assistance by all the means in their power'; those seeking to protect their traditional neutral status (such as Ireland, Austria and Sweden) which could be satisfied with the clause 'This shall not prejudice the specific character of the security and defence policy of certain Member States'; and those wanting to ensure that the article would not undermine NATO, which could be satisfied with the reminder that 'Commitments and cooperation in this area shall be consistent with commitments under the North Atlantic Treaty Organisation'. The debate also resulted in the insertion of a solidarity clause in the event of a terrorist attack or a natural or man-made disaster (Article 222 TFEU).

But the changes from the Constitutional Treaty (which never entered into force) to the Lisbon Treaty were, in fact mostly formal: they concerned the language rather than the substance.[48] There was also a debate on whether to retain CFSP or to merge it with all other external relations competences: the choice to merge them carried clear symbolic value, even though it was to the detriment of legal certainty (and possibly coherence and efficiency).[49]

The UK was particularly favourable to the maintenance of CFSP's distinctiveness.[50] This was because the UK government wanted the new Treaty to leave unaffected the UK's position in security and defence matters, as had been the case throughout the 90s. The Foreign Secretary at the time, David Miliband, identified on 11 October 2007 the Treaty provisions that ensured the UK's objective of retaining an independent foreign policy was achieved: they were (in the final version) Article 24 TEU ('the common foreign and security policy is subject to specific rules and procedures'); Article 275 TFEU (limiting the Court's jurisdiction); Declaration 13 and 14 on CFSP (stating that the policy 'does not affect the responsibilities of the Member States (...) for the formulation and conduct of their foreign policy')—and the FCO later identified Article 40 TEU as also meeting the objective.[51] Indeed, the non-affectation clause was re-formulated into Article

---

[47] Blanke and Mangiameli (2013), pp. 1201–1235.

[48] Italian Parliament (2007), p. 7; House of Commons (2008), p. para 219: 'We conclude that there is no material difference between the provisions on foreign affairs in the Constitutional Treaty which the Government made subject to approval in a referendum and those in the Lisbon Treaty on which a referendum is being denied.'

[49] Larik (2016), p. 40. See further Chap. 7.

[50] House of Lords (2008), p. 31: 'The Minister for Europe told us that the Government's position [on the Union's single legal personality] had changed because the Government was "able to secure the distinct treaty status for CFSP", retaining its special intergovernmental status.'

[51] House of Commons (2008), p. 52.

40 TEU, which provides that CFSP shall not affect other competences and vice-versa.

3.2.8 *Main Institutional and Legal Developments in CFSP Since the Lisbon Treaty*

The establishment of the EEAS—the EU's 'diplomatic body' foreseen in the Lisbon Treaty—is one of the main innovations of the Treaty and it is quite a singular institutional development, very specific to CFSP. Originally envisaged as a separate body reporting directly to the HR/VP, the EEAS was set to take on political affairs whereas more technical subjects (such as trade, development cooperation and enlargement negotiations) would remain as Directorates General within the Commission. The body was only created after the entry into force of the Lisbon Treaty, through a quadrilogue, between the Spanish presidency, Council, Commission and Parliament. The result was the Council Decision of 26 July,[52] a compromise between the EP and the Commission establishing the EEAS as a 'functionally autonomous body', including all EU delegations, and with budgetary oversight by the EP. Officially operative since 1 January 2011, the EEAS took over one year to become fully operational: the time necessary for a new building (in Rond-point Schuman, like the Commission and Council), new appointments, new personnel seconded by the Member States (40% of the fonctionnaires—the rest were transferred from the Council (one quarter) and the Commission (three quarters)).

The Brexit Referendum of June 2016 is an important caesura in the history of European integration, and it has had repercussion on the CFSP. For once, it became fashionable to talk about European defence—and not just of a 'common defence policy'. Already in July 2016, France and Germany encouraged the establishment of the Permanent Structured Cooperation, a scheme for cooperation foreseen as part of the CSDP. Closely following that development, in September the Commission's President Juncker announced the ambitious agenda of a fully-fledged Defence Union, and in November the Council decided to set up a Coordinated Annual Review on Defence, carried out by EDA and EUMS, with a view to harmonise national policies in the field of defence equipment and investment. Economic programmes also resulted also in a unified European Defence Fund as part of the latest multiannual financial framework, and an off-budget instrument, the European Peace Facility, to support external action with military or defence implication. In March 2017, the Council created a new Military Planning and Conduct Capability unit within the EEAS, which is the closest thing the EU has to a general head quarter—even though it controls only non-executive missions.

[52]Council Decision 2010/427/EU of 26 July 2010 establishing the organisation and functioning of the European External Action Service [2010] OJ L201/30.

As a matter of law, the most significant development was the establishment of the Permanent Structured Cooperation, officially launched in December 2017, whose geopolitical and legal significance is discussed in Chap. 5.

3.3 The Constitutional Architecture of Common Foreign and Security Policy

3.3.1 Institutional Arrangements

The **European Council** has, since Lisbon, a full-time president with a 2.5 year mandate, renewable once, who is expected 'at his level and in that capacity, [to] ensure the external representation of the union on issues concerning its common foreign and security policy, without prejudice to the powers of the HR/VP' (Article 15(6) TEU). By virtue of its composition (heads of state and government of the Member States), the European Council adopts positions defining the EU's approach, voting by unanimity to 'identify the strategic interests and objectives of the Union' (Article 22(1) TEU). In particular, in CFSP 'The European Council shall identify the Union's strategic interests, determine the objectives of and define general guidelines for the common foreign and security policy, including for matters with defence implications' (Article 26(1) TEU). European Council conclusions are not binding, but their existence has procedural consequences (essentially, if the European Council has reached agreement on an item, the Council can adopt a CFSP decision by unanimity).

The **Council** (in its composition as Foreign Affairs Council) is the main decision-maker:[53] the European Parliament has only a right to be informed, and it is not a co-legislator (unlike what occurs in the ordinary legislative procedure). The Council 'shall frame the common foreign and security policy and take the decisions necessary for defining and implementing it on the basis of the general guidelines and strategic lines defined by the European Council' (Article 26(2) TEU). Within the Council, a **Political and Security Committee** is entrusted with decision-making in CFSP crisis management operations (Article 38(1) TEU), and the distinctiveness of CFSP is reflected down to the working groups, separated between those who deal with CFSP and those who work with other external relations; the European External Action Service assists the HR.[54]

An institutional figure unique to CFSP is the **HR/VP**, who is both President of the Foreign Affairs Council and Vice President of the Commission, an institutional figure meant to bring coherence to EU external action by uniting the former 'community' pillar (Commission-led) to the 'intergovernmental' pillar (Council-led). Since (s)he is a member of the Commission, the rules for the election of the

---

[53] Wessel and Larik (2020), p. 296.

[54] An introductory overview is in (Marquardt, 2018, p. 22).

HR/VP are those for the election of commissioners. The role of this institutional figure is defined in Article 27 TEU. The HR/VP is to CFSP what the Commission is to most other EU policies, in so far as the HR/VP is in charge of initiative (and so are Member States) and implementation of the policy (Article 27(1) TEU). The HR/VP is also entrusted with representing the EU 'for matters relating to the common foreign and security policy. He shall conduct political dialogue with third parties on the Union's behalf and shall express the Union's position in international organisations and at international conferences' (Article 27(2) TEU).

The **European External Action Service** is the diplomatic body of the EU.[55] Its presence was envisaged by the Lisbon Treaty, in a succinct provision (Article 27(3) TEU). It was set up only during the mandate of the first HR, Catherine Ashton.[56] It has been operative—and growing—since 2010. It is a quintessentially 'EU' phenomenon: it is an institutional response to a political issue (the lack of coherence in EU foreign policy), and its composition reflects the hybridity between EU and Member States action (in so far as it is made up by officials seconded by diplomatic services of Member States, along with officials transferred from other EU institutions).

Delegations are formally integrated in the EEAS, even though the European Community started establishing them well before Lisbon (the first, to Washington, in 1973).[57] Delegations ensure the representation of the EU (as a bloc) in loco, in virtually all countries in the world. This is a significant advantage especially for those Member States who did not have the diplomatic outreach and network they can now enjoy by virtue of EU delegations. While there are few countries in which all Member States had an embassy (Tokyo, Moscow, New Delhi, Washington), the relationship between EU delegations and national embassies has given rise to issues of duplication and efficiency. Delegations also coordinate the representation of the EU in certain multilateral fora or international organisations. In addition to delegations, the EU avails itself of special representatives. These are political appointees with a geographical or thematic mandate (Article 33 TEU).

The establishment of the **European Defence Agency** (EDA) in 2004 had strategic and economic factors,[58] and was an important innovation in European security and defence. The EDA is as old as the failed Constitutional Treaty, and at the time of its establishment it was hoped that it would be one of 'the three main elements of the CSDP',[59] together with the mutual defence clause and independent crisis management capabilities (the latter two would only come into being with the Lisbon Treaty, whereas the establishment of the EDA was decoupled from the entry into force of the

---

[55] For a legal perspective, Gatti (2016); Blockmans et al. (2013). For an assessment of the first 10 years, see the Volume 26, Issue 1 (February 2021) of the European Foreign Affairs Review.

[56] Council Decision 2010/427/EU of 26 July 2010 establishing the organisation and functioning of the European External Action Service [2010] OJ L201/30.

[57] Austermann (2014).

[58] Bátora (2009), p. 1076.

[59] Trybus (2006), p. 667.

Constitutional Treaty). Apart from a coordinating role in the defence sector, the EDA has the important task of organising training and military exercises. Strategically, the Agency was set up primarily with consistency in mind. Joint Action 2004/551/CFSP[60] established the European Defence Agency with the aim 'to support the Member States in their effort to improve European defence capabilities in the field of crisis management and to sustain the ESDP as it stands now and develops in the future'. The consistency rationale was also meant to facilitate the creation of an EU security and defence 'identity'.[61] From an economic point of view, the EDA was expected to help with the fragmentation of the EU defence sector, by providing consistency especially when it comes to research and development programmes.

Currently, there are three **other independent agencies** established by a CFSP measure and operating within this policy. These are the European Union Institute for Strategic Studies (EUISS),[62] the European Defence Agency (EDA),[63] and the EU Satellite Centre (SATCEN).[64] The EU has made vast recourse to specialised agencies,[65] and CFSP ones are by no means exceptional nor new in the administrative practice of EU specialised decision-making, and judicial review was more of a theoretical possibility than a reality, so the EU did not design in peculiar arrangements for the review of their acts.[66]

3.3.2 Decision-Making

EU action in CFSP is, by definition, non-legislative (Article 24 TEU). It means that the EU cannot adopt the ordinary instruments (regulations and directives) pursuant to the ordinary legislative procedure. The Council adopts Decisions, instead. All of the CFSP acts discussed in this book are, therefore, technically Decisions (and for this reason their official name takes the form of **Body* Decision **Year*/**Sequential Number*/CFSP: for example, Political and Security Committee Decision 2022/100/CFSP[67]).

---

[60] Council Joint Action 2004/551/CFSP of 12 July 2004 on the Establishment of the European Defence Agency OJ 2004 L 245/17.

[61] Bátora (2009), p. 1076.

[62] Council Joint Action of 20 July 2001 on the establishment of a European Union Institute for Security Studies Official Journal L 200.

[63] Council Joint Action 2004/551/CFSP of 12 July 2004 on the establishment of the European Defence Agency OJ L 245/17.

[64] Council Decision 2014/401/CFSP of 26 June 2014 on the European Union Satellite Centre and repealing Joint Action 2001/555/CFSP on the establishment of a European Union Satellite Centre OJ L 188/73.

[65] Craig (2018), pp. 147–149.

[66] Butler (2022).

[67] This is the standard format for all EU acts published in the L Series of the Official Journal.

In particular, Article 25(a) TEU mandates that the Union shall conduct its CFSP by 'defining' general guidelines. These are adopted by the European Council, which shall, for this purpose adopt the necessary decisions (Article 26(1)). Article 25 (b) TEU distinguishes three kinds of decisions: actions to be undertaken by the Union; positions to be taken by the Union; and arrangements for the implementation of the first two. The first two of these three kinds of decision find further articulation, respectively, in Article 28 and 29 TEU.[68]

The Council decides by unanimity (Article 31(1) TEU), except for the adoption of:

- decisions 'defining a Union action or position' on the basis of a previous decision by the European Council (Article 31(2)): in other words, when the Member States already agreed unanimously in the European Council
- implementing or amending acts (Article 31(2) TEU): in other words, when modifying decisions already adopted previously. This is a very important and broad exception. Sanctions are often adopted by means of update of previous acts, and the rule of Article 31(2) could be construed as implying that no unanimity is required for the imposition of *further* sanctions, when the basic ones were already unanimously agreed.[69]
- When appointing a special representative.

In addition, as an 'exception' to unanimity, each country can decide to abstain from a vote, without thereby blocking the adoption of the act in question and without being bound by it. This form of differentiation, foreseen in Article 31(1) TEU as long as the members of the Council qualifying their abstention in this way represent at least one third of the Member States comprising at least one third of the population of the Union, was used most rarely.

In fact, studies on voting behaviour in the Council suggest that the institution (and its committee) decides mostly by consensus, even when the rule is QMV.[70] But the CJEU confirmed that the practice of the Council to adopt certain conclusions by consensus—that is, by unanimity—even in cases where the Treaty provides that it shall deliberate by QMV cannot derogate from the rules of the Treaty and cannot therefore create a precedent that is binding on the EU institutions.[71] The Court established that the Council cannot decide by unanimity when it ought to do so by QMV. First, in the Commission's submission, a search for consensus in the Council, instead of a qualified majority, is likely to lead to a different result, negatively affecting European Union policy. This is the first time that EU institutions explicitly

[68] A more detailed discussion of these is in the next section.

[69] More on this in Chap. 7.

[70] Novak (2013), p. 1091.

[71] Case C-687/15 *Commission v Council (CMR-15)* ECLI:EU:C:2017:803 par 42. See, to that effect, judgment of 6 May 2008, *Parliament* v *Council*, C-133/06, EU:C:2008:257, paragraph 60 and the case-law cited, and *Opinion 1/08 (Agreements modifying the Schedules of Specific Commitments under the GATS)* EU:C:2009:739 paragraph 172 and the case-law cited.

pleaded before the Court that the requirement of unanimity may be detrimental to the Union's policy. While the fact is widely uncontested in legal scholarship, EU institutions had never grounded a plea in law on it. The Court did not decide upon the specific issue, and rightly so, since the Commission had not brought any evidence for the claim that unanimity 'negatively affect[s] European Union policy'. Second, the Court did not share the view—proposed by the Commission—that the requirement of unanimity is exceptional in the Council's voting rules. Instead, it reached the same conclusion as the Commission, but through different reasoning. It simply reasoned that, applying the sources of EU law, Treaties are superior to practice, and therefore 'a practice which is contradicted by the position maintained by the Commission in this action, cannot alter the rules of the Treaties that the institutions are obliged to respect'.[72]

The carrying out of the CFSP imposes (weak) obligations on Member States. These can be grouped in three categories, depending on the stage of decision-making: information, consultation, and implementation obligations.

Information and consultation obligations are contained in Article 32 TEU ('Member States shall inform and consult one another within the European Council and Council on any matter of foreign and security policy of general interest'). Absent further specification of what is a matter 'of general interest', in practice it is Member States who decide on what they want to consult. As Wessel and Larik write, 'On the one hand, Member States are obliged to inform and consult one another, whereas, on the other hand, they are given the individual discretion to decide whether a matter is of 'general interest'. Hence, once Member States do not agree that a matter is of general interest (for instance, because one Member States considers it to be of national interest only) it becomes very hard for the Union to develop a policy in that area'.[73]

Implementation obligations are even less straightforward as the effects of CFSP acts are not obvious from the wording of the Treaty, to the point that it could be seriously questioned whether CSDP decisions enjoy the hallmark features of EU law (namely the fact that they produce direct effect in the legal system of Member States, and that they take precedence over domestic law of Member States). One could take the view that CFSP acts may only bind Member States (but, as the next section illustrates, they are hardly justiciable), not individuals, on pain of breaching Article 40 TEU. First, there are textual arguments to this effect. The wording of several provisions entail, rather than obligations with direct effect for individuals, duties of cooperation or solidarity[74] which are addressed to the Member States and to EU institutions and bodies.[75] In Article 24 (2) TEU the Union is called on to 'conduct,

[72] Case C-687/15 *Commission v Council* (*CMR-15)* para 42.

[73] Wessel and Larik (2020), p. 292.

[74] Klamert (2014), p. 38.

[75] Thus AG Wahl in H para 37: 'The Union is not meant, in the field of the CFSP, to adopt acts that lay down general abstract rules creating rights and obligations for individuals' (even though the AG derived this conclusion from the fact that legislative acts cannot be adopted).

define and implement a common foreign and security policy, based on the development of mutual political solidarity among Member States . . .'; in Article 32 TEU, 'Member States shall ensure, through the convergence of their actions, that the Union is able to assert its interests and values on the international scene'. Article 42(2) TEU logically implies that the decision of the European Council leading to a common defence cannot have direct effect, not even for individuals, as the European Council 'shall in that case recommend to the Member States the adoption of such a decision in accordance with their respective constitutional requirements'. Second, from the standpoint of judicial protection, it would be worrisome if CFSP acts, which are in principles subtracted from the jurisdiction of the Court, could confer rights and obligations to individuals; and third, following on from that, it is hard to conceptualise the direct effect of CFSP acts if national courts do not have jurisdiction. Yet, the General Court has taken a different view in the recent decision in *RT France*, concerning the EU ban on Russian-sponsored outlets. On that occasion, the GC took the view that Article 28 TEU enables the EU to take action which affects the rights of individuals.[76] Since it is phrased in these broad terms, the finding in unconvincing, especially for the second reason mentioned above. It appears to create the space for a CFSP decision which affects (indirectly or not individually) the rights of a natural or legal person, but on which it is not clear why the Court would have jurisdiction.

The lack of supremacy and pre-emption amounts to making most CFSP acts very fragile, and subjects to the spirit of loyal cooperation of the Member States.

3.3.3 *Objectives and Boundaries*

As a result of the split in EU external relations law between CFSP and other 'external' powers of the EU (trade, environment, development cooperation), it is difficult to identify the correct substantive 'legal basis' for a foreign policy act. To appreciate the significance of this difficulty, it is necessary to introduce the concept of legal basis in EU law.

A legal basis is an Article of the Treaties conferring powers to the EU to adopt measures in a certain policy domain. There are two kinds of legal bases: substantive and procedural. An example of substantive legal basis is Article 29 TEU, according to which: 'The Council shall adopt decisions which shall define the approach of the Union to a particular matter of a geographical or thematic nature.' This article empowers the Council to adopt such decisions. The substantive legal basis determines what is the correct procedural basis (and, therefore, the correct procedure for the adoption of an act). So, an act adopted on a CFSP (substantive) legal basis will be adopted pursuant to the procedure for the adoption of CFSP act. This is also

[76]Case T-152/22 RT *France v Council* ECLI:EU:T:2022:483 Para 51: 'décisions prévoyant des mesures de nature à modifier directement la situation juridique de particuliers'.

confirmed by Article 40 TEU. An example of procedural legal basis is Article 31(1) TEU, according to which 'decisions under this Chapter shall be taken by the European Council and the Council acting unanimously'. This procedural legal basis is of crucial importance. Unlike in other policy fields, in CFSP decisions are adopted, as a rule, by unanimity in the Council. In fact, CFSP decisions are adopted by the Council or the PSC pursuant to a number of legal bases, or on any combination thereof: Article 26(2) when implementing European Council guidelines; Article 28 when adopting a decision of operational character; Article 29 for decisions on a position; Article 31 for implementing decisions; Article 32 for actions 'strengthening systematic cooperation'; Article 33 when appointing a special representative; Article 37 for the conclusion of international agreements; Article 38 for the decisions of the Political and Security Committee; Article 39 for decisions on the protection of individuals with regard to the processing of personal data; Article 41 for the urgent financing of CFSP activities; CSDP legal bases; or procedural legal bases (such as 37 TEU or Article 218 TFEU for the conclusion of international agreements[77]); and, occasionally, pursuant exclusively to previous CFSP acts.

The importance of getting the legal basis 'right' is crucial, because of the nature of the EU. The EU is an organisation to which powers have been conferred by the Member States in order to achieve common goals. The Member States have struck a constitutional bargain, expressed in the Lisbon Treaty, to the effect that *the EU can only act in so far as powers have been conferred to it* (this fundamental 'principle of conferral' is codified in Article 5(2) TEU[78]).

The difficulty (for the Council, the Commission, the Court, etc) lies in understanding *what decision* exactly should be adopted on a CFSP legal basis (as opposed to another legal basis). Is financial assistance to the Economic Community of West African States (ECOWAS) for the purposes of eliminating traffic in small and light weapons a security measure (to be adopted under CFSP rules) or a development measure?

In other words, what are the boundaries of CFSP? Where does security and defence end, and where does trade, or development cooperation begin?

The Treaties provide no solution. One approach to ascertain the boundaries of CFSP is to consider the list of eight objectives for EU external action contained in Article 21(2) TEU, to check which of the objectives can be pursued by CFSP measures.

Article 21(2) TEU reads:

> The Union shall define and pursue common policies and actions, and shall work for a high degree of cooperation in all fields of international relations, in order to:

---

[77] Article 218 TFEU is one of those provisions applying across policies – including to CFSP. It details procedures for the conclusion of international agreements to which the EU is a party.

[78] The English text uses the word 'competences', a direct translation from the French, but what it means is 'powers': 'Under the principle of conferral, the Union shall act only within the limits of the competences conferred upon it by the Member States in the Treaties to attain the objectives set out therein. Competences not conferred upon the Union in the Treaties remain with the Member States.'

(a) safeguard its values, fundamental interests, security, independence and integrity;
(b) consolidate and support democracy, the rule of law, human rights and the principles of international law;
(c) preserve peace, prevent conflicts and strengthen international security, in accordance with the purposes and principles of the United Nations Charter, with the principles of the Helsinki Final Act and with the aims of the Charter of Paris, including those relating to external borders;
(d) foster the sustainable economic, social and environmental development of developing countries, with the primary aim of eradicating poverty;
(e) encourage the integration of all countries into the world economy, including through the progressive abolition of restrictions on international trade;
(f) help develop international measures to preserve and improve the quality of the environment and the sustainable management of global natural resources, in order to ensure sustainable development;
(g) assist populations, countries and regions confronting natural or man-made disasters; and
(h) promote an international system based on stronger multilateral cooperation and good global governance.

Advocates General and scholars have attempted to rationalise this uncertainty by proposing a classification of those objectives. AG Bot has for example taken the view that objectives (a) through (c) should be 'assigned to' CFSP;[79] this is supported by the fact that those are CFSP-specific objectives that had already appeared in the previous version of the Treaty on the European Union (in Article 11). In his opinion in a later case, however, the same Advocate General also included letter (h) as a CFSP objective.[80] Eeckhout instead regards only letter (c) as being undoubtedly a CFSP objective—and regards (d) through (g) as decidedly TFEU competences, with (a), (b) and (h) being of a cross-sectoral nature.[81] Van Elsuwege has suggested that letters (a) through (c) imply that CFSP rules must be followed.[82] Finally, Koutrakos excludes the economic and social objectives in Article 21(2) from being covered by CFSP.[83] As detailed in the rest of this section, the Court has not conclusively determined which if any of the eight objectives listed in Article 21(2) TEU fall under CFSP.

As shown elsewhere in further detail,[84] even though acts do not usually refer to specific letters directly,[85] institutions have used the wording of letters (a), (b), (c), (d), (g) and (h) for CFSP measures (whereas all the objectives have been used for TFEU measures). CFSP acts, in other words, have pursued nearly all of the possible objectives of Article 21(2) TEU. The sole exceptions are purely economic or environmental objectives (letter (e): encourage the integration of all countries into the world economy; and letter (f) help develop international measures to preserve

---

[79] Case C-130/10 AG Opinion para 63. Similarly, (Larik, 2016, p. 215).
[80] Case C-658/11 para 87.
[81] Eeckhout (2013), p. 169.
[82] Elsuwege (2010), p. 1006.
[83] Koutrakos (2013), p. 420.
[84] Lonardo (2018).
[85] This makes a quantitative analysis highly impractical.

and improve the quality of the environment and the sustainable management of global natural resources).

The conflation between policy objectives is most evident in the interface with the Area of Freedom Security and Justice. Article 21(2)(c) TEU stipulates as an objective the preservation of peace and international security. This objective can be pursued by both CFSP and AFSJ acts. Examples of the former are the sanctions against the Islamic State and Al Qaeda.[86] Examples of the latter are the Passenger Name Record Directive for the prevention, detection, investigation and prosecution of terrorism which provides for the transfer and processing of passenger data of flights to or from outside the EU,[87] and the traceability of money transfers Regulation which sets rules on information regarding providers and recipients of funds in order to prevent, detect, and investigate terrorism financing.[88]

The distinction between CFSP and other areas of external action is neither semantically nor practically tenable. It is an idiosyncrasy, a *caprice* of EU external relations law. It is semantically untenable since, if CFSP covers 'all areas of foreign policy' (Article 24 TEU), then there should be no other areas of foreign policy left, making the TFEU competences redundant. The argument that the Treaties distinguish between 'foreign policy' and 'external action' is hardly persuasive, as the Treaties seem to use the phrases interchangeably: Article 18 TEU talks about 'foreign affairs' instead of 'foreign policy' (the institutional figure who conducts CFSP is called the High Representative for the Union Foreign Affairs and Security Policy), and it is not clear what the difference between 'external' and 'foreign' may be, since Article 21(2) TEU merges *foreign* policy objectives under those for *external* action. A possible solution would be to try to redefine the scope of CFSP, narrow it down, so as to encompass only the purely political and security aspects of external action.[89]

3.3.4 Judicial Protection in Common Foreign and Security Policy

The rule of Article 19 TEU that the Court of Justice of the European Union 'shall ensure that in the interpretation and application of the Treaties the law is observed'

[86] Council Decision (CFSP) 2016/1693 of 20 September 2016 concerning restrictive measures against ISIL (Da'esh) and Al-Qaeda and persons, groups, undertakings and entities associated with them and repealing Common Position 2002/402/CFSP, 8th recital.

[87] Directive (EU) 2016/681 of the European Parliament and of the Council of 27 April 2016 on the use of passenger name record (PNR) data for the prevention, detection, investigation and prosecution of terrorist offences and serious crime.

[88] Regulation (EU) 2015/847 of the European Parliament and of the Council of 20 May 2015 on information accompanying transfers of funds and repealing Regulation (EC) No 1781/2006.

[89] According to Dashwood, CFSP consists of the 'political, security and defence aspects' of foreign policy. Dashwood (2014).

finds an important limitation in the domain of Common Foreign and Security Policy. Article 24 TEU, in the relevant part, reads 'The Court of Justice of the European Union shall not have jurisdiction with respect to these provisions, with the exception of its jurisdiction to monitor compliance with Article 40 of this Treaty and to review the legality of certain decisions as provided for by the second paragraph of Article 275 of the Treaty on the Functioning of the European Union.'

Article 275 TFEU second paragraph reads as follows: 'the Court shall have jurisdiction to monitor compliance with Article 40 of the Treaty on European Union and to rule on proceedings, brought in accordance with the conditions laid down in the fourth paragraph of Article 263 of this Treaty, reviewing the legality of decisions providing for restrictive measures against natural or legal persons adopted by the Council on the basis of Chapter 2 of Title V of the Treaty on European Union'.

That Article merges grounds for review, content of the act, and procedural requirements (standing). The procedural requirement (standing under the fourth paragraph of Article 263 TFEU) is linked to the content of the acts (restrictive measures); the ground for review of legality is as well linked to restrictive measures, but the ground of Article 40 TEU is independent from either procedure or content of act challenged. Upon a literal reading, Article 275 TFEU thus would have envisaged a system whereby CFSP acts can be reviewed, in general, only on one ground: compliance with Article 40 TEU. There are no procedural requirements specified for this action. Compliance with Article 40 TEU can be reviewed by the Court in direct actions, preliminary rulings on the validity of acts, infringement proceedings, etc. Always on a literal reading of Article 275 TFEU very special category of CFSP acts, decisions establishing restrictive measures, could be reviewed also for their legality. In this case, however, the Treaty prescribed a procedural restriction: the action must be an action for annulment brought in accordance with Article 263 fourth paragraph TFEU. A literal interpretation would have entailed that the action for the review of the legality of those measures could not stem from a preliminary ruling (because that procedure is Article 267, not 263), unless, that is, the applicant challenges the decision on the grounds of Article 40 TEU. Finally, a literal reading of that provision would have led to the conclusion that the Court does not have jurisdiction to rule on actions for non-contractual liability brought for damages allegedly arising out of CFSP acts.

The decisions of the Court paint a different picture, discussed in the next chapter. In a nutshell, the Court interprets its own jurisdiction broadly, departing sometimes significantly from the text of Article 24 TEU and 275 TFEU. The case law of the Court is probably the most significant legal development of CFSP since Lisbon.

3.4 Conclusion

CFSP is characterised by legal distinctiveness. The institutional machinery, the limited involvement of the Court, and the unanimity for decision-making are the salient feature of that make this competence 'special'. These rules are largely due to path-dependence. Ever since, for accidental reasons related to domestic French politics (and not for an ideological or principled objection), the federal project of European Defence Union failed in the early 50s, Western European states have always resorted to keep foreign security and defence policy cooperation separate from the economic integration they started pursuing through the European Economic Communities. Even when the two were eventually merged, at the end of the Cold War, Common Foreign and Security Policy remained separate to a significant extent. A further merge was attempted with the Lisbon Treaty, but it is far from complete.

Legal scholarship has studied this phenomenon in some depth. What is missing, at least in explicit terms, is a debate on the desirability of the legal distinctiveness. With a view to contribute to that debate, the rest of the book will survey the highlights of the EU's action since Lisbon, highlighting achievements, tensions, and issues.

References

Austermann, F. (2014). *European Union delegations in EU foreign policy: A diplomatic service of different speeds*. Palgrave Macmillan.

Bátora, J. (2009). European defence agency: A flashpoint of institutional logics. *West European Politics, 32*(6), 1075–1098.

Bindi, F. (2012). European Union foreign policy. In F. Bindi & I. Angelescu (Eds.), *The foreign policy of the European Union* (2nd ed., pp. 11–39). Brookings Institution Press.

Blanke, H.-J., & Mangiameli, S. (Eds.). (2013). *The treaty on European Union (TEU): A commentary*. Springer.

Blockmans, S., Hillion, C., Cremona, M., Curtin, D., De Baere, G., Duke, S., Eckes, C., Van Vooren, B., Wessel, R. A., & Wouters, J. (2013). *EEAS 2.0: A Legal Commentary on Council Decision 2010/427/EU Establishing the Organisation and Functioning of the European External Action Service*. CEPS Paperbacks.

Butler, G. (2022). Hidden administrative review in EU law: The BoAs of EU agencies in the common foreign and security policy. In M. Chamon, A. Volpato, & M. Eliantonio (Eds.), *Boards of appeal of EU agencies* (pp. 122–150). Oxford University Press.

Craig, P. P. (2018). *EU administrative law* (3rd ed.). Oxford University Press.

Cremona, M. (2018). The position of CFSP/CSDP in the EU's constitutional architecture. *Research Handbook on the EU's Common Foreign and Security Policy*.

Dashwood, A. (2014). The continuing bipolarity of EU external action. In I. Govaere, E. Lannon, P. van Elsuwege, & S. Adam (Eds.), *The European Union in the World*. Brill | Nijhoff.

Duquette, E. (2001). The European Union's common foreign and security policy: Emerging from the US Shadow. *UC Davis Journal of International Law and Pollicy, 7*, 169.

Eeckhout, P. (2013). *EU external relations law*. Oxford University Press.

Elsuwege, P. V. (2010). EU external action after the collapse of the pillar structure: In search of a new balance between delimitation and consistency. *Common Market Law Review*, 987–1019.

Gatti, M. (2016). *European external action service: Promoting coherence through autonomy and coordination*. Brill Nijhoff.

Giegerich, B. (2017). *Foreign and security policy*. Oxford University Press.

Gosalbo Bono, R. (2006). Some reflections on the CFSP legal order. *Common Market Law Review*, 337–394.

Hofmann, H., & Türk, A. (2006). *EU administrative governance*. Edward Elgar.

House of Commons. (2008). *Foreign Policy Aspects of the Lisbon Treaty*.

House of Lords. (2003). *The Future of Europe - The Conventions' Draft Constitutional Treaty.*
House of Lords. (2008). *The treaty of Lisbon: An impact assessment.* House of Lords.
Italian Parliament. (2007). *Report on the Ratification of the Lisbon Treaty.*
Kiso, J. O. (1997). Coreper and the political committee: Damaging for CFSP? *Cambridge Review of International Affairs, 10*(2), 141–154.
Klamert, M. (2014). *The principle of loyalty in EU law.* Oxford University Press.
Koskenniemi, M. (Ed.). (1998). *International law aspects of the European Union.* Kluwer Law International.
Koutrakos, P. (2013). *EU international relations law.* Hart.
Larik, J. (2016). *Foreign policy objectives in European constitutional law.* Oxford University Press.
Lonardo, L. (2018). Common foreign and security policy and the EU's external action objectives: An analysis of Article 21 of the treaty on the European Union. *European Constitutional Law Review, 14*(3), 584–608.
Loth, W. (2020). The EC and foreign and security policy: The dream of autonomy. In U. Krotz, K. K. Patel, & F. Romero (Eds.), *Europe's cold war relations: The EC towards a global role* (pp. 145–163). Bloomsbury.
Marquardt, S. (2018). The institutional framework, legal instruments and decision-making procedures. *Research Handbook on the EU's Common Foreign and Security Policy.*
Martinez, J. S. (2019). The constitutional allocation of executive and legislative power over foreign relations: A survey. In C. A. Bradley (Ed.), *The Oxford handbook of comparative foreign relations law* (pp. 96–114). Oxford University Press.
Novak, S. (2013). The silence of ministers: Consensus and blame avoidance in the council of the European Union: The silence of ministers. *JCMS: Journal of Common Market Studies, 51*(6), 1091–1107.
Parsons, C. (2017). The triumph of community Europe. In D. Dinan (Ed.), *Origins and evolution of the European Union.* Oxford University Press.
Trybus, M. (2006). The New European defence agency: A contribution to a common European security and defence policy and a challenge to the community *acquis*? *Common Market Law Review, 43*(3), 667–703.
Tuori, K. (2015). *European constitutionalism* (1st ed.). Cambridge University Press.
Wallace, W. (2017). European foreign policy since the cold war: How ambitious, how inhibited? *The British Journal of Politics and International Relations, 19*(1), 77–90.
Wessel, R. A., & Larik, J. (Eds.). (2020). *EU external relations law: Text, cases and materials* (2nd ed.). Hart Publishing, Bloomsbury Publishing Plc.
Wessels, W. (2013). CFSP progress or decline after Lisbon? *European Foreign Affairs Review*, 449–469.
Woolcock, S. (2017). *Trade policy policy-making after the treaty of Lisbon.* Oxford University Press.

Part II
Common Foreign and Security Policy after Lisbon

Chapter 4
Restrictive Measures: Constitutional Issues, Classification, Judicial Review

Contents

4.1 Introduction

Restrictive measures, or sanctions, are the most used—and, according to some, the most effective—instrument of EU foreign policy. This chapter provides an overview of the EU sanctions regimes. Sparsely used by the Community Member States during the Cold War (against the Soviet Union, the Community adopted trade restrictions in 1982; against Argentina after the invasion of the Falklands and against South Africa, in line with UN sanctions, for the apartheid; against China in 1989 following the Tiananmen massacre), since the 90s international sanctions have acquired prominent as a coercive but not military means of solving international disputes. The increased adoption of such sanctions by the UN Security Council[1] has in fact helped develop the practice also among other actors, including the EU.

[1] Cassese et al. (2020), pp. 310–311.

L. Lonardo, *EU Common Foreign and Security Policy After Lisbon*,
https://doi.org/10.1007/978-3-031-19131-2_4

This chapter aims to show some of the threads and the issues in this domain. Some of these are horizontal themes of constitutional nature, such as the procedure for the adoption, the issue of secrecy that arises therein, and the effectiveness of this foreign policy tool (Sect. 4.1). The chapter proposes two possible ways to categorise sanctions: one is to distinguish between country sanctions one the one hand, and individual sanctions on the other hand (this is what Article 215 TFEU does); this distinction does not reflect the practice of the Council, and it is in fact also possible to classify sanctions depending on the rationale for their adoption: terrorist sanctions, counterproliferation sanctions, cybersanctions, sanctions against democratic back-sliding or in conflict situation (Sect. 4.2).

In the light of the variety (and complexity) of the political and legal issues involved, and of major developments in the case law of the CJEU in the period under analysis, the chapter then concentrates on the case law of the Court to highlight salient features of judicial protection afforded against restrictive measures and CFSP acts more broadly (Sect. 4.3).

4.2 Constitutional Issues: Adoption, Secrecy, Effectiveness

4.2.1 Adoption

The procedure to adopt EU sanctions consists of two steps.[2] First, the Council of the European Union adopts a decision, whose legal basis is Article 29 TEU.[3] Second, it adopts a regulation, usually, but not exclusively, under Article 215 TFEU.[4]

[2] 'The Treaty of Maastricht [. . .] allowed the EU to engage in a more proactive approach with regard to the projection of its values via the imposition of sanctions. This was an important turning point, but one which required a *legal* response to the question of how to connect the non-legally enforceable CFSP with the mainstream legal order. The response was found in the practices which initially emerged during the 1980s, by adopting a decision in the framework of EPC, followed by a Regulation concluded via the familiar Community method in the domain of the Common Commercial Policy. This arrangement continued to provide the basis for the settlement at Maastricht by transferring the practice to a combination of measures: a CFSP instrument which 'paves the way' for a Regulation.' (Cardwell 2015), the internal quotation is from Hoffmeister (2008), p. 91.

[3] 'The Council shall adopt decisions which shall define the approach of the Union to a particular matter of a geographical or thematic nature. Member States shall ensure that their national policies conform to the Union positions.'

[4] 'Where a decision, adopted in accordance with Chapter 2 of Title V of the Treaty on European Union [=CFSP}, provides for the interruption or reduction, in part or completely, of economic and financial relations with one or more third countries, the Council, acting by a qualified majority on a joint proposal from the High Representative of the Union for Foreign Affairs and Security Policy and the Commission, shall adopt the necessary measures. It shall inform the European Parliament thereof. 2. Where a decision adopted in accordance with Chapter 2 of Title V of the Treaty on European Union so provides, the Council may adopt restrictive measures under the procedure referred to in paragraph 1 against natural or legal persons and groups or non-State entities. 3. The acts referred to in this Article shall include necessary provisions on legal safeguards.'

This two-tier system is a 'relic' of the procedure that existed under the EPC.[5]

As far as the first step is concerned, the CFSP Decision is adopted by unanimity, except in the (important) cases in which the Treaties foresee QMV (when it implements a conclusion of the European Council, or when it amends or implements a previous decision). The measures are usually prepared by COREPER II, and they may be based on intelligence sources. Sanctions are the only substantive area of CFSP over which the Court has jurisdiction (in addition to the 'procedural' provision of Article 40 TEU). It is therefore of primary importance to identify what exactly constitutes a restrictive measure: the case law on the identification of a reviewable CFSP sanction is discussed in Sect. 4.4 below.

As far as the second step is concerned, the CFSP Decision is usually implemented by a Regulation adopted, by the Council, on Article 215 TFEU—hence this is not a CFSP act (and on this implementing Regulation the CJEU has jurisdiction). As a matter of law, the existence of a CFSP Decision does not oblige the Council to adopt the 'TFEU' Regulation, and in fact the text of the Decision and of the implementing Regulation may not be identical.[6]

The restrictive measures thus adopted may implement UN Security Council resolutions, or they can be 'autonomous sanctions', that is, unilaterally decided by the EU. Examples of the former are measures adopted after 9/11 to target people affiliated with Al Qaeda or other terrorist organisations. Examples of the latter are measures adopted against politicians in Egypt and Tunisia, in the wake of the so-called Arab uprisings, in order to support democracy and the rule of law in those countries.[7] On the other hand, the EU appears to have claims to regional leadership in this domain, in the sense that when it imposes sanctions, its partners tend to follow suit.[8]

4.2.2 Secrecy

Some authors have maintained that the adoption of sanctions (especially terrorist sanctions) on the basis of intelligence information (which is valuable only in so far as it is secret, inaccessible to the target of the measure as well as to the courts), leads to a circumvention of the traditional criminal justice procedure.[9] Indeed, this has led some authors to talk about the overcriminalisation of terrorism.[10] The impossibility

---

[5] See the comprehensive analysis by Beaucillon (2018).

[6] Case C-134/19 P *Bank Refah* ECLI:EU:C:2020:793 para 41.

[7] These are all discussed in Sect. 4.2.2.

[8] Cardwell and Moret (2022).

[9] de Goede (2011).

[10] Mitsilegas (2018).

of an independent review of intelligence information constitutes one of the main obstacles to the safeguard of human rights in the context of terrorist listing.[11]

Restrictive measures, in so far as they can be scrutinised by courts, need to provide reasons for their adoption. In *Kiselev,*[12] the General Court held that the obligation to state reasons on which an EU sanction is based is an essential *procedural* requirement, to be distinguished from the question whether the reasons given are well founded, the latter question pertains to the *substantive* legality of the contested act.[13] On the first, the obligation to state reasons, corollary of the right of the defence, is enshrined in Article 296(2) TFEU and according to established case-law,[14] it has a twofold purpose. Firstly, to provide the person concerned with sufficient information to make it possible to ascertain whether the act is well founded or whether it is vitiated by a defect which may permit its legality to be contested before the EU courts. Secondly, to enable those courts to review the legality of that act.[15] For this reason, the GC has established that addressees of EU sanctions are entitled to obtain, as far as feasible, the evidence used against them when receiving notification of the imposition of the sanction.[16] On the second, since EU courts may not substitute their assessment of the evidence, facts and circumstances justifying the adoption of such measures to that of the Council, the review carried out by those Courts must be restricted to checking that the rules governing procedure and the statement of reasons have been complied with, that the facts are materially accurate and that there has been no manifest error of assessment of the facts or misuse of power. That limited review applies, especially, to the assessment of the appropriateness of the evidence on which such measures are based.[17] The CJEU held that Article 47 Charter, providing the right to an effective remedy, requires the EU courts to ensure that a decision which affects that person individually is taken on a sufficiently solid factual basis.[18] That entails a verification of the factual allegations underpinning that decision, with the consequence that judicial review cannot be restricted to an assessment of the cogency in the abstract of the reasons relied on. On the contrary, it must check whether those reasons, or, at the very least, one of those reasons, deemed sufficient in itself to support that decision, are substantiated by sufficiently specific and concrete evidence.[19]

---

[11] Hayes and Sullivan (2010).

[12] Case T-262/15 *Kiselev v Council of the European Union* EU:T:2017:392.

[13] Ibid Para 52.

[14] See e.g. Case T-200/14 *Ben Ali* v *Council* EU:T:2016:216, para 94 and case law there cited.

[15] See e.g. Case C- 176/13 *Bank Mellat*, EU:C:2016:96, para 74; Case T-307/12 and T-408/13 *Mayaleh v Council*, EU:T:2014:926, para 105.

[16] Case T-181/08 *Pye Phyo Tay Za v Council of the European Union* EU:T:2010:209.

[17] Case T-408/13 *Mayaleh v Council*, EU:T:2014:926.

[18] Judgments of 18 July 2013, *Commission and Others* v *Kadi*, C-584/10 P, C-593/10 P and C-595/10 P, EU:C:2013:518, paragraph 119; of 18 June 2015, *Ipatau* v *Council*, C-535/14 P, EU:C:2015:407, paragraph 42; and of 18 February 2016, *Council* v *Bank Mellat*, C-176/13 P, EU:C:2016:96, paragraph 109.

[19] As held by constant case law, e.g. Joined Cases C-584/10 P, C-593/10 P and C-595/10 P *Kadi II*, EU:C:2013:518, para 119; Case T-331/14 *Azarov*, EU:T:2016:49, para 43.

The balance between the secrecy of the information on which the measures may be based, and the rights to due process of the addresses of the measures is a particularly delicate one. It is struck on a case by case basis by EU courts—even though, by and large, Member States are very reluctant to disclose evidence, even confidentially.[20]

4.2.3 *Effectiveness*

What aims do restrictive measures pursue? By adopting restrictive measures, the Union spreads its fundamental values and pursues its objectives[21] in the international arena. At a very abstract level, it can be stated that 'sanctions are used as a means to promote a change in behaviour, as a punishment or a means to isolate a state, or a combination thereof.'[22] But the reasons for the adoption of restrictive measures, and therefore their intended consequences, vary significantly. A useful model was proposed by Giumelli, who suggests a distinction between coercing, constraining, and signalling as possible aims of EU sanctions.[23]

The debate on the effectiveness of sanctions is old and fierce.[24] Here, two interesting mechanisms on the effects of sanctions in third countries may be singled out: sanctions can produce the desired effect of coercing into submission, or constraining a foreign country, if the asymmetry in power between the entities is such as to prevent the addressee from carrying on with a certain behaviour (due to lack of resources, opportunities, motivation); the same sanctions may fail if, instead, they generate hatred or resentment against the entity imposing them. Thus, in 2014 Putin's popularity raised concomitantly with the imposition of EU sanctions.[25] It is probably impossible to predict what effect sanctions will have, and when.

4.3 The Types of Sanctions

A possible taxonomy of EU sanctions is to distinguish between country sanctions and individual sanctions—which is what Article 215 TFEU does—but this distinction is more blurred in practice. Another way to slice the cake is to consider the rationale for the adoption of restrictive measures: one can thus distinguish 'thematic'

[20] Abazi and Eckes (2018).

[21] For a discussion of the EU objectives as related to EU sanctions (Larik, 2016, pp. 169–171).

[22] Cardwell (2015), p. 12.

[23] See Giumelli (2011).

[24] Vines (2012) and Hawkins and Lloyd (2003).

[25] Fokht (2019).

sanctions, aimed at counter nuclear proliferation, terrorism, cyberattacks, or democratic backsliding.

4.3.1 Classification by Target: Country Sanctions and Individual Sanctions

Legally (in Article 215 TFEU), there is a theoretical distinction between 'country sanctions' and 'individual sanctions'—and the case law has in fact addressed different legal issues.[26] The difference lies in the individuation of the targets of the measures. Thus, when sanctioning Venezuela, the EU adopted measures addressed at *EU* companies, prohibiting them from supplying certain technologies to the Venezuelan government, offices, agencies etc. Thus, formally, the addressees of those country sanctions were not Venezuelan companies;[27] whereas terrorist sanction, for example, or sanctions for violations of human rights, list (in an annex), the name and surname of addressees—and crucially for the purposes of judicial protection—a statement of the (public) reasons for the listing. Often, the CFSP Decisions adopting restrictive measures, or the implementing Regulation, contain a mix of the country sanctions and individual sanctions. The Court thus draws a distinction between provisions 'of a general nature, their scope being determined by reference to objective criteria and not by reference to identified natural or legal persons'[28] on the one hand; and on the other hand, 'measures targeting identified natural or legal persons, in practice, entities individually named in the provisions of the act concerned'.[29]

In *Kala Naft* an Iranian company owned by the National Iranian Oil Company sought the annulment of Council Decision (2010/413/CFSP) concerning restrictive measures against Iran. The General Court (upheld on appeal by the Court of Justice) considered that Article 4 of the Decision—prohibiting the sale, supply or transfer to Iran of key equipment and technology as well as the supply technical and financial assistance in the oil and natural gas industries—were of a general nature and, therefore, of the kind on which the Court does not have jurisdiction (the ECJ nonetheless found jurisdiction because it considered that the measures the applicant was challenging derived from the implementation of Article 20 of Decision 2010/413, which provided asset freeze for certain entities specified in the annex, including Kala Naft).

[26] On which see Beaucillon (2018).

[27] The Court has then clarified that this formalistic reading does not change the fact that, by prohibiting EU companies from contracting with Venezuelan companies, the sanction does in fact impose a restriction to Venezuelan companies.

[28] *Manufacturing Support & Procurement Kala Naft v Council* para 99.

[29] Heliskoski (2018), p. 13.

A similar reasoning was repeated in *Rosneft*, where the Court distinguished between measures prohibiting EU companies from providing financial assistance or technical expertise to the Russian oil sector[30] (provisions on which the Court did not have jurisdiction) and those providing for asset freeze or similia *against specific addressees* (including, in that case, the Russian government-owned company Rosneft).

Portela identified a pattern of escalation and sequencing in the imposition of sanctions: 'The beginning of the actual imposition of sanctions is sometimes preceded by the passing of the legislation enacting sanctions—a so-called 'sanctions framework'—with an empty annex, indicating that the Council is ready to include entries but that it will initially refrain from doing so. [. . .] The first stage in the actual sanctions exercise consists of the blacklisting of a number of individuals on which a visa ban and an asset freeze is applied, often accompanied by a few companies and agencies. [. . .] A second stage includes an embargo on the supply of arms, equipment for internal repression and surveillance and dual-use items, in addition to a ban on the provision of related services and of any form of military cooperation. The next stage in the escalation prohibits the export or import of certain products and commodities, and encompasses the imposition of financial sanctions'.[31] This, however, is neither a set policy nor a rule without exception. As discussed below, the 2022 sanctions against Russia and Belarus are not sequenced at all.

4.3.2 Classification by Rationale: Anti-Terrorism, Counterproliferation Sanctions, Cybersanctions, Democratic Backsliding and Conflict Situations

Terrorist sanctions target individuals or entities suspected of terrorist acts (as defined in article 1(3)of the Common Position 2011/931/CFSP). The 9/11 attacks firmly placed terrorism at the top of the international security agenda of the EU. Ever since, the EU's fight against terrorism has resulted in a vast array of legal instruments, including sanctions that take the form of asset freezes, travel bans and other restrictions to the fundamental rights of suspected terrorists. The (legal) literature on EU sanctions to fight terrorism has provided an extensive assessment of the (negative) impact of restrictive measures on the fundamental rights of individuals (most notably, related to due process and the right of defence). Another strand of

---

[30] Articles 4 and 4a of Council Decision 2014/512 of 31 July 2014 concerning restrictive measures in view of Russia's actions destabilising the situation in Ukraine' providing for a system of prior authorisation for the sale, supply, transfer or export of certain technologies suited to specific categories of oil exploration and production projects in Russia and for a prohibition on the provision of associated services necessary for those projects.

[31] Portela (2022), p. 3.

literature (mostly deriving from critical security studies) has criticised the negative repercussions of such measures on the human rights of the targets. Authors have highlighted the political as well as stigmatising functions of terrorist listing. While due process guarantees were often not respected in the initial days of terrorist sanctions and the adoption of such measures on intelligence information was harshly criticised in the literature, judicial protection against these measures has significantly improved the situation, prompting a process of constitutional dialogue in which the Council modifies its practices of listing and de-listing in order to comply with the criteria established in the Court's judgments.[32]

Counterproliferation sanctions are directed against individuals (mostly, legal persons such as companies) for taking part in or helping with processes deemed to be contrary to a counterproliferation regime. In practice, the same distinction explained in the paragraph on country sanctions holds. Iran had been developing a civil nuclear programme since the 1950s. In 2002, serious doubts arose about the scope of its research when two unknown nuclear sites were discovered, including a uranium enrichment site. Tensions ensued between Iran (supported by Russia) and the United States, supported by several European Union countries, which suspected Tehran of maintaining secret programmes for the development of military capabilities.[33] The UN imposed sanctions (for the first time in 2006), and the EU implemented them, and further adopted other autonomous measures (imposing inter alia restrictions on trade and on the Iranian banking sector: the judgment in *Bank Refah* a particularly significant case discussed in Sect. 4.4 of this chapter, arose out of these sanctions).[34] On 14 July 2015, a historical agreement ('the Iran deal') was signed between Iran and the 5+1 (the Members of the UNSC + Germany). One of the successes of Mogherini's time as HR/VP, the deal provided for the limitation of Iran's nuclear programme to the civilian sphere and a strengthening of controls in return for the lifting of some UN and autonomous sanctions. North Korea, after withdrawing from the Non-Proliferation Treaty (NPT) in 2003, has conducted several nuclear tests in breach of international law. Since 2006, the EU has imposed sanctions, both autonomously and in implementation of UN ones.

While regimes of terrorist sanctions and counterproliferations sanctions often originate in the UN (and the EU merely follows), 'the UN lacks a mandate to address situations of democratic regression, such as *coups d'état*. This constitutes the main scenario that attracts the imposition of sanctions by the EU, alongside the United States and other partners'.[35] EU sanctions of this kind are found in the neighbourhood, to promote the rule of law (such as in Tunisia and Egypt, sanctioning politicians responsible for the misappropriation of state funds; or in Belarus, sanctioning non-independent prosecutors who brought fabricated charges against political opponents etc), or further afield (Myanmar, Venezuela).

---

[32] Heupel (2009). Many of these insights draw on the monograph by Nanopoulos (2019).

[33] Cattaruzza (2017), p. 84.

[34] Since 2011, the EU adopted measures against Iran to end human rights violations.

[35] Portela (2022), p. 2.

A brief mention of cybersanctions is also in order. The cyber-attacks sanctions framework regulation[36] allowed for the adoption, in July 2020, of the EU's first sanctions against cyber-attacks. Significantly, the framework regulation allows for the adoption of measures even in the absence of an attribution of the attack to a country. In the case of the 2020 sanctions, the individuals and entities targeted were allegedly involved in an attempted cyber-attack against the Organisation for the Prohibition of Chemical Weapons, in Cloud Hopper, in WannaCry and NotPetya. The last three are among the most devastating cyber-attacks in history: they affected public services and critical infrastructures, had a far-reaching geographical spread, and the estimated damages amount to several billions of dollars.[37]

In terms of conflict situation, after the 2022 invasion of Ukraine, the EU reacted swiftly, with an unprecedented level of unity (at least initially) in overcoming for example initial reticence by certain Member States to impose sanctions against Russian banks and luxury goods but encountering more difficulties with the imposition of sanctions on the import of Russian energy. In extreme synthesis,[38] the EU adopted individual restrictive measures such as asset freezes and travel restrictions against hundreds of Russians and Belarusians; restrictions against dozens of Russian and Belarusian companies (including SWIFT bans for some banks); economic sanctions against sectors of the Russian and Belarusian economies (including transports, space, banking, oil refining and metallurgical industries), trade restrictions for certain products (such as weapons, dual-use goods, construction products, luxury goods, as well as oil and gas imported by sea); a ban on certain Russian media companies; restrictions on economic relations with the non-government-controlled areas of Donetsk and Luhansk; and even though it is not a restrictive measure for the purposes of EU law, the EU has also partially suspended the EU-Russia agreement on visa facilitation.[39] The 2022 sanctions against Russia are contained in acts amending the March 2014 and July 2014 measures ('the 2014 sanctions'), and are therefore contained in the consolidated version of those acts.[40] Compared to the 2014 sanctions, the 2022 sanctions are heavier because they are broader: they target greater sectors of the Russian economy and more individuals. Contrary to usual practice, the 2022 sanctions were also adopted in quick succession and not, as in 2014, by gradually increasing the pressure on Russia over the course of four months.

---

[36] Council Regulation (EU) 2019/796 of 17 May 2019 concerning restrictive measures against cyber-attacks threatening the Union or its Member States (OJ L 129/1).

[37] See e.g. Nash et al. (2018).

[38] Lonardo (2022).

[39] Decision 2022/333 on the partial suspension of the application of the Agreement between the European Community and the Russian Federation on the facilitation of the issuance of visas to the citizens of the European Union and the Russian Federation [2022] OJ L 54/1.

[40] Council Decision 2014/145/CFSP of 17 March 2014 OJ 2014 L078 and Council Regulation (EU) 269/2014 of 17 March 2014 OJ 2014 L 078, p. 6.); Council Decision 2014/512/CFSP of 31 July 2014 OJ 2014 L 229, p. 13; Council Regulation (EU) 833/2014 of 31 July 2014 OJ 2014 L 229, p. 1.

4.4 Judicial Review: The Role of the Court in CFSP

As mentioned in Chap. 3 on the legal context, the Court's understanding of its own power to hear CFSP cases is possibly the most significant developments in the interpretation of the legal provisions of CFSP and thus deserves closer scrutiny.

The post-Lisbon case law in this area is in fact characterised by a teleological reasoning aimed at the protection of fundamental rights and the rule of law, in particular in its declension as effective judicial protection. The need to ensure a complete system of legal remedies despite the express constitutional limitations of Article 24 TEU and 275 TFEU has also resulted in decisions which are more or less a major departure from the text of the Treaties, in so far as the Court has established an overall broad jurisdiction over CFSP acts (including acts which do not provide for restrictive measures) in direct and indirect actions, as well as in actions for damages.

The rest of the section will outline procedural avenues, including rules on standing, through which cases involving CFSP provisions or articles adopted thereupon can reach the Court; it will then discuss grounds of review by the Court; and the effects of the Court's judgments. The section is thus not exclusively about restrictive measures, but, following the movement of Court's case law, it zooms out from sanctions to CFSP decisions more broadly.[41]

4.4.1 Procedural Avenues to Challenge CFSP Acts

4.4.1.1 Direct Actions: Article 263 TFEU

Article 263 TFEU empowers certain institutions and Member States to bring direct actions for the annulment of acts of EU institutions, bodies, offices, agencies. Several cases have been brought by institutions (the Commission and the European Parliament) seeking the annulment of acts by the Council which were based on a substantive CFSP legal basis.[42] These cases involve the identification of the correct legal basis for the conclusion of an international agreement or related matters (the issue is addressed again in the section dedicated to Article 40 TEU).

Pursuant to the fourth paragraph of Article 263 TFEU, natural or legal persons may challenge measures of general application. The Court recognised standing to challenge restrictive measures for natural persons (Rotenberg), companies (Bank Refah), including companies controlled by third countries (Rosneft, Export Development Bank of Iran), and holders of public offices in third countries (Azarov,

[41] The short narrative provided below is fully developed in Butler (2017); Koutrakos (2018); Heliskoski (2018); Van Elsuwege (2021).

[42] C-130/10 *Parliament v Council* ECLI:EU:C:2012:472 paras 43 and 44; C-658/11 *European Parliament v Council (Mauritius)* EU: C:2014:2025; C-263/14 *European Parliament v Council (Tanzania)* EU: C:2016:435; C-244/17 *Commission v Council (Kazakhstan)* ECLI:EU:C:2018:662; Case C-180/20 *Commission v Council (Armenia)* ECLI:EU:C:2021:658.

Yanukovych). The Court even recognised that a third country is a legal person for the purposes of the fourth paragraph of Article 263 TFEU (Venezuela). These applicants encounter the *TWD* limitation,[43] meaning that they are barred from challenging via preliminary rulings the validity of measures they could challenge via direct action, once the terms for introducing the latter have expired.

4.4.1.2 Preliminary References: Article 267 TFEU

Rosneft was the first case in which the Court had to consider whether the legality of restrictive measures can be challenged through a preliminary reference procedure. The Court grounded its jurisdiction on several textual and teleological arguments, the first of which was the consideration of the architecture of judicial protection under EU law. Such a system, the Court recalled, consists of both the action for annulment and the preliminary ruling procedures: an applicant can avail itself of both in order to challenge the validity of an act of the institutions, and these include CFSP acts.[44]

In addition, declaring jurisdiction on preliminary rulings of measures falling within CFSP—the Court's argument goes—avoids the potential deterioration of the protection of fundamental rights which would derive from each national court being able to monitor CFSP decisions in the absence of a centralised mechanism. If national courts had jurisdiction when the Court of Justice of the EU does not, this might lead to diverging and potentially even conflicting interpretations of the same CFSP measure (para. 78).[45] Furthermore, as the Court noted (para. 71), preliminary rulings on the validity of a decision providing for restrictive measures might be necessary, since implementation is in part the responsibility of the Member States. Completely excluding the Court's jurisdiction from an area of EU law such as CFSP would seriously hinder the system of judicial protection (para. 75 and case law there cited). Even though it is left to the discretion of national courts to decide whether to make a reference for a preliminary ruling as well as what are the questions to be referred, completely ruling out the opportunity for an applicant (or the national court) to make such a request is indeed against Article 47 Charter.

The Court has never heard a request for preliminary reference involving exclusively a question of interpretation of a CFSP provision or act based thereupon.

[43] C-188/92 - TWD v Bundesrepublik Deutschland ECLI:EU:C:1994:90.

[44] This is the 'complete system of legal remedies and procedures designed to ensure judicial review of the legality of acts of the institutions'. Court of Justice, Case C-50/00 P *UPA* ECLI:EU:C:2002:462, para 40. See also *Rosneft* para 71.

[45] This is also one of the concerns of the referring court in Rosneft. See *Rosneft*, AG Opinion para. 27. For this reason, the AG suggested that the Court can issues preliminary rulings in CFSP (para. 61–62 Opinion).

4.4.1.3 Infringement Actions: Article 258 TFEU

AG Tanchev mentions that the Commission could begin an action for failure to fulfil an obligation against a Member State, even in the context of CFSP.[46] So far, this action has not been brought.

4.4.2 Grounds of Review

4.4.2.1 The Boundaries of the Policy

By providing that TFEU competences shall not affect the competence provided for in the chapter on Common Foreign and Security Policy (CFSP), Article 40 TEU establishes a boundary between the CFSP and other EU competences (including, for example, other 'external relations' competences such as the Common Commercial Policy, Development and Cooperation, etc). Similarly, albeit not exactly symmetrically, the Article provides that the CFSP shall not affect other competences of the EU (the lack of symmetry lies in the fact that other competences can affect CFSP provisions, as long as the latter are not contained in Chapter V TEU: it is the case, arguably, of provisions such as Article 218 TFEU, which also applies to CFSP).

Article 40 TEU empowers the Court to check that an EU measure has been adopted pursuant to the correct (either procedural or substantive) legal basis. Thus, for example, if a measure is to be adopted pursuant to a CFSP substantive legal basis, the Council decides by unanimity. Conversely, other voting rules will apply (depending on the decision-making procedure foreseen by the Treaties) if the measure is to be adopted pursuant to a TFEU legal basis.

In a series of interinstitutional disputes[47] that have taken place since the entry into force of the Lisbon Treaty, the Court confirmed that the mechanism to monitor that the proper procedure for the adoption of an act has been followed is this: the substantive legal basis of a measure is to be ascertained by applying a centre of gravity test.[48]

[46] Case C-619/18 *Commission v Republic of Poland (Rule of Law)* ECLI:EU:C:2019:325 para 48.

[47] C-130/10 *Parliament v Council* ECLI:EU:C:2012:472 paras 43 and 44; C-658/11 *European Parliament v Council (Mauritius)* EU: C:2014:2025; C-263/14 *European Parliament v Council (Tanzania)* EU: C:2016:435; C-244/17 *Commission v Council (Kazakhstan)* ECLI:EU:C:2018:662. The Court adopts the same approach in direct or indirect actions brought by individuals for the annulment of restrictive measures, such Case C-72/15 *Rosneft* ECLI:EU:C:2017:236 para 86; Case T-290/17 *Stavitsky* ECLI:EU:T:2019:37 paras 64 and following.

[48] C-244/17 *Commission v Council (Kazakhstan)* para 37. Case C-377/12 *Commission* v *Council (Framework Agreement with the Philippines)* EU:C:2014:1903, para 34; case C-263/14, *Parliament* v *Council (Tanzania)* EU:C:2016:435, para 44; C-244/17 *Commission v Council (Kazakhstan)* ECLI:EU:C:2018:662 AG Opinion para 58; Case C-180/20 *Commission v Council (Armenia)* ECLI:EU:C:2021:658 para 35.

Due to this line of litigation, Article 40 TEU has become an area of constitutional dialogue: at stake, in cases involving this provision, are not only the prerogatives and decision-making of EU institutions, but also, in light of the new generation of free-trade agreements and of a prospective accession of the EU to the ECHR, the role of the Court, and of judicial protection afforded by an international agreement to individuals. So far, the Court has never found a breach of Article 40 TEU.

4.4.2.2 Legality Control of Restrictive Measures: Article 275 TFEU

In *Rosneft*, the Court needed to ascertain what constitutes a decision proving for restrictive measures, for the purposes of establishing the Court's jurisdiction under Article 24 TEU and 275 TFEU. It drew a distinction between measures of general application—over which it found it lacked jurisdiction—and measures defining their subject by reference to specific natural or legal persons.

In *Rosneft*, for example, the Court did not scrutinise the Council's political choice to target the Russian oil sector by making the provision of certain services to Russian companies subject to prior authorisation, because it considered such restriction to be a measure of general application, not targeting specific entities but only an abstract and general category of operators.[49]

The ECJ instead exercised its jurisdiction over other provisions because 'it is clear that the persons and entities subject to those measures are defined by reference to specific entities. Those provisions prohibit, inter alia, the carrying out of various financial transactions with respect to entities listed in [the CFSP measure at issue]'.[50]

Nulla quaestio that a Regulation, adopted under Article 215 TFEU, implementing a CFSP Decision falls under the jurisdiction of the Court of Justice (because it is a TFEU act).[51] Furthermore, in *Rosneft*, the Court ruled that Article 215 acts as a 'bridge' between CFSP and TFEU,[52] and thus it appears that CFSP decisions which need implementation via Article 215 are also subject to the Court's jurisdiction, because they have 'crossed the bridge' (AG Whatelet's expression).[53]

4.4.2.3 Other Provisions

In previous cases, the Court had taken the view that it only had jurisdiction to review a CFSP act in two cases: either if it is a restrictive sanction, or to monitor compliance with Article 40 TEU.

---

[49] ECJ 28 March 2017, Case C-72/15 *Rosneft*, para. 99.

[50] ECJ 28 March 2017, Case C-72/15 *Rosneft*, para. 100.

[51] C-72/15 *Rosneft* para 106.

[52] *Rosneft* par 89; see also case C-310/10 par 59.

[53] *Rosneft* par 104.

This case law is occasionally followed by the General Court, but not by the ECJ. The case law is still developing and, as Opinion 2/13 aptly summarised it, 'as EU law now stands, certain acts adopted in the context of the CFSP fall outside the ambit of judicial review by the Court of Justice'.

The recent case law appears to suggest that the Court will interpret the exclusion of its jurisdiction narrowly. And that, if there is a measure of general application conferring jurisdiction to the Court, this is sufficient to enable it to exercise jurisdiction over CFSP acts, even when these are not restrictive measures or where there is no issue of compliance with Article 40 TEU.

In *Elitaliana*,[54] the ECJ reviewed a decision relating to public procurement, adopted under the CSDP and in the context of EULEX Kosovo, on the grounds that it had financial implications which are to be managed through non-CFSP competences. In the context of CSDP naval operations off the Somali coast,[55] the EU has concluded treaties with Mauritius and Tanzania, for the trial and transfer of suspected pirates. In *Mauritius* and *Tanzania*,[56] the European Parliament brought actions for annulment before the ECJ, claiming in both cases that its procedural right under Article 218(10) TFEU[57] was infringed (it was, in fact, informed after the conclusion of the agreements). The Court found it had jurisdiction to review the validity of the agreement in question as it derived from Article 218(10) TFEU, which is a provision of general application and thus is not excluded from its review—and held that the Parliament's prerogative had been breached. In *H*,[58] the Court reviewed a decision, adopted pursuant to a CFSP instrument, by the Head of an EU Mission. The Court did so because, despite the decision not being a restrictive measure, it was considered to be of staff management (a matter on which the Court has jurisdiction pursuant to Article 268 TFEU). Again, in *SatCen*,[59] the GC found that it had jurisdiction over decisions of the CFSP agency (the European Union Satellite Centre) whereby an employee of that agency the was disciplined, suspended and ultimately dismissed. The GC found that it had jurisdiction under Article 263 TFEU as regards the review of the legality of the contested decisions and under Article 268 TFEU, read in conjunction with the second paragraph of Article 340 TFEU, in relation to claims for non-contractual liability, taking into account Article 19(1) TEU and Article 47 of the Charter: this was notwithstanding the fact that SatCen is established on a CFSP legal basis and operates within that framework.[60] In *KS v Council*, the General Court dismissed an action brought against the Council, the

[54]C-439/13 P *Elitaliana SpA v EULEX Kosovo* EU:C:2015:753.

[55]These CSDP missions and operations are discussed in Chap. 5.

[56]C-658/11 *European Parliament v Council (Mauritius)* EU: C:2014:2025 and C-263/14, *Parliament* v *Council (Tanzania)* EU:C:2016:435.

[57]Article 218(10) TFEU stipulates that 'The European Parliament shall be immediately and fully informed at all stages of the procedure'.

[58]Case C-455/14 P *H v Council and Commission* (2016) ECLI:EU:C:2016:569.

[59]Case T-286/15 *KF v The European Union Satellite Centre* EU:T:2018:718.

[60]Ibid para 99.

Commission and the EEAS by family members of victims of war crimes in Kosovo on the grounds that it lacked jurisdiction. The applicants sought to establish the non-contractual liability of the EU for its failure to equip EULEX Kosovo with sufficient resources to properly investigate those crimes. That case is currently pending in appeal as case C-44/22 and is discussed again in Chap. 7.

4.4.3 *Effects*

4.4.3.1 Annulment

Even though the Court has annulled Decisions authorising the conclusion of international agreements by the EU, it is constant practice that the effects of that annulled decision be maintained into force. The annulment of an act adopted, in the context of international agreements, pursuant to a CFSP legal basis thus has chiefly the effect of modifying *pro-futuro* the practice of EU institutions.

The annulment of decisions providing for restrictive measures has instead the effect of depriving those measures of effects *ex tunc*. It is constant case law that the annulment of a restrictive measure only benefits the applicant.[61]

4.4.3.2 Non Contractual Liability

In *Bank Refah*, the Court reasoned that systemic and teleological considerations mandate the extension of its jurisdiction to actions for damages based on CFSP Decisions providing for restrictive measures. The action for damages has a 'specific purpose' dictating conditions for its use;[62] and the fundamental value of the rule of law (Articles 2 and 21 TEU) and the principle of effective judicial protection (Article 47 of the Charter of Fundamental Rights of the EU) make the jurisdiction of the CJEU necessary. In that regard, the Court found that the coherence of the system of remedies would be jeopardized if the Court only had jurisdiction over implementing regulations, and not over CFSP Decisions.[63] This is because the two may not be identical.[64] The ECJ nevertheless rejected the appeal on the substance, in that the substantive conditions necessary to give rise to the non-contractual liability of the Union were not met.[65]

---

[61] The 'Kadi' annulment does not benefit other people included in the sanctions list; Tridimas (2020), p. 459.

[62] Case C-134/19 P *Bank Refah Kargaran*, para. 33.

[63] Case C-134/19 P *Bank Refah Kargaran*, para. 39.

[64] Case C-134/19 P *Bank Refah Kargaran*, para. 41.

[65] See further Chap. 5 for the exportability of this judgment to CSDP.

4.5 Conclusion

Restrictive measures are probably the key instrument through which the EU has conducted its CFSP in the period under analysis. From targeting terrorists affiliated with Al Qaeda to sanctioning politicians who permitted or organised the referendum on Crimean independence in 2014, the scope and geographical reach of these measures have been far reaching. While an overall assessment of their effectiveness runs the risk of not capturing the varieties in the objectives that such measures pursue, focus on the case law of the Court reveals how this institution has been active and influential in shaping the EU sanctions landscape.

The Court's interpretation of the provisions relating to CFSP is far from literal. The landmark cases such as *Kala Naft* and *Rosneft* have contributed to delimiting the jurisdiction of the Court, but in other instances (*H*), the ECJ found jurisdiction on CFSP measures other than sanctions. The grounds for review, which should in principle consist only of Article 40 TEU, have been expanded so as to include the general principles, the Charter, and Article 218. Crucially, the procedure for the review of legality of restrictive measures has been extended to preliminary ruling.

These developments are, from the perspective of the protection of individual rights, entirely commendable. They afford not only EU citizens, but in fact third country national and legal persons alike the standard of protection offered by EU law. This is particularly obvious in the case law on the right of fair trial, with decisions that go so far as to mandate that EU institutions check the compliance of third countries authorities with EU standards.[66] These normative considerations on the Court's jurisdiction are discussed again in Chap. 7.

References

Abazi, V., & Eckes, C. (2018). Closed Evidence in EU Courts: Security, secrets and access to justice. *Common Market Law Review, 55*(3), 753–782.

Beaucillon, C. (2018). Opening up the Horizon: The ECJ's new take on country sanctions. *Common Market Law Review*, 387–415.

Butler, G. (2017). The coming of age of the Court's Jurisdiction in the common foreign and security policy. *European Constitutional Law Review, 13*(4), 673–703.

Cardwell, P. J. (2015). The legalisation of European Union foreign policy and the use of sanctions. *Cambridge Yearbook of European Legal Studies, 17*, 287–310.

Cardwell, P. J., & Moret, E. (2022). The EU, sanctions and regional leadership. *European Security*, 1–21.

Cassese, A., Gaeta, P., Viñuales, J. E., & Zappalà, S. (2020). *Cassese's international law* (3rd ed.). Oxford University Press.

---

[66] Judgments in Joint Cases T-244/16 *Yanukovych v Council*, T-285/17 *Yanukovych v Council*, Joint cases T-245/16 and T-286/17 *Yanukovych v Council* and cases T-274/18 *Klymenko v Council*, T-284/18 *Arbuzov v Council*, T-285/18 *Pshonka v Council*, T-289/18 *Pshonka v Council* and T305/18 *Klyuyev v Council*.

Cattaruzza, A. (2017). *Atlas Des Guerres et Conflits. Un Tour Du Monde Géopolitique*. Éditions Autrement.

de Goede, M. (2011). Blacklisting and the Ban: Contesting targeted sanctions in Europe. *Security Dialogue, 42*(6), 499–515.

Fokht, E. (2019). Russia and Putin: Is President's Popularity in Decline? *BBC News* (19 June 2019).

Giumelli, F. (2011). *Coercing, constraining and signalling: Explaining UN and EU sanctions after the Cold War*. ECPR Press.

Hawkins, D., & Lloyd, J. (2003). Questioning comprehensive sanctions: The birth of a norm. *Journal of Human Rights, 2*(3), 441–454.

Hayes, B., & Sullivan, G. (2010). *Blacklisted: Targeted sanctions, preemptive security and fundamental rights*. European Center for Constitutional and Human Rights.

Heliskoski, J. (2018) 'Made in Luxembourg: The fabrication of the law on Jurisdiction of the Court of Justice of the European Union in the field of the common foreign and security policy'. *Europe and the World: A Law Review, 2*(3), 2–20.

Heupel, M. (2009). Multilateral sanctions against terror suspects and the violation of due process standards. *International Affairs (Royal Institute of International Affairs 1944-), 85*(2), 307–321.

Hoffmeister, F. (2008). The contribution of EU practice to international law. In M. Cremona (Ed.), *Developments in EU external relations law* (pp. 37–127). Oxford University Press.

Koutrakos, P. (2018). Judicial review in the EU's common foreign and security policy. *International and Comparative Law Quarterly, 67*(1), 1–35.

Larik, J. (2016). *Foreign policy objectives in European constitutional law*. Oxford University Press.

Lonardo, L. (2022). Weapons, humanitarian assistance, sanctions: A legal analysis of the EU's immediate response to the Russian Invasion of Ukraine of 2022. *European Law Review, 47*.

Mitsilegas, V. (2018). European criminal law and the dangerous citizen. *Maastricht Journal of European and Comparative Law, 25*(6), 733–751.

Nanopoulos, E. (2019). *The juridification of individual sanctions and the politics of EU law*. Hart Publishing.

Nash, K., Castellanos, S., & Janofsky, A. (2018) One year after NotPetya cyberattack, firms wrestle with recovery costs. *Wall Street Journal* (27 June 2018).

Portela, C. (2022) *Sanctions, conflict and democratic backsliding*. European Union Institute for Security Studies.

Tridimas, T. (2020). Economic sanctions, procedural rights and judicial scrutiny. *Cambridge Yearbook of European Legal Studies, 22*, 455, 459.

Van Elsuwege, P. (2021). Judicial review and the common foreign and security policy: Limits to the gap-filling role of the Court of Justice. *Common Market Law Review*, 1731–1760.

Vines, A. (2012). The effectiveness of UN and EU sanctions: Lessons for the twenty-first century. *International Affairs (Royal Institute of International Affairs 1944-), 88*(4), 867–877.

Chapter 5
Common Security and Defence Policy in Action

Contents

5.1 Introduction

How does the EU operationalise its Common Foreign and Security Policy? In addition to sanctions, discussed in the previous chapter, what concrete measures can the EU adopt—and has adopted—in order to carry out its security and defence policy?

Precisely with a view to equip the EU to act increasingly more in the defence domain, the Lisbon Treaty updated the 'toolbox' of policy and legal instruments available to the EU, with a sub-policy called Common Security and Defence Policy (CSDP).[1] CSDP is, in turn, the evolution of the European Security and Defence Policy established in the 90s. CSDP is defined in Article 42(1) TEU as follows:

> The common security and defence policy shall be an integral part of the common foreign and security policy. It shall provide the Union with an operational capacity drawing on civilian and military assets. The Union may use them on missions outside the Union for peace-keeping, conflict prevention and strengthening international security in accordance with the principles of the United Nations Charter. The performance of these tasks shall be undertaken using capabilities provided by the Member States.

[1] For a comprehensive legal treatment, see Koutrakos (2013).

L. Lonardo, *EU Common Foreign and Security Policy After Lisbon*,
https://doi.org/10.1007/978-3-031-19131-2_5

This chapter provides an overview of what the EU has done through its CSDP, with a special focus on its civilian missions and military operations, and the Permanent Structured Cooperation.

Section 5.2 provides a narrative overview of EU missions since 2003, and discusses recurrent issues in the practice of—and debate about—CSDP missions. These involve issues of horizontal coherence; the assessment of the performance of CSDP; and accountability. The chapter recalls some criteria against which previous studies have assessed these missions (including coherence, match between declared and achieved objective as well as 'degree of match between mission launch and EU interests at stake',[2] and budgetary issues). The chapter then delves into a discussion of legal accountability. CSDP missions are of a hybrid nature, because both personnel and authorities from the EU and from the Member States are involved. This creates complex legal issues including the identification of the source of authority for a decision, as well as accountability (who is responsible for damages created in the course of a CSDP mission: the EU—because it authorised the mission—or the Member State—because it carried it out?).

The chapter then offers and overview of the other policy innovation brought about by the Lisbon Treaty. These are the Permanent Structured Cooperation (Sect. 5.3), the mutual defence clause (Article 42(7) TEU), the solidarity clause (Article 222 TFEU), and the opportunity of launching missions with only few participating Member States (Sect. 5.4).

The main recurring themes of this chapter are that of accountability for CSDP missions and operations, as well as consistency, defined in two dimensions: differentiation and ambition.

- Differentiation: within CSDP, the Treaty (Article 42 TEU) offer a number of options for differentiation, including the possibility of conferring a task to "a group of Member States which are willing and have the necessary capability" (Article 44); the establishment of a dedicated agency for capability development—the European Defence Agency (EDA)—'open to all Member States wishing to be part of it' (Article 45); and, most significantly, the creation of a dedicated format for enhanced cooperation in defence, known as Permanent Structured Cooperation (PeSCo) (Article 42 and 46 TEU and additional protocol 10).
- Ambition (objectives): 'In response to the challenges it faces, the EU and its member states have invested in a range of policy mechanisms that are designed to pull governments closer together on defence. While it is certainly true that there is nothing comparable in the history of EU security and defence to the hyperactivity that has been observed in this domain since 2016, the reality today is that the 'alphabet soup' of EU security and defence – CSDP, PESCO, EDF, CARD, CDP, MPCC, EPF, etc. – has not yet led to any tangible shift in the Union's capability base or readiness for deployment'. [3]

[2] Meyer (2020).

[3] European Union Institute for Security Studies (2020), p. 3.

5.2 Civilian Missions and Military Operations

The choice to consider missions since 2003 is justified because although the Lisbon Treaty formally reshaped Common Foreign and Security Policy—of which CSDP is a part—the changes did not alter the substance of EU powers to carried out a security and defence policy through the deployment of (civilian) missions or (military) operations. It shall be recalled that the origins of the CSDP lie in the St Malo Declaration of 1998, a Franco-British declaration launching the European Security and Defence Initiative (which then evolved into a European Security and Defence Policy, and eventually, since 2009, acquired its current name of CSDP). The St Malo Summit resulted in a declaration that called for the Union to have 'the capacity for autonomous action',[4] and 'backed up by credible military forces'.[5] The relationship of such an initiative with the NATO commitments of some Member States was highlighted earlier in Chap. 3. The actions were to be carried out within the EU Treaty framework (through the freshly adopted Amsterdam Treaty), meaning by making use of the EU's institutional framework for decision making. This point is of great significance: France and the UK decided that it would be *through the EU*, and not outside the EU Treaties, that defence initiatives shall be carried out. It is not always the case that major defence policies, including those agreed between EU Member States, use Treaty framework: this was of course true until the Single European Act, and it is still partly true. Consider for example the intervention in Libya in 2011, which was undertaken by a 'coalition of the willing', that is some Member States acting outside the EU Treaties, *because* the EU could not agree on a CSDP operation.[6] A more recent example is the European Intervention Initiative (EI2), launched by France to foster a common European strategic culture, which consists of activities formally independent from the EU Treaties and thus in principle not governed by EU law.

This chapter therefore discusses the CSDP 'in action' by considering some developments that have progressed since 2003. However, it is important to bear in mind that 2009 is an important *caesura*, conceptually. The shift in the institutional framework meant a momentary halt in the number and ambition of missions launched—momentum for new operations was taken up in the 2010s, once the EU bodies (HR/VP and EEAS) became more comfortable in their newly acquired role, and once the economic crisis that hit the EU in 2008 subsided to push foreign policy matters again to the top of political agendas. In addition, it shall be recalled that in the second electoral cycle since the Lisbon Treaty (2014 elections) there have been several 'significant initiatives to substantially reinvigorate'[7] the CSDP, including the launch of new missions.

---

[4] Joint Declaration on European Defence Joint Declaration issued at the British-French Summit (Saint-Malo, 4 December 1998), available at https://www.cvce.eu/obj/franco_british_st_malo_declaration_4_december_1998-en-f3cd16fb-fc37-4d52-936f-c8e9bc80f24f.html.

[5] Ibid.

[6] The episode is considered in detail in Chap. 6.

[7] Meyer (2020), p. 6.

It is customary to talk about civilian *missions* and military *operations*. Overall, the balance has increasingly shifted toward more civilian missions, and this was not least due to the preferences of some Member States (notably the Nordics).[8] Meyer observes an additional factor: 'Civilian missions were also less costly and less politically divisive for the EU, especially as public opinion across most Member States had grown increasingly sceptical about military interventions following deployments to Iraq and Afghanistan.'[9]

Missions vary widely in aims, size (of personnel or participating third countries), duration, and of course geographical reach. For the latter, a pattern clearly emerges, and it is that the distance of the missions from EU territory has been generally increasing. Consider that the first CSDP missions and operations were in the Balkans:[10] what is today North Macedonia and Bosnia Herzegovina[11] (but the first autonomous military operation was in the Democratic Republic of Congo[12]). The 2010s saw instead missions in Somalia,[13] Central African Republic,[14] and the Sahel.[15]

The variance in the other aforementioned characteristics of CSDP missions—aims, size, duration—is more difficult to reconduct to a simplified pattern.[16] A few words can be said on each.

The tasks of the EU's CSDP are defined in Article 43 TEU: 'The tasks [. . .] in the course of which the Union may use civilian and military means, shall include joint disarmament operations, humanitarian and rescue tasks, military advice and assistance tasks, conflict prevention and peace-keeping tasks, tasks of combat forces in crisis management, including peace-making and post-conflict stabilisation. All these tasks may contribute to the fight against terrorism, including by supporting third countries in combating terrorism in their territories.' They are the so-called 'expanded Petersberg Tasks', as they add to the those foreseen in 1992 by the Council of the Western European Union (WEU): peace management, peace keeping, peace enforcement. The name is derived from the fact that the Member States met in Petersberg, close to Bonn (Germany). The mandate of civilian missions is identified by the acronym in their name: EUCAP for capacity building mission, EULEX for rule of law mission, EUAM for advisory mission etc. Civilian missions may have, broadly speaking, advisory roles: examples of these are the various EUBAM, such as

[8]On which see Jakobsen (2009).

[9]Meyer (2020), p. 5.

[10]Meyer (2020), p. 5.

[11]On which see the next section.

[12]ARTEMIS 2003.

[13]EUCAP Somalia 2012.

[14]EUTM RCA 2016.

[15]EUCAP Sahel Niger 2012 and EUCAP Sahel Mali 2014.

[16]Meyer (2020), p. 6 notes that 'This diversity makes any overarching and comparative assessment of the EU's performance in this respect difficult'.

the one assisting with border control in Libya,[17] or in Moldova and Ukraine,[18] or in Rafah.[19] Other civilian missions may instead have supporting role (such as police assistance, help with security sector reforms or capacity building). This was the case, for example, of EUPOL RD Congo (2007–2014) in support of the National Congolese police's programme of reform.[20] Often, civilian missions actually have a combination of both support and advise tasks.

The variance in personnel size has also been very significant. Military missions have a higher number of personnel, in general terms. EUFOR Althea, a military operation, reached a maximum of 7000 people at one time (this was the biggest EU CSDP operation in terms of size), whereas the abovementioned EUBAM Rafah comprised 16 people.

When it comes to the duration of CSDP missions and operations, these have ranged from a few months (Artemis in the Democratic Republic of Congo, EUFOR in the Democratic Republic of Congo), to a couple of years (EUFOR Chad; EUFOR Central African Republic) to several years (EUPOL DRC—7 years). In the latter case, the mandate is usually renewed, and the objectives of the CSDP action in question can be shaped *in fieri*. This is often the case for military operations.

Akin to the civilian missions, the military operations launched by the EU must be aimed toward the objectives in Article 43 TEU. There are, of course, also other limitations deriving from international law (these are binding on the EU both as they reflect customary international law and, as far as the obligations contained in the UN Charter, because of explicit references to it in the EU Treaties). Use of force must be compliant with the UN Charter: the current international security system, institutionalised at the end of WW2, introduced a presumption that uses of force are unlawful.[21] The presumption is rebuttable, but it must be shown that force was used in self-defence, or pursuant to an authorisation by UN Security Council, or—but this is far from uncontentious in the international law community—that it was

---

[17] Decision 2013/233/CFSP of 22 May 2013 on the European Union Integrated Border Management Assistance Mission in Libya (EUBAM Libya).

[18] This mission helps Ukraine and the Republic of Moldova to harmonise border control, customs, and trade procedures with those in EU Member States—an obligation deriving from the Association Agreements those countries signed with the EU.

[19] After Israel's unilateral disengagement from the Gaza Strip in summer 2005, the Palestinian authorities signed an agreement containing rules for passing the Rafah (Ghaza) crossing point. Under the agreement, the crossing point was supposed to be under the joint control of Israel, the Palestinian Authority, and a third party—the EU, indeed. Joint Action 2005/889/CFSP of 12 December 2005 on establishing a European Union Border Assistance Mission for the Rafah Crossing Point (EU BAM Rafah).

[20] Joint Action 2007/405/CFSP of 12 June 2007 on the European Union police mission undertaken in the framework of reform of the security sector (SSR) and its interface with the system of justice in the Democratic Republic of the Congo (EUPOL RD Congo).

[21] Article 2(4) is the basic prohibition on the use of force by States. It provides that 'All Members shall refrain in their international relations from the threat or use of force against the territorial integrity or political independence of any State, or in any other manner inconsistent with the Purposes of the United Nations.

consistent with the purposes of the UN (for example, that use of force was used for humanitarian purposes, to stop gross violations of human rights et similia).

Military operations require a headquarter. This is located in the territory of the leading Member State of each mission (and it entailed, after Brexit, moving headquarters of some UK-led operations).

5.2.1 *The First Missions and Operations: The Pre-Lisbon Period*

Pre-Lisbon, security had only become part of EU constitutional structure, formally, in 1992. It shall be recalled that while the EU had an intergovernmental foreign and security policy, defence as such was not in the picture, at least not before the St Malo Declaration. The tasks the EU had decided to take up in the 90s were related to crisis management—and were in fact left to the otherwise dormant Western European Union (The Western European Union was established in 1954 by the six founding Member States and the United Kingdom, closely following the failure of the European Defence Community). It is in that context that the first mission was launched, but NATO was determinant, which is why Javier Solana and the Member States activated the ESDP by continuing a UN police mission in Bosnia which ran in parallel to a NATO mission (SFOR). The EU launched its first ever mission to be directed by the EU, EUPM, after it was approved by the Council in March 2002. It would start its operations in 2003, with around 500 officers for an initial duration of three years.

EU-NATO cooperation had entered a new era since the so-called Berlin-plus agreements of 1999,[22] the first major result of which was the launch of the first EU military operation, EUFOR Concordia, between April and December 2003. Its objective was to guarantee security on the ground in North Macedonia, after the tensions of the previous year, and to ensure the respect of the Ohrid agreements signed in 2001 between the country's ethnic groups. The operation could count on the support of 26 countries (including some future Member States), who contributed a total of 400 military personnel. At the end of the year, EUFOR Concordia was replaced by a smaller police operation, EUPOL Proxima (around 170 officials).

In spring 2003, the EU also had its own autonomous military operation (autonomous from NATO, that is), when France seized the chance to 'Europeanise' its planned operation in substitution of the UN mission MONUC in the DRC.

But the most geopolitically consequential and symbolically important operation was EUFOR Althea, in Bosnia-Hercegovina. Launched at the end of 2004 again

[22] Whose integral text is still classified at the time of writing. The agreement, was reached also thanks to the newly elected Erdogan in Turkey, enabling the EU to take advantage of NATO planning and command capabilities and even some military equipment (such as the radar airplanes AWACS).

within the context of the Berlin-plus agreements, the relevance of this operations lies in the fact that it was the largest military operation yet (7000 members of staff), and that it was the first large-scale EU operation (under UK command and ultimately under Deputy SACEUR). Needless to say, the operation was launched after negotiating with NATO, and in fact it succeeded NATO's operation SFOR. The EU's involvement in the country has been significant since, with each High Representative for Bosnia and Herzegovina, who occasionally acted almost as de facto President of the country since the figure was created with the Dayton Agreement (1995), being from EU countries.

The first EU naval operation, EUNAVFOR Atalanta was launched in November 2008, and headed by the UK. It had as mandate the patrolling of the Gulf of Aden, protecting the World Food Programme humanitarian aid cargos as well as local fishermen from pirates—the latter constituting a significant security threat in that key region, where maritime traffic to and from the Suez Canal is bound to pass.

By far the most delicate mission of the EU is EULEX Kosovo. The country declared independence from Serbia in February 2008—a declaration which the EU had long pushed to postpone, as several Member States had already made it clear they would not recognise Kosovo (Cyprus,[23] Greece, Romania, Slovakia and Spain[24]); which the US welcomed, but Russia and Serbia rejected. It is in this context that the EU approved EULEX Kosovo, a civilian mission with the initial objective to train Kosovo's police and assist the country's judiciary. The operation took place in parallel to the UNMIK mission and the NATO KFOR mission. The mission was led by France but under the supervision of the Dutchman Pieter Feith, concomitantly appointed special representative of the EU in Kosovo.

5.2.2 *Narrative Overview of EU Missions and Operations Since Lisbon*

The first HR/VP of the Lisbon era, Catherine Ashton, developed the 'comprehensive approach' to crisis management, meaning that the EU would be keen not only on the military aspects thereof, but also to other perspectives, from conflict prevention to post-conflict state building. This was also in line with the mutating policy of the US, which, under the new Obama administration, was drawing on the lessons learnt (or so they thought) in Afghanistan and Iraq about state building. And while the HR/VP was 'busy' setting up the EEAS and the EU's priority quickly shifted away from security and defence to focus on the impending financial crisis, there were significant developments in the CSDP. In terms of civilian missions, there were fewer EUPOL/EUPM missions, and more border control (EUMM/EUBAM), rule of

[23]Which also abstained from voting on the Decision establishing EULEX Kosovo.

[24]These countries voted in favour of establishing EULEX Kosovo but declared they would not participate in it.

law support (EULEX/EUJUST), security sector reform (EUSEC/EUSSR), and capacity-building (EUCAP). In terms of military operations, sizes shrunk but the EU intervened with assistance (EUAM) or train and equip (EUTM) operations. As an example of the 'comprehensive approach', one may recall that two operations in the Horn of Africa were set up in coordination with EUNAVFOR Atalanta against piracy: EUTM Somalia was established with the objective to train Somali security forces; and EUCAP Nestor, based in Djibouti, had the objective to train Somalia's coast guard. A further example is constituted by the capacity-building missions which played an important support role in EU foreign policy in the Sahel region of Western Africa in the past decade. When, at the end of 2012, the Malian government reached out for help against the threat of Islamist separatist groups, the French President Holland launched operation Serval (later operation Barkhane) whereby a French military contingent provided support to Bamako; and the EU launched EUTM Mali (2013) and EUCAP Sahel Mali (2014) and EUTM CAR (2016, in the Central African Republic), adding to international presence in loco in addition to UN (MINUSMA) and AU (MISAHEL) missions. These EU missions did not have direct military objectives but rather had the goal to contribute to strengthening the countries' capabilities to face the hybrid (weaponization of migration, people and drug smuggling) or terrorist threats (from Al Qaeda to Boko Haram) in that pivotal region. It is in fact this geopolitical dimension of the Sahel, which is the land corridor connecting sub-Saharian Africa to the shores of the Mediterranean, that enabled President Hollande to frame security threats in that region as a threat for the EU's security as a whole.

Inevitably, one of the great geopolitical surprises since Lisbon, the Arab uprisings, also resulted in CSDP missions—albeit not as successfully as one could have hoped for.[25] The southern and eastern shores of the Mediterranean Basin were shaken by political turmoil (Morocco, Tunisia) or war (Libya, Syria, Iraq) from the first half of the past decade. One direct consequence of these was the substantial increase in immigrants trying to reach EU borders from those countries, as well as those from sub-Saharian Africa and Afghanistan. The main migratory route (at least until 2014) was through Libya, via the Italian island of Lampedusa between Malta and Tunisia. Italy's naval operation Mare Nostrum (2013-2014) was later substituted by an EU one (*Triton*)—established not under the CSDP but the AFSJ—and promoted by the EU agency Frontex. Since 2015, a CSDP operation, EUNAVFOR MED Sophia was established until 2020 with a view to counter networks of migrants smuggling in the Mediterranean. EUBAM Libya is a CSDP mission for the training of Libyan border patrol units—a mission whose achievements are highly dubious, especially in the context of the ongoing civil war in the country.

The von der Leyen 'geopolitical' Commission had not only ambitions of strategic autonomy (in trade, security and defence, and technology) or climate regulation (with the Green New Deal) but also renewed attention to the Mediterranean basin. Once Sophia's mandate ended—and the operation had anyways encountered serious

[25] See Chap. 6.

political difficulties due to the strong opposition by the Italian interior minister—in 2020 the EU launched EUNAVFOR MED Irini (led by Italy and Greece), with a more limited scope (arms control).

5.2.3 *Some Recurrent Key Issues*

5.2.3.1 Horizontal Coherence

Horizontal coherence requires EU action to be consistent *across EU policies*.[26] The word coherence is oftentimes used synonymously with consistency, and so it will be used in this chapter, even though some have sought to distinguish the terms, point out that consistency 'refers to the character of an outcome or state', while coherence 'rather specifies the quality of a process'.[27]

Several studies have addressed issues of horizontal coherence in CFSP[28] and CSDP in particular.[29] Mention shall be made here of operations in the Mediterranean Sea to face the so-called migrant crisis of 2015: these were conducted, by the EU and the Member States, through both CSDP and non-CSDP structures.

CSDP operations, in fact, do not include the operations coordinated by Frontex (such as Triton, Triton+, Themis) in the Mediterranean, even though there is a significant overlap with the objectives that a CSDP (naval) operation or border patrol mission can carry out. Those three Frontex-coordinated operations—which, as far as EU law is concerned, fall under the Area of Freedom Security and Justice—are in fact *border control* missions. The EU NAVMEDFOR Sophia (2015–2020),[30] was established, after the Italian operation Mare Nostrum, to undertake systematic efforts to identify, capture and dispose of vessels and enabling assets used or suspected of being used by migrant smugglers or traffickers, in order to contribute to wider EU efforts to disrupt the business model of human smuggling and trafficking networks in the Southern Central Mediterranean. Those 'wider efforts' comprise precisely of AFSJ activities, such as the abovementioned Frontex operations.

There is, therefore, significant overlap because they both concern security (area of freedom security and justice and CFSP have that element in common). This thread, of the conflation between CFSP and AFSJ, is discussed further in Chap. 7.

---

[26] Gauttier (2004), p. 23.

[27] Gebhard (2017), p. 106.

[28] Duke (2011).

[29] Koenig (2011).

[30] Later Operation Irini (since 2020).

5.2.3.2 Assessing Performance

Assessing CSDP missions is a recurrent concern of the scholarship of the topic, as well as, more broadly, a key theme of this book. Painting with very broad strokes, two criteria can be used to assess effectiveness: an internal one (effectiveness of missions 'in their own terms'[31]) and an external one (effectiveness of missions with regard to EU interests at stake). In addition, other criteria may be used to assess the performance, more broadly understood, of CSDP missions. These criteria include coherence with other EU policies (horizontal coherence discussed above), or consistency with EU values, or the level of democratic legitimacy.

Assessing CSDP may entail checking the alignment between declared and achieved objectives. This form of 'internal' effectiveness (effectiveness on the missions' own terms) leads to a fairly positive evaluation. CSDP missions have, by and large, achieved their own objectives. Often, however, political objectives change and shape an operation *in fieri*. This is especially true of military operations.

Assessing CSDP missions may also entail verifying the alignment between declared objectives and EU interests at stake: for example, one may consider 'how quickly operations were agreed and resources deployed in relation to the crisis'.[32] This is relevant to assessing the performance of CSDP missions because a quick response is presumably more in line with EU's objective of avoiding crises rather than of intervening through crisis management measures once the situation has escalated. Speed, in other words, is considered to be conducive *eo ipso* to an alignment with EU interests.

5.2.3.3 Budgetary Issues

Article 41(2) TEU draws a distinction between military and civilian missions.

> [T]he Operating expenditure to which the implementation of this Chapter [i.e. on Common Foreign and Security Policy] gives rise shall also be charged to the Union budget, except for such expenditure arising from operations having military or defence implications and cases where the Council acting unanimously decides otherwise

It is well acknowledged in the literature that difficult access to budgetary resources is a hindrance to the launch of CSDP missions. Article 41(2) TEU makes it clear that the cost of military operations cannot be charged to the EU budget, and thus it is borne by Member States (unlike civilian missions) under the 'costs lie where they fall' principle. 'This is a substantial disincentive for Member States to contribute their assets unless they have significant national interests at stake, or pivot nations or EU leaders can 'compensate' or in other ways induce them to commit'.[33]

[31] Meyer (2020), p. 8.

[32] Meyer (2020), p. 8.

[33] Meyer (2020), p. 8.

There is an exception to this 'cost lie where they fall' rule: the European Peace Facility (EPF).[34] This is an assistance mechanism that is part of the Common Security and Defence Policy (CSDP). It is an instrument that finances operations with military or defence implications. The costs are borne by all Member States. This is the innovative feature of the EPF (and of its predecessors, the Athena mechanism and the African Peace Facility): it streamlines budget management in so far as, contrary to the general rule of the CSDP, costs are not borne only by the specific Member States or third countries participating in a CSDP military operation. It can finance actions to strengthen the capacities of third states and regional or international organisations relating to military and defence matters. Assistance to third countries is another innovation of the EPF (not present in the Athena mechanism).

5.2.3.4 Accountability

It is possible to identify several criteria for accountability, depending on the subject of accountability (institution, body, individual); the means (legal, political); or the forum (parliamentary, judicial). By and large, there are important studies on most of these dimensions of CSDP missions and operations. The topic is of special importance because CSDP missions are a form of 'Europeanized intergovernmentalism' due to the hybrid nature of these operations (in which both EU authorities/personnel and Member States authorities/personnel are involved). The resulting hybrid structure runs the risk of being unaccountable to both national and EU level (perhaps, this problem of collective action is an instance of the proverbial wisdom conveyed in many languages: the more the shepherds, the less the sheep are watched).

Legal Accountability

Due to the hybridity of CSDP missions and operations—proposed by Member States, adopted by the Council, implemented by Member States through a mix of EU and Member States' personnel—the attribution of a measure or of an act in the context of such missions is far from straightforward, and the matter is further complicated by the lack of jurisdiction of the CJEU over CFSP.

The General Court in *H*, [35] for example, found that the decision of an EU diplomat, adopted on the powers conferred by a CFSP act, was attributable to

---

[34] Council Decision (CFSP) 2021/509 of 22 March 2021 establishing a European Peace Facility, and repealing Decision (CFSP) 2015/528. With minor innovations mentioned below, the EPF replaces the 'Athena mechanism', introduced in 2004. The complete list of costs covered by Athena (including transport, infra- structure, medical services, lodging, fuel, etc.) is stated in the annexes to the Council decision 2015/528, which abrogates Council Decision 2011/871/CFSP and its predecessors.

[35] T-271/10 *H v Council* ECLI:EU:T:2014:702.

Italy. Civil or military personnel may be seconded by Member States to EU missions or operations. In that case, the act of national authorities is dispositive of an EU status. H, an Italian magistrate, was seconded by Italy to the European Union Police Mission ('EUPM') in Bosnia and Herzegovina.[36] EUPM fosters the rule of law in Bosnia and Herzegovina, and as part of its activities it requires judges on the territory. H was redeployed, by the Head of Mission, to a different region of the country, and sought to annul such an act before the General Court. The General Court had to consider its own jurisdiction over the act of the Head of Mission. The Decision setting up EUPM states, in Article 5(4): 'All seconded staff shall remain under the full command of the national authorities of the seconding State or EU institution concerned. National authorities shall transfer Operational Control (OPCON) of their personnel, teams and units to the Civilian Operation Commander'. Article 8(2) establishes that 'The State or EU institution having seconded a staff member shall be responsible for answering any claims linked to the secondment, from or concerning the staff member. The State or EU institution in question shall be responsible for bringing any action against the seconded person'. After acknowledging this responsibility, the General Court took the view that 'only the national courts have jurisdiction to deal with any issue concerning the secondment of national members of staff, whereas the judicature of the European Union has jurisdiction in respect of EU members of staff who have been seconded'.[37] In that case, therefore, the General Court's position followed legal orthodoxy:[38] contrary to what the applicant maintained, an act of Italian authorities cannot be annulled by EU courts—Italian courts could grant effective remedies, instead.[39] The reasoning of the General Court, however, was problematic on the issue of attribution.[40] Why would the act of the Head of an EU Mission be attributable to Italy? The General Court's answer was the powers exercised in that circumstance were only delegated by the Italian authorities (because they concerned seconded personnel), and thus were, in principle, attributable to them.[41] The ECJ reached a different conclusion. It found that the decision of the Head of Mission was attributable to the EU, because 'by virtue of the second sentence of Article 5(4) of [EUPM] decision, national authorities have transferred operational control of their personnel, teams and units to the Civilian Operation Commander, who, pursuant to Article 5(2), exercises command and control of the EUPM in Bosnia and Herzegovina at the strategic level and, in that capacity, issues instructions to the Head of Mission'.[42]

[36] First set up by Council Joint Action 2002/210/CFSP of 11 March 2002 for a period of one year, and was subsequently prolonged several times.

[37] Case C-455/14 P *H v. Council and Commission*, para 46.

[38] On a relatable composite procedure see Case C-202/18 *Rimsevics v Latvia*, EU:C:2019:139.

[39] Case C-455/14 P *H* para 53.

[40] See also Klabbers (2018).

[41] Case C-455/14 P *H* para 50.

[42] Ibid., para. 51. On this basis, despite hermeneutic difficulties arising from the fact that the decision would be adopted pursuant to CFSP—on which the CJEU ought not to have jurisdiction—

Under EU law, another way to ensure legal accountability is the so-called 'action for damages' (technically, non-contractual liability). This entails some attribution (of the conduct giving rise to damages) to the EU.[43] The question of EU's responsibility for CSDP missions was put initially to national courts, such as in the case of *Tomanovic*,[44] litigated in front of UK courts. In that case the claimants (family members of Serbian victims of human rights violations which EULEX Kosovo would have failed to investigate properly) tried to establish the EU and its institutions' responsibility for human rights violations in the context of a Common Security and Defence Policy mission. The UK High Court, on that occasion, decided to dismiss the action and not to refer the question to the European Court of Justice.[45]

But while on the EU non-contractual liability in the context of CSDP missions the last word has not been said, a relatively recent development, recalled in Chap. 4, is the recognition that the CJEU is prepared to award damages created by the EU by the (unlawful) adoption of restrictive measures. This was established in *Bank Refah*. The question left open by that judgment, however, is whether the damages may stem only from the unlawful adoption of restrictive measures, or if they may stem also from unlawful conduct carried out in the context of other CFSP activities (and in the latter case, these would include CSDP missions and operations):[46] and this is precisely the question that the Court is called upon to answer in *KS and KD v Council, Commission, EEAS*. In that case, the applicants (family members of people disappeared and killed in the 90s) claimed that EULEX Kosovo failed in its mission when it insufficiently investigated the disappearance and killing of their family members. The General Court dismissed the action. It found that the activity in question was manifestly outside its jurisdiction, as it fell under CFSP: the proceedings arose 'from acts or conduct which fall within the scope of political or strategic issues connected with defining the activities, priorities and resources of the EULEX Kosovo mission',[47] but those acts or conduct are neither restrictive measure, nor they concern the monitoring of the boundaries of CFSP. The Commission appealed the finding, and the case is currently pending as C-44/22 P. It is discussed again in Chap. 7.

---

the Court went on to refer the judgment on the substance of the action against the Head of Mission decision to the General Court. In the new judgement, the General Court confirmed the validity of the Head of Mission decision, T-271/10 RENV, EU:T:2018:180.

[43]For the legal technicalities of EU 'contributing' to damages created by Member States see (Fink, 2019).

[44]*Tomanovic v. European Union* [2019] EWHC 263 (QB).

[45]For a discussion of that case (Johansen, 2019).

[46]For an argument in this sense, (Lonardo & Carrozzini, 2021) and (Eckes, 2016, p. 510). Contra (Poli, 2022, p. 1057).

[47]T-771/20 para 28.

Other Forms of Accountability

Parliamentary accountability was studied early on after the inception of the Lisbon Treaty. In 2012, Wouters and Raube, for example, contended that 'neither the EP nor national parliaments are in a position to hold decision-makers sufficiently accountable'.[48]

In her work on accountability of EU crisis management missions, Moser considered the legal, political, and administrative dimensions of accountability. Moser painted a brighter picture than the one outlined above. In the operational aspects of the crisis management missions, the quality, quantity, and capacity of the accountability mechanisms receive an overall positive evaluation.[49] The findings of Moser on *de facto* accountability arrangements in the civilian aspects of CSDP offer an authoritative corrective to the narrative on accountability in EU security and defence.

Moser's work also confirms that the legal dimension of accountability is lagging behind the practical (successful) developments of CSDP. This raises issues of legitimacy as well as normative questions about the proper role of EU institutions: again, these thread are discussed in Chap. 7.

5.3 Permanent Structured Cooperation[50]

Article 46 TEU (and Protocol 10, annexed to the TFEU), foresees a system whereby a *group* of Member States could set up a permanent framework for cooperation in the field of defence. Initially, this Permanent Structured Cooperation (known as PeSCo) was meant to be a flexible template for an avant-garde of Member States who met quantifiable target criteria of defence capabilities. This idea did not find its way into the Lisbon Treaty. Instead, participation in PeSCo was based on capability *commitments* (related to multinational forces and the activity of the EDA) rather than on quantified targets or strict criteria. Interested Member States simply notify their intention to participate to the Council. This shift (from an exclusive to an inclusive PeSCo) was mostly due to the concerns expressed by a number of Member States as to the potentially divisive nature of the original project. PeSCo does nonetheless contain an absolutely major innovation when it comes to decision-making: all deliberations related to the establishment of PeSCo as well as the admission of new or suspension of current participating countries are made by qualified majority.[51]

Despite its inclusive design, however, PeSCo would not be seriously considered for implementation long after the entry into force of the Lisbon Treaty. In fact, there

---

[48] Wouters and Raube (2012), p. 162.

[49] Moser (2020), p. 281.

[50] This section draws on (Missiroli & Lonardo, 2019).

[51] Fiott et al. (2017).

was no legal duty, nor time-frame, for Member States to set up PeSCo.[52] No opportunity or necessity seemed to arise to justify its activation. Early proposals for its establishment—such as the one tabled by the trio presidency of Belgium, Hungary, and Poland (June 2010), or the joint Italian-Spanish letter to HRVP Catherine Ashton asking for a debate in the Foreign Affairs Council (May 2011)—failed to generate momentum, with the Union as a whole then entirely absorbed by the financial and Eurozone crises, and the diplomatic and security communities busy with the establishment of the European External Action Service and the onset of the so-called 'Arab Spring'. A change of government in the UK, in 2010, also put a brake on CSDP ambitions at large.

It was only after the Brexit Referendum of June 2016 that some Member States considered it necessary to relaunch efforts in the domain of security and defence. This was also due to the fact that some saw not only the opportunity but also the necessity to relaunch the EU's role in this domain (as indeed the EU Global Strategy, released on the same week of the Brexit referendum, encouraged them to do). With the foreseeable departure of the UK—a proactive CSDP player between 1999 and 2009, a more reluctant one thereafter, but constantly sceptical of big leaps forward in institutional terms—the initiative was taken by France and Germany, who produced a first joint (non-)paper on PeSCo already in July 2016.

The paper represented a compromise between their respective approaches (the French being more ambitious and restrictive than the German one) but eventually received the approval of the European Council, who mandated the HR/VP to work on options for an "ambitious and inclusive" PeSCo based on a "modular" approach, and in January 2017 the EEAS circulated a Food for Thought paper along these lines. The election of Donal Trump to the US presidency also pushed some initially hesitant countries (e.g. Poland) to join in on the ongoing discussion about PeSCo. PeSCo was officially established by 25 Member States—"whose military capabilities fulfil higher criteria [..] and which have made commitments to one another in this area [..] with a view to the most demanding missions"—through a Council Decision on 12 December 2017.[53] Only Denmark (opt-out), the UK (Brexit) and Malta (still open to joining later on but reluctant as its constitution contains a neutrality clause) stayed out, but without opposing it. Paradoxically, what was originally intended as a

[52] The only potential deadline was set in the attached Protocol 10 (art.1.b) whereby eligible Member States were required "to have the capacity to supply by 2010 at the latest, either at national level or as a component of multinational force groups, targeted combat units for the missions planned, structured at a tactical level as a battle group, with support elements including transport and logistics [..]". Yet this requirement – set in 2007 at Lisbon, when the treaty was expected to enter into force quickly (and not, as it did eventually, in December 2009)—it was not in fact a deadline for activating PeSCo but for 'battlegroups'.

[53] Council Decision (CFSP) 2017/2315, establishing permanent structured cooperation (PESCO) and determining the list of participating Member States' (OJ L331/57). Portugal and Ireland joined the others on 7 December, after a supplement of consultation with their national parliaments. Ireland is a notable case in point as the country had previously struggled to ratify the Lisbon Treaty (two referenda were needed), i.a. due to its new provisions on defence.

form of closer integration for a small pioneer group of Member States ended up including almost all eligible Member States and being effectively supported by all.

A subsequent Council Decision (2018/909), in June 2018, laid out the governance of PeSCo projects—put under the joint supervision of the HR/VP, the EEAS (including the EU Military Staff) and the EDA (with a key screening and coordinating role), which together constitute the PeSCo 'Secretariat'.

A total of 61 projects have been approved by the Council—in three batches: March 2018 (17), November 2018 (17), and November 2019 (13) and November 2021 (14).[54] Projects concern land, maritime, air, cyber, space (and joint) operations aimed at developing capabilities.

To date none of the 25 Member States has taken part in *all* PeSCo projects, nor does any of the projects have *all* 25 on board. Membership varies from a minimum of two countries (for 10 projects) to a maximum of 24 (all bar Ireland) for the possibly most significant PeSCo initiative, namely Military Mobility. The average number of project participants also seems to decrease from the first to the fourth batch. It is also apparent that some projects have a primarily symbolic nature; that a few others do not appear particularly 'permanent' in their scope and may not even materialise; that membership of both PeSCo at large and its individual projects, too, is all but 'permanent', as the provisions allow not only later accession, but also suspension and even withdrawal of participating countries; and that there is still no identifiable common 'structure' among and across the projects. For their part, the "ambitious and more binding" common commitments formulated through the various projects are hardly binding in conventional EU legal terms, as there is no enforcement mechanism built into the PeSCo architecture: in essence, they remain voluntary ones, with incentives for compliance linked primarily to peer pressure and reputational risk, and all liable to the uncertainties of political support, national funding and, in some cases, industrial capacity. Finally, for most of the projects it is entirely conceivable that they could have also been launched also outside and independently of the PeSCo framework, raising the issue of the added value PeSCo will bring under the current conditions.

It is interesting to note that, alongside PeSCo, other initiatives were gaining traction also outside the EU, potentially in competition with the logic (and the commitments) of PeSCo. In September 2017, in a major speech on Europe delivered at the Sorbonne, France's President Emmanuel Macron launched the so-called European Intervention Initiative (EII or EI2), designed to create by 2020 'a common intervention force, a common defence budget and a common doctrine for action'. Macron's initiative, tangibly more exclusive and arguably conceived to keep the UK engaged in an operational European defence framework despite Brexit, was neither part of a NATO nor an EU construct and has not yet generated any significant action.[55]

---

[54] A complete and detailed list of the 47 PeSCo projects can be found at https://pesco.europa.eu.

[55] The nine EI2 'founding' members were—alongside France—Belgium, Denmark, Estonia, Germany, the Netherlands, Portugal, Spain and the UK. Finland joined in late 2018, Romania, non-EU Norway, Sweden and Italy (after a change of government) followed in 2019.

Within NATO, the Framework Nations Concept (FNC), had made headway, prompting the creation of three multi-national divisions led, respectively, by Germany, the UK and Italy.[56] And NATO's Enhanced Forward Presence in the Baltic states and Poland—deployed since 2016 to deter Russian activities in the region—was based on the same approach applied to battlegroup formations.

5.4 Other CSDP Tools

5.4.1 Qualified Security Guarantee (Art.42(7) TEU)

Article 42(7) TEU is an important 'mutual defence clause'. Pursuant to it, MSs have an obligation to assist another MS victim of an 'armed aggression' on its territory:

> If a Member State is the victim of armed aggression on its territory, the other Member States shall have towards it an obligation of aid and assistance by all the means in their power, in accordance with Article 51 of the United Nations Charter. This shall not prejudice the specific character of the security and defence policy of certain Member States.

Apart from the ambiguity of the phrase 'armed aggression', which does not recur elsewhere in European or international law,[57] the Article is phrased similarly to other clauses of collective defence, such as Article 5 NATO Charter or Article 4 of the 1948 Brussels Treaty, whereby Western European States agreed to make an alliance for the security of the continent.[58] EU Treaties heavily rely on United Nations obligations, on paper:[59] the very Article 42(7) TEU makes reference to Article

[56] NATO in fact subsumed the UK so-called Joint Expeditionary Force (JEF), launched already in 2012, that brought together Denmark, the Netherlands, Norway and the Baltic states (Sweden would join in 2018).

[57] General Assembly, Resolution A/RES/29/3314 of 14 December 1974 on the Definition of Aggression; its Art. 1 states: "Aggression is the use of armed force by a State against the sovereignty, territorial integrity or political independence of another State, or in any other manner inconsistent with the UN Charter, as set out in this Definition". The Resolution is not binding on the EU if not to the extent it reflects customary law.

[58] Respectively: "The Parties agree that an armed attack against one or more of them in Europe or North America shall be considered an attack against them all and consequently they agree that, if such an armed attack occurs, each of them, in exercise of the right of individual or collective self-defence recognised by Article 51 UN Charter, will assist the Party or Parties so attacked by taking forthwith, individually and in concert with the other Parties, such action as it deems necessary, including the use of armed force, to restore and maintain the security of the North Atlantic area.Any such armed attack and all measures taken as a result thereof shall immediately be reported to the Security Council. Such measures shall be terminated when the Security Council has taken the measures necessary to restore and maintain international peace and security' and 'If any of the High Contracting Parties should be the object of an armed attack in Europe, the other High Contracting Parties will, in accordance with the provisions of Article 51 UN Charter, afford the Party so attacked all the military and other aid and assistance in their power".

[59] Eeckhout and López Escudero (2016), p. 52.

51 of the UN Charter (the obligation for other Member States is to aid and assistance 'in accordance with' Article 51 UN Charter). It is therefore beyond doubt that EU Member States must comply with the UN Charter when they exercise their right to (collective) self-defence. But while this is clear as a matter of principle, the issue is far from settled in practice. International lawyers have long debated the meaning of Article 51 UN Charter, and in essence there are two reasonable and opposite interpretations of it: a permissive and a restrictive interpretation. The permissive one disregards the (literal) requirement that the armed attack must have occurred and allows, for example, for anticipatory self-defence. A permissive interpretation also relinquishes the requirement that the armed attack is committed by a State. A restrictive interpretation instead recalls that State practice points to the direction that self-defence can only be exercised against a state.[60] It is therefore debatable whether Art. 51 of the UN Charter—and consequently Article 42(7) TEU—extends the right to (collective) self-defence to a case of attack by non-State actors. In practice, Article 42(7) TEU was only used once in the history of the EU, when President Hollande called for its application after November 2015. The trigger of France's request were simultaneous shootings and killings in Paris, carried out by operatives of the Islamic State (IS), which later claimed responsibility for the attack. No State ever recognised IS as a State within the meaning, for example, of the Montevideo Convention. The application of Article 42(7) TEU in case of an attack by an entity that France considers a terrorist organisation is evidence, therefore, that the notion of 'aggression' in Article 42(7) TEU is interpreted broadly. When it was triggered after the 2015 Paris attack, the concrete use of that clause consisted in France concluding bilateral agreements with some other EU countries, with the aim of receiving troops for France's missions abroad and focus their soldiers on patrolling the country's territory.

5.4.2 *Solidarity Clause (Article 222 TFEU)*

The relationship of Article 42(7) TEU provision with Article 222 TFEU is worth of analysis. Even though the clause is in the TFEU, there are four grounds for considering it in relation to other CFSP instruments.

In *Anagnostakis*, the General Court held that Art. 222 TFEU "clearly does not relate to economic and monetary policy, or economic circumstances or the budgetary difficulties of the Member States"—thus implying that it might refer, instead, to the CFSP, or at least to EU's external action in general.[61] This was the opinion of AG Jääskinen in *Elitaliana*: EU's external action covers Article 222 TFEU.[62] Even more

[60] Milanovic (2010).

[61] General Court, judgment of 30 September 2015, case T-450/12, Anagnostakis v. Commission, para 60.

[62] Opinion of AG Jääskinen delivered on 21 May 2015, case C-493/13, P Elitaliana v. EULEX Kosovo, para. 17.

explicit was the Opinion of AG Bot in case C-130/10, that the Article relates to the CFSP, in particular in so far as concerns CSDP.[63] Finally, the Council Decision implementing Article 222 refers, in its fifth recital, to the structures developed under the CSDP as instruments developed pursuant to the solidarity clause.[64] However, the Council Decision implementing the solidarity clause does not provide a general framework for dealing with actions having military defence implications, because the joint proposal[65] excluded "defence implications".

Both Articles 42(7) TEU and 222 TFEU require that the event takes place on a Member State's territory. Both Articles shall be read in conjunction with Article 196 TFEU, which imposes duties on the EU to encourage cooperation to prevent and assist civilians in case of natural or man-made disasters. But these are, on paper, the only overlap in the scope of the two Articles.

While the mutual defence clause requires an armed aggression to trigger it, the mutual assistance clause requires a terrorist attack, a man-made, or natural disaster. While, as we saw, 'armed aggression' was interpreted so as to encompass a terrorist attack, the scope of application of the solidarity clause is wider.

Moreover, the mutual defence obligation is only incumbent upon other Member States, while Article 222 TFEU imposes an obligation on the EU as well. This means the opportunity to mobilise the Union's own resources such as police, funds, etc.[66] It is also important to recall that Article 42(7) TEU is subject to the exception that the provision "shall not prejudice the specific character of the security and defence policy of certain Member States", even though what the exception exactly means is object of debate.[67]

The obligations of solidarity are wider than those stemming from mutual defence. Obligations involve the prevention, protection, and assistance in case of such an event. Moreover, it is debated whether Article 222 TFEU could be used also to suppress social arrest (whether this is certainly not the case for Art. 42(7) TEU).

---

[63] Opinion of AG Bot delivered on 31 January 2012, case C-130/10, European Parliament v. Council of the European Union, para. 65.

[64] Council Decision 2014/415/EU of 24 June 2014 on the arrangements for the implementation by the Union of the solidarity clause.

[65] High Representative of the EU for Foreign Affairs and Security Policy and the European Commission, Joint proposal of 21 December 2012 for a Council Decision on the arrangements for the implementation by the Union of the Solidarity Clause presented, pursuant to Article 222(3) TFEU.

[66] M. FUCHS-DRAPIER, The European Union's Solidarity Clause in the Event of a Terrorist Attack: To- wards Solidarity or Maintaining Sovereignty?, in Journal of Contingencies and Crisis Management, 2011, p. 185 et seq.

[67] P. HILPOLD, Filling a Buzzword with Life: The Implementation of the Solidarity Clause in Article 222 TFEU, in Legal Issues of Economic Integration, 2015, p. 217.

5.4.3 Missions by Only Some Member States (Article 44 TEU)

Article 44(1) TEU allows for a form of enhanced cooperation by some MSs to carry out, on a voluntary basis, specific tasks entrusted to them by the Council. The reasons why the European Parliament and other authors have not called for these legal bases is that the permanent structured cooperation, in the eyes of its supporters, offers two distinctive advantages: it can be used for external action, and, as the name suggests, it is permanent.

References

Duke, S. (2011). Consistency, Coherence and European Union external action: The path to Lisbon and beyond. In P. Koutrakos (Ed.), *European foreign policy: Legal and political perspectives*. Edward Elgar Pub.

Eckes, C. (2016). Common foreign and security policy: The consequences of the court's extended jurisdiction: CFSP: Consequences of extended jurisdiction. *European Law Journal, 22*(4), 492–518. https://doi.org/10.1111/eulj.12183

Eeckhout, P., & Escudero, M. L. (2016). *The European Union's external action in times of crisis*. Hart Publishing. https://doi.org/10.5040/9781509900589

European Union Institute for Security Studies. (2020). *The CSDP in 2020: The EU's legacy and ambition in security and defence*. Publications Office. https://data.europa.eu/doi/10.2815/22734

Fink, M. (2019). EU liability for contributions to member states' breaches of EU law. *Common Market Law Review*, 1227–1264.

Fiott, D., Missiroli, A., & Tardy, T. (2017). *Permanent structured cooperation: What's in a name?* Chaillot Papers. EUISS. https://www.iss.europa.eu/content/permanent-structured-cooperation-what%E2%80%99s-name.

Gauttier, P. (2004). Horizontal Coherence and the external competences of the European Union. *European Law Journal, 10*(1), 23–41. https://doi.org/10.1111/j.1468-0386.2004.00201.x

Gebhard, C. (2017). Coherence. In C. Hill, M. Smith, & S. Vanhoonacker (Eds.), *International relations and the European Union* (3rd ed.). Oxford University Press.

Jakobsen, P. V. (2009). Small states, big influence: The overlooked Nordic influence on the civilian ESDP*. *JCMS: Journal of Common Market Studies, 47*(1), 81–102. https://doi.org/10.1111/j.1468-5965.2008.01833.x

Johansen, S. Ø. (2019). Suing the European Union in the UK: Tomanović et al. v. the European Union et al. Text/html,PDF. *European Papers - A Journal on Law and Integration, 4*(May):345357. https://doi.org/10.15166/2499-8249/295.

Klabbers, J. (2018). Too much, too little, too late? Reflections on law and ethics in the EU's foreign policy. In S. Blockmans & P. Koutrakos (Eds.), *Research handbook on the EU's common foreign and security policy, Research handbooks in European law*. Edward Elgar Publishing.

Koenig, N. (2011). The EU and the Libyan crisis – In quest of Coherence? *The International Spectator, 46*(4), 11–30. https://doi.org/10.1080/03932729.2011.628089

Koutrakos, P. (2013). *The EU common security and defence policy. Oxford University Press*. https://doi.org/10.1093/acprof:oso/9780199692729.001.0001

Lonardo, L., & Carrozzini, A. (2021). Non-contractual liability For EU sanctions: Towards the normalization of CFSP. *European Foreign Affairs Review, 26*(3), 459–476. https://doi.org/10.54648/EERR2021037

Meyer, C. (2020). *CSDP, Missions and Operations: In Depth Analysis*. European Parliament Publications Office. https://data.europa.eu/doi/10.2861/08725

Milanovic, M. (2010). Self-defense and non-state actors: Indeterminacy and the Jus Ad Bellum. *EJIL: Talk!* (blog). 21 February 2010. https://www.ejiltalk.org/self-defense-and-non-state-actors-indeterminacy-and-the-jus-ad-bellum/.

Missiroli, A., & Lonardo, L. (2019). The evolution of enhanced cooperation in the EU: From EnCo to PeSCo (2009-2019) | Coleurope. *Bruges Research Papers*. https://www.coleurope.eu/fr/research-paper/evolution-enhanced-cooperation-eu-enco-pesco-2009-2019.

Moser, C. (2020). *Accountability in EU security and defence: The law and practice of peacebuilding*, 1st edn. Oxford Studies in European Law. Oxford University Press.

Poli, S. (2022). The right to effective judicial protection with respect to acts imposing restrictive measures and its transformative force for the common foreign and security policy. *Common Market Law Review*, 1045–1080.

Wouters, J., & Raube, K. (2012). Europe's common security and defence policy: The case for inter-parliamentary scrutiny. *SSRN Electronic Journal*. https://doi.org/10.2139/ssrn.2274804

Chapter 6
The Silence of Foreign Policy

Contents

6.1 Introduction

Calls for the EU to 'do more' in foreign policy have been heard over the decades—and certainly since the EU equipped itself with foreign policy 'tools' through the CFSP legal-institutional machinery. The political appetite for EU foreign policy action may either increase or decrease at times of external shocks, such as the three geopolitical surprises from which this book commended (the Arab uprisings, the 2014 seizure of Crimea, and the 2022 Russian war against Ukraine). One authority on the subject, in an analysis for the European Parliament, wrote that 'One shortcoming [of Common Security and Defence Policy] is a failure to launch in response to emerging or manifest crises, even though it can be contested which CSDP operations should have been launched in specific cases as well as whether they would have been effective. This raises questions about why there has not, at times, been a greater convergence of views regarding the need for an EU operation and a willingness to provide national assets for it.'[1]

With this background, the chapter is dedicated to a counterintuitive topic. The topic is counterintuitive, or rather impossible, because the chapter sets out to discuss and explain non-events. To say that something 'did not happen' is hardly

[1] Meyer (2020), p. 7.

L. Lonardo, *EU Common Foreign and Security Policy After Lisbon*,
https://doi.org/10.1007/978-3-031-19131-2_6

meaningful unless it implies—and this is the only sense relevant throughout the chapter—that it should or might have happened, that it was expected to happen, or that its not happening has some 'specifiable consequences'.[2] As in Conan Doyle's story, the fact that the dog did not bark is only significant because the dog should have barked. The notion of inaction in this chapter operates *in concreto*. The aim is not to identify an abstract threshold below which we can talk about 'inaction'. One could consider that the EU sending a military mission is action, but only issuing a strategic document is inaction. Or one could consider a strategy to be action, but anything below that, for example a declaration, is inaction. And so on and so forth: is a tweet by the High Representative enough? And by a Commissioner? What about a spokesperson? This chapter tries to consider instances in which the inaction, of whatever kind, was consequential. For example, the EU's inaction in the South China Sea allows great-power politics games to be played by China and the US. EU inaction in Libya in March 2011 (which was of an entirely different nature altogether) meant that only some Member States intervened in the country.

Sometimes social scientists do (seek to) explain non-events.[3] In essence, such explanations must rely, at some point, on a positive event: on something that actually happened. This event can be a choice, such as a decision not to act (this is discussed in Sect. 6.2) or any other choice which resulted, perhaps not deliberately, in setting up a constraint which later impeded the behaviour whose absence we are trying to explain (this is the case of 'structural constraints' which are sometimes invoked: of which law is a special kind). Geography can contribute to the choice not to act: for example, because some geographical feature made it impossible, or excessively difficult. Mistakes can also explain inaction through that framework. In other cases, when there was no positive choice of the actor in question (or of someone else creating a constraint), the only likely form of explanation will be a residual one, i.e. the most plausible explanation of the inaction may be found by reference to why *some other actor* instead acted.[4] If it is possible to explain why NATO acted in a scenario but not the EU, the 'difference' is likely the best approximation we can get to explaining why the EU did not act.

The chapter recalls theoretical accounts and methodological issues with the explanation of non-events, including the notion of counterfactuals (Sect. 6.1). It posits that one should distinguish conceptually between instances of inaction motivated by a choice not to act, and other instances (failures to act). It then focuses on case studies of great geopolitical significance, selected to illustrate the distinction.[5]

[2]Lukes (2004), p. 53.

[3]Elster (2015), p. 6; Evans and Newnham (1998), p. 440 listing inaction as part of policy-making.

[4]Elster (2015), p. 6; This method is a comparison. It implies that there are sufficient similarities between the two actors (the one who acted and the one who, *ceteris paribus*, did not act). What are 'sufficient similarities' is to be ascertained by reference to the underlying theory. See Elster (1978), p. 218 fn 3.

[5]Rather than an empirical confirmation of the validity of the framework, they are used as illustrations thereof.

Section 6.2 presents examples of choices not to act, by reference to EU policy in the Indo-Pacific region and in Latin America. In those areas, for example, the EU had only two CSDP missions (both in the Indo-Pacific: the Aceh Monitoring Mission (AMM) in Indonesia and the EUNAVFOR operation Atalanta off the Somali coasts). Section 6.3 presents what it argues to be instances of the failures to act: the role of the EU in Libya in March 2011 and in Ukraine in 2014. As far as Libya is concerned, 'Member States could not agree on undertaking EU military missions to impose a no-fly zone or to provide humanitarian and evacuation assistance.'[6] As far as Ukraine (2014) is concerned, the EU as such was unable to decisively manage the conflict, and its (slow) response was by way of restrictive measures rather than through CSDP missions.

6.2 The Theory

Due to the methodological difficulties in explaining non-events, political scientists and historians are generally weary of venturing into this territory.[7]

When it comes to assessing failures of foreign policy, the literature does not refer to inaction, but rather to unsuccessful action. For example, Baldwin sought to define a framework by which to analyse foreign policy. He defines various parameters by which policies should be considered and by which it should be ascertained what is closer, on the spectrum, to a success or to a failure.[8] Rather than explaining inaction, therefore, foreign policy analysis explains action by comparing it to alternative policy options. This is essentially a 'utility framework' set at determining what are the best policy choices available to an actor given the constraints. This implies some form of rationality and of rational choice:[9] an actor will choose the best option for her, given the constraints. The issue on why rational choice proponents disagree is, of course, the determination of what constitutes the 'best' option. Thus, Baldwin correctly points out that policymakers may choose policies that are generally ineffective, provided that they are at least more effective than the alternatives: 'the question of whether a technique of statecraft is likely to work is different from the question of whether it should be used'.[10] The absolute chances of success are not relevant, only relative ones are. One will therefore not be surprised to see

[6] Meyer (2020), p. 6.

[7] To repeat, the kind of non-events this chapter is interested in are those that should have, or could reasonably be expected to have happened. Nobody should be seriously interested in explaining why Napoleon was not born in Russia (or one of the other infinite non-events concerning the life of Napoleon). One could instead ask why Napoleon was not successful in Russia (whereas he was in Italy and Germany).

[8] Baldwin (2000).

[9] Elster (1986); Spittaels (2022) for an example of interaction between rational choice theory and geopolitics, see.

[10] Baldwin (2000), p. 186.

deployment of restrictive measures over and over even though their effectiveness is low: a rational actor could choose them if they had the highest relative chances of 'success' (if they work better than civilian missions, for example). In this sense, the 'best' policy is not necessarily choosing one that will work but one that had the best chance of working given the constraints.[11]

But this leads to the question of what success is. It was argued that pursing success by reaching easily attainable goals is not success[12] and that it is better to use the concept of net costs vs net gain to ascertain it. In the words of a commentator:

> Leaders expecting a larger net gain through diplomacy than through war ... should rationally elect to pursue their goals through diplomatic bargaining and negotiating. This is true even if the expected gross gain from war is larger than the gross gain from diplomacy, provided that the cost differential is large enough (as it frequently is) to make the net effect of diplomacy preferable to war.[13]

This synthetic discussion of some rational theoretical explanations of foreign policy choices enables to attempt an answer to the interesting question 'when is it rational not to act?' One answer is when the net marginal gain of inaction is superior to the net marginal gain achievable through all other feasible options. This explanation is elegant and synthetic (as rational choice theory generally is), albeit somewhat speculative as it attributes rational design to collective entities (such as institutions) rather than to the individual.[14] This explanation also has the advantage of accounting for cases in which inaction has a net cost higher than the net gain, such as the health impact of inaction on air pollution. It also enables us to understand why it can be a rational strategy to *wait*, until a situation is ripe for action[15] (either because strong emotions have subsided, or because meanwhile more information has arisen[16]).

But that is akin to a decision not to act, which is relevant for the examples discussed in Sect. 6.3 of this chapter. It is of course also possible to talk about 'imposed' inaction, or failure to act. Scholars have also tried to understand inaction by policymakers in this latter sense (albeit the research concerns policy in general, not foreign policy specifically).[17] An important exception, discussed at length

---

[11] Thiel (2019), p. 48 'in 2014 EU states exhibited differences over whether aid to Gambia over an anti-LGBTI rights law should be frozen. While the Northern member states, which are generally forceful advocates of LGBTI rights globally, were strongly in favor of such action, the Southern ones pointed out that a reduction in aid may well lead to more displacement of Africans moving to their shores in search of a better life. In the end, financial sanctions were imposed'.

[12] Baldwin (2000), pp. 171–172.

[13] de Mesquita (1981), p. 183.

[14] To say that an institution acts rationally is a shortcut, a second best explanation.

[15] See the work of Zartman (1989).

[16] Plutarch, in the life of Fabius (the Roman dictator appointed to face Hannibal), thus describes a crucial episode: 'Fabius was not ignorant of this danger of his countrymen; he foresaw what would happen from the rashness of Minucius, and the cunning of Hannibal; and, therefore, kept his men to their arms, in readiness to wait the event; nor would he trust to the reports of others, but he himself, in front of his camp, viewed all that passed.'

[17] McConnell and 't Hart (2019).

below, is Sergio Fabbrini's analysis, asking 'Why was the EU as such unable to pursue an effective, coherent and accountable intervention in the 2011 Libya crisis?'[18]

One strand of the literature identified that the inaction may be due to an actor preventing a meaningful policy alternative from entering the political agenda[19] (a double non-event). Here, it is possible to explain the inaction (by institution A) by pointing to the choice of actor B to manipulate the belief of A. In the words of Lukes,

> is it not the supreme and most insidious exercise of power to prevent people, to what- ever degree, from having grievances by shaping their perceptions, cognitions and preferences in such a way that they accept their role in the existing order of things, either because they can see or imagine no alternative to it, or because they see it as natural and unchangeable, or because they value it as divinely ordained and beneficial?.[20]

The (Gramscian) preoccupation of Lukes is with the power of preventing the people from doing something, but the mechanisms of 'shaping their perceptions, cognitions and preferences' can have the more general result of preventing institutions from acting, for example through agenda-setting.

Another strand of the literature considered a different manner of constraints, those which are not imposed directly or deliberately, but arise as unintended consequences of some other choice, that is they arise either because of path dependency, or because they are part of a system that grows incrementally into a level of unmanageable complexity. The failure to intervene in Libya is probably an instance of the latter. In Fabbrini's words, it arose 'from the difficulties of an intergovernmental regime in solving basic structural and institutional dilemmas of collective action.'[21] These are not meant to be explanations, because '[t]o say that something may happen by accident, is not to provide an explanation'.[22] But the analysis is very helpful. It shows that what is to be explained here is the origin of the legal framework rather than the failures it results in.

The discussion of failure to act implies counterfactual thinking in the selection of the non-event: this is what it means to say that inaction must have specifiable consequences. More generally, statements about causations always involve counter-factuals.[23] Needless to say, counterfactuals are far from being theoretically uncontentious,[24] but they are a very useful tool for applying a hypothesis. Once a hypothesis has been generated, in other words, a counterfactual may rely on it. The

---

[18]Fabbrini (2014), p. 178.

[19]Cobb and Elder (1971).

[20]Lukes (2004), p. 28.

[21]Fabbrini (2014), p. 178.

[22]Elster (1984), p. 304.

[23]Elster (1978), p. 176 discussing whether causation necessitates or is simply non-definitionally bound to counterfactuals.

[24]See Lukes (2004), p. 49 for a discussion of methodological difficulties in the context of policy inactions, and Hansel and Oppermann (2014) for a recent application. The literature of the

other way round cannot work; nor can a counterfactual be used to prove a hypothesis. Counterfactuals are hypothesis-bound (or, in Elster's words: 'both Mill and Weber neglect the importance of having a specific theory that can circumscribe the set of legitimate counterfactual assumptions'[25]).

This book does not suggest a theory to explain EU institutions' behaviour. It does, however, try to apply some hypotheses identified thanks to the insights of the scholars mentioned above. The first insight is that if institutions act rationally, it is expected that they will refrain from acting when it serves them best to do so. Inaction can therefore be the result of a deliberate, rational choice of the actor (this is meant to be exemplified by the next section). The second is that it can be the result of the deliberate choice of another actor. The third is that it can be the result of unintended consequences, such as a structural, systemic constraint (this is meant to be exemplified by the analysis of Sect. 6.3). In that case, as the conclusion clarifies, it is not the inaction what is to be explained, but rather the existence of the constraint.

6.3 Decision Not to Act

A decision not to act by EU institutions is not usually advertised publicly. It flows instead rather naturally from strategic interests of the Union. Thus, in areas with limited geostrategic interests the EU is not particularly active, but this is not flagged as deliberate inaction. Instead, the EEAS is keen to emphasise the geostrategic relevance of all the partnerships the EU has with various regions in the world. The diplomatic language is everything here. Some regions have 'relevance', others have 'importance', others yet have 'key importance'.

The EU has in place several strategic documents spanning several areas of the world, including those which pose only an indirect security threat to the EU's territory. These strategies are produced by the EEAS or the Commission, but they are not necessarily 'operationalised', that is, they are not always followed up by EU action in the form of civilian missions, military operations, sanctions, or other kind of diplomatic means. But this is not a 'failure': it reflects, instead, EU interests and priorities.

In terms CSDP inaction pre-Lisbon, one could mention the war in Lebanon in 2006 (when the EU decided not to intervene as such, but to leave the task to a UN mission, already present on the territory, so-called UNIFIL II); as well as the great divisive moment: the intervention in Iraq in 2003. The EU would only participate, since 2005, through a rule of law training mission (EUJUST LEX), carried out outside Iraqi territory with a view to train judges and fonctionnaires in the security sector.

---

metaphysical impossibility of the counterfactual is very vast indeed. Reference can be made to (Elster, 1978) chapter six and to the first chapter of Tetlock and Belkin (2021).

[25] Elster (1978), p. 180.

Consider, for example, the Indo-Pacific region, in which France takes a keen interest (not least due to former imperial[26] and cultural[27] presence in what used to be called Indochina).[28] One of the EU's strategic documents is the 2021 Strategy for Cooperation in the Indo-Pacific. It is probably best read in conjunction with the 2020 joint communication by Commission and High Representative *Towards a Comprehensive Strategy with Africa* and of course with the 2019 EU-China strategy, in a context in which patters of global reach and dynamics between China and the US are changing.[29] Despite the increased institutional links between EU and ASEAN, and the EU's involvement in regional construction there,[30] when it comes to security the EU's interest in the Indo-Pacific region is mostly indirect. An exception to this is the perceived threat of disinformation, and of cyber threats more generally, which know no geographical boundaries. Economic interests (consider for example multilateral trade and investment) are instead very significant. Threats to maritime security in the Western Indian Ocean are a persistent security issue. Already several years before the adoption of the Indo-Pacific strategy, and under UN Security Council auspices, these were tackled by an EU naval operation (Atalanta). It is fair to state that the EU has been particularly active in countering piracy in the region of the Gulf of Aden, through its CSDP machinery. This is due to the key geopolitical importance of the area, linking the Indo-Pacific region to the Mediterranean through two choke-points: the first is Bab-el-Mandeb (between Djibouti and Yemen) from which access to the second, the Suez Canal, can be gained. The same EU presence is not found in other parts of the Indo-Pacific, such as the Indian subcontinent itself or South-East Asia. In fact, the further we go from the EU borders the more difficult it becomes to justify, legally and politically, an EU presence through a CSDP mission to help counter drug or human trafficking (which are real plagues in parts of the region). China is a regional hegemon and the US is the only power that can stretch its military might to even compete in that region. However, the role of an EU coordinated response in case of humanitarian catastrophes and disasters should also not be underestimated - and this is of course facilitated by a naval presence.

Another region where EU action is limited is South America (but with the important exception of Venezuela, mentioned below). The legacy of the Spanish and Portuguese empires results in close linguistic and cultural ties with Southern American countries, and it is those two Member States who take the keenest interests, among EU countries, in the region. Since 1999, the two regions have a bi-regional strategic partnership. Areas of cooperation are on largely

[26]France established a presence in what used to be called *Cocinchine* (south Vietnam) in 1787 which, one century later, became part of the colony of French Indochina together with Cambodia (1860), Tonkin and Annam (1884), Laos (1893).

[27]Consider the role of the Societé des Missions Étrangères funded in 1663 in Paris for the evangelisation of non Christian lands of East Asia.

[28]La stratégie de la France dans l'Indopacifique (2020) https://www.elysee.fr/admin/upload/default/0001/10/c3852600ccbecbccb2fa05ecf147fa307a79ac17.pdf.

[29]Beeson and Biscop (2021); on US-China relations, Friedberg (2012) remains excellent.

[30]Beeson (2013).

non-contentious issues such as sustainable development, climate change and protection of biodiversity. A Joint Communication to the European Parliament and the Council European Union, Latin America and the Caribbean: joining forces for a common future (April 2019) sets out the current policy framework for relations between the two regions.

Venezuela is somewhat an exception: it has no preferential trade agreement with the EU and it is affected by a perduring economic and political crisis. 2017 was a particularly turbulent year. After months of protests and political stalemate between the government and the opposition-controlled National Assembly, in July President Maduro called for a new Constituent Assembly. This was perceived by the EU as an illegitimate move, undermining the rule of law in Venezuela—and it resulted in the imposition of restrictive measures.[31] Those sanctions were challenged by Venezuela in front of the Court of Justice of the European Union, resulting in a significant judgment confirming that a third country can in fact bring such actions for annulment of EU sanctions, as mentioned in Chap. 4. Toward the end of the past decade, the EU took a strong stance on the leadership issue of that country, 'contended' by former President Maduro and the EU-backed opposition leader Guaidó. In January 2019, the European Parliament, in a non-binding document, stated that it '[r]ecognises Mr Guaidó as the legitimate interim president of Bolivarian Republic of Venezuela'.[32] Unlike countries such as the US, Australia, and indeed most of Latin America, the EU only recognised Guaidò as interim president, calling for new elections. The stance was not uncontroversial, as it found the opposition of some European right-wing parties.

If what was said so far is correct, it should also be the case that EU action will follow Member States' changing priorities. The Arctic would seem to illustrate the point. If it is defined as the area within the Arctic Circle—very roughly, this is where trees stop growing due to low temperatures—Finland and Sweden have 25% and 15% of their territory in it,[33] Denmark is the third EU 'Arctic state', and Norway and Iceland are two European Economic Areas Members. In other words, the EU is in the Arctic.[34] Due to climate change,[35] the region has acquired great geopolitical relevance. It was also relevant before, of course. Russia would trade with Englishmen, Scots, and the Dutch via the Arctic and the Nordic port of Arkhangelsk since the sixteenth century.[36] But the Arctic's geopolitical weight has increased dramatically

[31] Decision (CFSP) 2017/2074 of 13 November 2017 concerning restrictive measures in view of the situation in Venezuela. This was implemented On 13 November 2017, by Regulation (EU) 2017/2063 concerning restrictive measures in view of the situation in Venezuela (OJ 2017 L 295, p. 21), on the basis of Article 215(2) TFEU and Decision 2017/2074.

[32] European Parliament (2019) https://www.europarl.europa.eu/doceo/document/TA-8-2019-0061_EN.html.

[33] Dodds and Nuttall (2019), p. 31.

[34] Coninsx (2019), p. 237.

[35] Tamnes and Offerdal (2016).

[36] The commerce between Russia and Norway on the same route gave rise to an interesting linguistic phenomenon: a pidgin language called Russenorsk.

in the past few years. The EU has not stood idle.[37] This was not due exclusively to the three Member States with most immediate interests (fisheries, tourism, energy). The geopolitics of the Arctic—a most fascinating subject as it involves the nexus between climate change, foreign policy and imperialism, 'indigenous' cultures, and geography—touches instead many other states, indeed the EU.[38] The conservation of marine biological resources, for example, are an exclusive competence of the EU. The EU also enjoys competence in the areas of fisheries and energy, not to mention climate policy. While the first EU document on the region dates to 1999, the current Arctic policy is from 2016 (and it is centred on climate change, development, and multilateralism).[39] These are all areas to which indigenous geopolitics can contribute. EU Arctic policy is only partly foreign policy, and as the EU is ready to tell third countries how to deal with their indigenous people, it should also consider how the EU itself does it internally.[40]

6.4 Failure to Act

The Arab uprisings were a defining moment for EU foreign policy—both because they were the first geopolitical surprise after Lisbon, and due to the EU's failure to achieve a coordinated, effective response. There seems to be widespread opinion in academic and policy commentary that EU (in)activities in Libya (and the intervention by a group of Member States) were a failure.[41] Obviously, something that looks like a failure in a given moment may be rationalised as a great success later. And Libya was, it seems, a 'lesson learnt' for the EU, at least judging to its handling of later geopolitical surprises.[42]

6.4.1 Libya

Until 2010, Libya seemed to get on relatively well with its neighbours on the other shore of the Mediterranean. After the 9/11 attacks, Libya had started to exit from the international isolation which Qaddafi had imposed. The colonel's attitude became

[37] Chuffart et al. (2021).

[38] Coninsx (2019), p. 237.

[39] *JOINT COMMUNICATION TO THE EUROPEAN PARLIAMENT AND THE COUNCIL An Integrated European Union Policy for the Arctic* (2016).

[40] See e.g. European Parliament session of 15 March 2017, intervention by Pietikäinen, Rapporteur of the Commission for EU Arctic policy, available at https://www.europarl.europa.eu/doceo/document/CRE-8-2017-03-15_ET.html.

[41] Fabbrini (2014), p. 177; Puri (2016).

[42] See again conclusions of this chapter.

more open toward Western countries (refusing to condemn the 2003 invasion of Iraq, renouncing the goal of acquiring weapons of mass destruction, recognising Libyan involvement in terrorist acts). Geopolitics meant that Libya provided oil to Europe, and gas through a pipeline (the Greenstream) across Italy. Italy was indeed Libya's privileged interlocutor with Libya. This was due also to a reconciliation in the form of a payment from Italy to make good the colonial past[43]—a gesture no doubt favoured by the close relationship between the leaders of the two countries (Berlusconi and Qaddafi)—as well as to Libyan investments in Italian companies (such as the bank Unicredit, the energy company Eni, the car manufacturer FIAT, and the defence company Finmeccanica). Libya was also part of the *Union pour la Mediterranée*, Sarkozy's 2008 institutional creation grouping leaders of countries on both shores of the sea.

It is then understandable that, by and large, in February 2011, Member States (with the exception of Germany) were hesitant to take a hard line against Qaddafi once the riots started.[44] However, by 20 February, about 5 days after the beginning of the protests, the EU began reacting to the crisis with general condemnations and calls to limit violence.[45] Six days later, the UNSC also announced sanctions against Qaddafi with resolution 1970. In the early phases of the crisis, the EU was mostly aligned and coherent in denouncing the violent repression and supporting the Libyan people's quest for democracy. At this stage, the EU arguably displayed a relatively high level of *horizontal coherence* in its crisis management policies.[46] However, as the crisis progressed, the EU *as such* did not continue with a coherent stance, particularly when the potential use of force was beginning to be considered.

It was in the UNSC that decisions were made. While the UK and France adopted a more aggressive tone and began pushing for military intervention, Germany, initially supportive of armed intervention, shied away from the use military force and abstained in voting for UNSCR resolution 1973 on 17 March.

The intervention in Libya was eventually by NATO, implementing the abovementioned resolution (after initial operations and the enforcement of no-fly zones by the UK, Canada, France, and US), with heavy involvement of the Italian and French navies.

The EU did not launch a CSDP military operation to Libya, but the Council adopted restrictive measures[47] and, on 21 March, it announced it was prepared to 'provide support' to humanitarian assistance if called to do so by the UN Office for the Coordination of Humanitarian Affairs (OCHA).[48] OCHA never requested the

[43] Treaty of friendship, partnership and cooperation between the Italian Republic and Great Socialist People's Libyan Arab Jamahiriya, done in Benghazi on 30 August 2008.

[44] Fabbrini (2014), p. 183.

[45] Fabbrini (2014), p. 183.

[46] Koenig (2011), pp. 17–18.

[47] Decision 2011/137/CFSP and, following the adoption of UNSC Resolution 1973, EU Council Decision 2011/178/CFSP.

[48] Council (2011) 8.

mission. The EU was also able to launch lower-level missions outside of CSDP such as a FRONTEX operation (Joint Operation Hermes) to assist Italy with migrant flows.[49] As mentioned in the previous chapter, the EU did intervene with CSDP missions in Libya, but only later: EUBAM, assisting with border control in Libya (launched in 2013).

How did these issues arise? Why did the EU not operationalise its CSDP? The literature has identified structural problems inhibiting decision making at EU level, proposing various classifications of the issues.[50] For our purposes, it is sufficient to highlight problems of inter-institutional coherence, vertical coherence, and multilateral coherence.

More analytically, questions about *inter-institutional coherence* are exemplified by the fact that, while the European Council president began stating that the role of any intervention in Libya should be regime change, the HR/VP maintained a considerably less aggressive tone.[51] Further inconsistencies can be found between other institutions such as the Commission and the EEAS which faced significant hurdles in coordinating their policy. This is due no doubt due to the multiplication of bodies with partially overlapping competences involved in crafting EU foreign policy: their competition or disagreements can decrease effectiveness.[52]

The EU had significant shortfalls in its *vertical coherence*,[53] as shown by Member States votes in the UN Security Council. This is further complicated by the fact that the EU suffers from a lack of democratic accountability since in the context of CFSP the European Council and Foreign Affairs Council do not have political checks against them, giving member state governments more influence.[54] It was the case that on the Libyan issue it was hard to reconcile the preferences of influential Member States over the use of military force. Germany's decision to avoid the use of military force is due to the fact that Germany did not see a major threat to itself nor a large national interest in Libya,[55] and to a belief among German authorities that the intervention was not well planned.[56] Germany's stance was also influenced by domestic politics.[57] Further demonstrating the divide between member states was the fact that France chose to recognize the Transitional National Council before there was any agreement among EU members. The European Parliament

---

49 Koenig (2011), p. 15.

50 For example, some have argued that the EU tends to fair poorly in new circumstances but tends to improve over time as their engagement and experience with a region increases (Kundnani & Vaisse, 2011). However, France's continued tendency to go its own way, defying the preferences of the EU and the rest of the member states, contradicts this idea and highlights the collective action problem that the EU faces (Harchaoui, 2017).

51 Koenig (2011), p. 19; Fabbrini (2014), p. 184.

52 As the saying goes, too many cooks spoil the broth.

53 Koenig (2011), pp. 20–22.

54 Fabbrini (2014), p. 191.

55 Miskimmon (2012), p. 402.

56 Miskimmon (2012), p. 397.

57 'Analysis - Domestic Concerns Drive German Caution on Libya' (2011).

viewed the European Council decision to recognise the TNC as a failure of leadership: rather than guiding member states, EU institutions on that occasion merely waited for a consensus to form among major states and then adopted that consensus.[58] Despite disagreements among member states about the resolution and the use of force, the Council of the EU still endorsed resolution 1973 and pledged the EU's support in implementing it.

In general, the EU maintained a high level of *multilateral coherence* with the UN and generally had initiatives that supported the NATO mission in Libya, though its interaction and cooperation with the latter was much more limited.[59]

6.4.2 Ukraine 2014

Significant EU involvement in Ukraine can be traced back to the launch of the European Neighbourhood Policy (ENP) in 2004, which was in turn a result of the expansion in EU membership. This meant that, for the first time, Ukraine bordered with the EU (with Romania, Hungary, Slovakia and Poland).

There are several factors for Russia's increased interest in Ukraine in the new century, an examination of which is beyond the scope of this chapter. Among these were the fact that the EU eastern 'enlargement' and influence came to be seen as more threatening by Moscow; the belief that the 2008 Russo-Georgian war showed that the EU was unwilling to intervene to support its normative positions; and a perceived increase in anti-Russian attitudes within the EU. In this context, the negotiations between the EU Commission and Ukraine for the conclusion of an Association Agreement and a Deep and Comprehensive Free Trade Agreement (DCFTA) must be examined.

Once Russia began to perceive EU negotiations with Ukraine as threatening, it increased its support and encouragement of pro-Russian politicians and movements in Ukraine and began to present east-looking political alternatives, like the Eurasian Customs Union, to Ukraine and other countries in central and Eastern Europe.[60] Through a combination of carrots and sticks, Moscow eventually convinced Yanukovych not to sign the agreement negotiated with the Commission. This resulted in an Europhile protest movement in November and December of 2013. On 22 February 2014, Yanukovych and the opposition agreed to hold general elections in May. On that occasion, the Ukrainian Parliament accused Yanukovych of human rights violations and removed him from his position. Following these events, in March 2014 Russophile forces seized control of strategic strongholds in Crimea, essentially controlling the peninsula by 6 March. The Supreme Council of the autonomous republic of Crimea voted to secede from the republic and to become

58 Helwig (2013), p. 247.

59 Koenig (2011), pp. 22–23.

60 Howorth (2017), p. 127; Nitoiu and Sus (2017), p. 75.

part of the Russian Federation. This was also confirmed by a popular referendum in the region (passed with 97% of consents). The international community did not recognise the annexation of Crimea by Russia, which took the form of a Treaty signed on 18 March 2014. Eventually, gunmen without insignia began occupying important buildings in Eastern Ukraine in a similar manner to what had previously occurred in Crimea. This culminated in Donetsk and Luhansk claiming independence on 7 April, leading commencement of hostilities in Eastern Ukraine. In response to the increasing violence, Germany and France engaged with Russia and Ukraine on the sides of a celebration of the allied landings in France in a process termed the 'Normandy Format'. Eventually, this format led to the first Minsk Agreement in February 2015, when the parties came to agree an unstable ceasefire.

The EU's cumbersome intergovernmental foreign policy structure arguably resulted in a failure by the EU to understand the views of Russia and the motivations of Ukrainian leaders, resulting in Yanukovych being pressured into not signing the agreement, which is what triggered the initial protests.[61] Negotiations for the agreement were conducted by the Commission—the subject matter being trade and other 'TFEU competences'—not by the EEAS. One way to understand the argument is to say that the Commission officials, who are competent experts in technicalities of trade, lacked the diplomatic expertise of considering Ukraine's past and geopolitics. Starting in early 2014, the EU's initial pronouncements were relatively minor and mainly condemned the use of violence, urged peace and a democratic solution, and sought to encourage Ukraine to accept the association agreement. However, this changed when Ukrainian government forces fired on protestors who had gathered in Maidan Square, leading to the imposition of targeted sanctions on key figures in Ukraine by the EU and its partners. Howorth argues that the EU's efforts in mediating between government and opposition were uncoordinated and incoherent with different bodies working against each other.[62] On 3 March, the FAC condemned Russian aggression, expressed support for the new Ukrainian government, and suspended the EU and its MSs from participating in the G8 until the crisis was resolved. Following Russia's annexation, the EU imposed sanctions against Russian and Crimean political leaders (the March sanctions). The EU and US also suspended Russia from the G8 summit. Some argue that despite this response, the EU continued to approach the crisis in a disorganised and incoherent fashion with MSs presenting different views and preferences. Howorth emphasises the stark divide between CEE MSs and Western Member States, and, as the crisis progressed, the divides forming between CEE MSs (where Hungary and the Czech Republic were issuing reportedly pro-Russian statements while States like Lithuania were emphasizing their support for NATO).[63] Orenstein and Kelemen take a different approach and argue that the EU's response was enabled by a common perception of Russia as a threat by the 'Big Three' and by other member states in Central and

---

[61] Kuzio (2017), p. 107.

[62] Howorth (2017), p. 128.

[63] Howorth (2017), pp. 129–130.

Eastern Europe.[64] They emphasise that the main reason that the EU was able to overcome its normal collective action problems was because of the perception of a large threat from Russia. Others disagree with the idea that Russia was seen as an overwhelming threat to most member states because Russia did not directly threaten states that were not in CEE. They argue instead that Russia's annexation of Crimea was a key point in aligning Member States towards supporting sanctions and taking a hard line against Russia because the annexation violated the norms of sovereignty and self-determination within Europe's borders.[65]

On the Normandy format, Natorski and Pomorska saw the willingness of Member States within the EU to delegate the diplomatic responsibilities of negotiating to Germany and France as an important sign of trust within the EU.[66] Overall, they viewed trust as an integral part of the EU's ability to function and saw this as vindication that the EU was able to exercise influence and control in this instance. Interestingly, Natorski and Pomorska saw that while member states initially chose to lead in their response to the crisis, they delegated more responsibilities to the EU as the crisis progressed. Howorth opposes this view and argues that by taking the lead, larger states demonstrated that they recognized the impotence of the EU as a foreign policy actor. The same author further points to the fact that the Minsk Agreements were signed through the OSCE rather than the EU as evidence that the EU was not seen by member states as a viable vehicle for foreign policy,[67] and that there is "no hard evidence . . . that [Russia's intentions in Eastern Ukraine] have been affected in any discernible way by the exercise or expression of 'EU Power.'"[68]

On 17 July, Malaysian Airlines flight MH17 was shot down by Ukrainian rebel groups using a Russian supplied Surface-to-Air missile leading to the deaths of a large number of EU citizens. This is when the Eu adopted a further round of heavier sanctions (the May sanctions). Kuzio argues that the severity of the event enabled the EU to get around the EU's slow, "unwieldy structure" by encouraging certain member states who would normally have blocked action to apply tough sanctions.[69] He argues that this event was the impetus for putting significant, punishing, sectoral sanctions on Russia and that before, MSs had been unwilling to apply truly punitive sanctions.[70] Natorski and Pomorska, emphasizing the role that trust and empathy between member states played in the crisis, also agree that the downing of flight MH17 was critical to allowing the EU to pass a punishing, third round of sanctions.[71]

---

[64] Orenstein and Kelemen (2017), p. 89.

[65] Sjursen and Rosén (2017), p. 30.

[66] Natorski and Pomorska (2017), p. 64.

[67] Howorth (2017), p. 131.

[68] Howorth (2017), p. 131.

[69] Kuzio (2017), p. 115.

[70] Kuzio (2017), p. 116.

[71] Natorski and Pomorska (2017), p. 63.

There is broad agreement in the literature that EU response to the initial phase of the crisis was slow and irresolute, but that the situation had changed by mid-2014.[72] However, here there is disagreement as to which event (the annexation of Crimea and the downing of MH17 being the most plausible candidates) allowed the EU to overcome its deadlocks.

Indeed, the EU did manage to impose several sanctions that severely impacted the Russian economy even though this also entailed losses (though not to the same degree) to the EU. Natorski and Pomorska also emphasize the manner in which the EU dealt with this threat. They argue that the EU created a dual track approach to deal with Russia whereby the EU engaged with Russia diplomatically to try to mediate conflict while also condemning Russian actions and applying sanctions.[73]

Issues of coherence were raised once again. In their introduction and conclusion to the 2017 special issue of the Journal of Common Market Studies dedicated to the Ukraine crisis, Cross and Karolewski argue that even the most cohesive states can show different foreign policy preferences between bureaucratic bodies, interest groups, or political parties and thus, argue that the EU should be seen as a valid foreign policy actor (2017; 138). Orenstein and Kelemen, on the other hand, argue that the EU's consensus based design in the foreign policy field incentivises external actors to cultivate 'Trojan Horses' within the EU who will oppose other members in taking certain actions. They argue that during the Ukraine crisis, these Trojan Horses could be seen as Cyprus, Greece, Hungary, and to some degree Italy (2017: 92). Howorth also seems to disagree that the EU acted as a coherent actor give that he repeatedly brings up the uncoordinated and occasionally counterproductive work that different institutions, bodies or member states were undertaking at the same time (2017; 128). The structural problems presented by the EU's foreign policy design were also briefly touched upon by Zarembo who, while conducting a comparative study of two missions found that the Commissionled, EU Border Assistance Mission may have been more adaptable because it was not subject to the same intergovernmental approach that traditional CSDP missions are.

It is also possible to account for EU action (or inaction) by understanding it as unintended consequence of another choice: long term decisions constrain short term responses. As Karolweski and Cross put it "structural dependencies are likely to impact EU power, but might be quite specific given the nature of the crisis".[74]

6.5 Conclusion

The study of the literature presented in this chapter shows that inaction may be explained either by a deliberate choice to refrain from acting (it is suggested that this may be due to most Member States lacking political priorities or strategic interests in

[72] Contra, Howorth, who argues the EU exhibited a poor response to a crisis of its own making.

[73] Natorski and Pomorska (2017), p. 58.

[74] Karolewski and Cross (2017), p. 142.

specific regions); or by a deliberate choice to withdraw information or preventing another actor from acting; or it can be explained 'residually', that is as a by-product of the explanation of someone else's action (arguably, the Normandy format allowed some Member States to act over the Ukrainian conflict because that format was more efficient thus preventing the need for independent EU action); or, finally, if the non-event is only explained by virtue of structural constraints or similar concepts (cumbersome decision-making process and incoherent institutional framework hindering EU action in Libya and, initially, Ukraine), then it is those constraints which need explanation.

This suggests two avenues of research. One is to find possible solutions to enhance the effectiveness of the EU's CSDP. In fact, some forms of institutional engineering were common suggestions by commentators already at the time of the Libyan crisis or shortly thereafter. Among these, there was the idea of concentrating more power in the HR/VP or the EEAS by giving them a greater role for leadership on foreign policy, planning, and information sharing among member states.[75] Or fostering a common strategic outlook among Member states, between Member States and EU institutions, and between EU institutions responsible for foreign policy.[76] While this proved ineffective in the context of the Arab uprisings, the EU had learnt something by the time of the Russian seizure of Crimea in 2014. It is undeniable, however, that the EU responded very differently to the 2022 war of Russia against Ukraine. At least in its initial phases, the EU's response was consist, and somewhat effective. What had changed in the ten years intervening between the Arab uprisings and the Russian invasion was not the law. The differences are to be found in the strong emotions that Putin triggered in Europe; in the sensitivity of the political border; and in the uses of CFSP as laboratory for constitutional experimentation. We shall return to this discussion in the next chapter and in the conclusions.

The other avenue is more theoretical perhaps but equally valuable, and it consists of the quest for an explanation of the structural constraints singles out in this chapter. It will be recalled that the explanation for a non-event must rely, at some point, on an event: to say that the EU did not launch a CSDP mission in Libya because there are structural constraints is useful but not an exhaustive explanation. It simply shifts the *explanandum*: why are there structural constraints? From what and whose choices did they flow? Some scholars argue that the foreign policy apparatus of the EU presents structural constraints 'by design'.[77] To answer, a historian will probably be needed.

---

[75]Helwig (2013), p. 251: Lehne (2017), pp. 12–14: Koenig (2011), p. 25.

[76]Helwig (2013), pp. 252–253: Koenig (2011), pp. 27–28.

[77]Menon (2008).

References

'Analysis - Domestic Concerns Drive German Caution on Libya'. (2011). *Reuters* (18 March 2011).
Baldwin, D. A. (2000). Success and failure in foreign policy. *Annual Review of Political Science, 3*(1), 167–182.
Beeson, M. (2013). Living with giants: ASEAN and the evolution of Asian regionalism. *TRaNS: Trans -Regional and -National Studies of Southeast Asia, 1*(2), 303–322.
Beeson, M., & Biscop, S. (2021). EU–Asia security relations in a global context: Geoeconomics and geopolitics. In T. Christiansen, E. Kirchner, & S. S. Tan (Eds.), *The European Union's security relations with Asian partners* (pp. 29–49). Springer International Publishing.
Chuffart, R., Raspotnik, A., & Stępień, A. (2021). Our common arctic? A more sustainable EU-Arctic nexus in light of the European green deal. *The Polar Journal, 11*(2), 284–302.
Cobb, R. W., & Elder, C. D. (1971). The politics of Agenda-building: An alternative perspective for modern democratic theory. *The Journal of Politics, 33*(4), 892–915.
Coninsx, M.-A. (2019). The European Union: A key and reliable partner in the arctic and beyond. *European Foreign Affairs Review*, 237–241.
de Mesquita, B. B. (1981). Risk, power distributions, and the likelihood of war. *International Studies Quarterly, 25*(4), 541.
Dodds, K., & Nuttall, M. (2019). *The arctic: What everyone needs to know*. Oxford University Press.
Elster, J. (1978). *Logic and society: Contradictions and possible worlds*. Wiley.
Elster, J. (1984). The contradictions of modern societies. *Government and Opposition, 19*(3), 304–311.
Elster, J. (Ed.). (1986). *Rational choice*. New York University Press.
Elster, J. (2015). *Explaining social behavior: More nuts and bolts for the social sciences* (2nd ed.). Cambridge University Press.
Evans, G., & Newnham, J. (1998). *The penguin dictionary of international relations*. Penguin Books.
Fabbrini, S. (2014). The European Union and the Libyan crisis. *International Politics, 51*(2), 177–195.
Friedberg, A. L. (2012). *A contest for supremacy: China, America, and the struggle for mastery in Asia*. W.W. Norton & Company.
Hansel, M., & Oppermann, K. (2014). Counterfactual reasoning in foreign policy analysis: The case of German nonparticipation in the Libya Intervention of 2011. *Foreign Policy Analysis*, p. n/a-n/a.
Harchaoui, J. (2017). How France is making Libya Worse: Marcon is Strengthening Haftar. *Foreign Affairs, 20*.
Helwig, N. (2013). EU foreign policy and the high representative’s capability-expectations-gap: A question of political will. *European Foreign Affairs Review, 18*(2).
Howorth, J. (2017). "Stability on the Borders": The Ukraine crisis and the EU's constrained policy towards the Eastern Neighbourhood. *JCMS Journal of Common Market Studies, 55*(1), 121–136.
Joint Communication to the European Parliament and the Council An Integrated European Union Policy for the Arctic (2016).
Karolewski, I. P., & Cross, M. K. D. (2017). The EU's power in the Russia–Ukraine crisis: Enabled or constrained? *JCMS: Journal of Common Market Studies, 55*(1), 137–152.
Koenig, N. (2011). The EU and the Libyan crisis – In quest of coherence? *The International Spectator, 46*(4), 11–30.
Kundnani, H., & Vaisse, J. (2011). *The European foreign policy scorecard*. European Council on Foreign Relations.
Kuzio, T. (2017). Ukraine between a constrained EU and assertive Russia: Europe's hybrid foreign policy. *JCMS: Journal of Common Market Studies, 55*(1), 103–120.
Lehne, S. (2017). *Is there hope for EU foreign policy?* Carnegie Europe.

Lukes, S. (2004). *Power: A radical view* (2nd ed.). Palgrave Macmillan.
McConnell, A., & 't Hart, P. (2019). Inaction and public policy: Understanding why policymakers "Do Nothing". *Policy Sciences, 52*(4), 645–661.
Menon, A. (2008). *Europe: The state of the Union*. Atlantic.
Meyer, C. (2020). *CSDP, missions and operations: In depth analysis*. European Parliament Publications Office.
Miskimmon, A. (2012). German foreign policy and the Libya crisis. *German Politics, 21*(4), 392–410.
Natorski, M., & Pomorska, K. (2017). Trust and decision-making in times of crisis: The EU's response to the events in Ukraine. *JCMS: Journal of Common Market Studies, 55*(1), 54–70.
Nitoiu, C. and Sus, M. (2017) The European Parliament's Diplomacy – A tool for projecting EU power in times of crisis? The case of the Cox–Kwasniewski mission. *JCMS: Journal of Common Market Studies*, Vol. 55, No. 1, pp. 71–86.
Orenstein, M. A., & Kelemen, R. D. (2017). Trojan horses in EU foreign policy. *JCMS: Journal of Common Market Studies, 55*(1), 87–102.
Puri, H. S. (2016). *Perilous interventions: The security council and the politics of Chaos*. Harpercollins Publishers India.
Sjursen, H., & Rosén, G. (2017). Arguing sanctions. On the EU's response to the crisis in Ukraine. *JCMS: Journal of Common Market Studies, 55*(1), 20–36.
Spittaels, S. (2022). Mapping greed as a conflict motivation: Evidence from armed conflicts in Sudan and Libya on the complexity of armed groups' interactions with natural resources. In D. Criekemans (Ed.), *Geopolitics and international relations: Grounding world politics anew*. Brill | Nijhoff.
Tamnes, R., & Offerdal, K. (Eds.). (2016). *Geopolitics and security in the arctic: Regional dynamics in a global world*. Routledge, Taylor & Francis Group.
Tetlock, P., & Belkin, A. (2021). Counterfactual thought experiments in world politics: Logical, methodological, and psychological perspectives. In *1. Counterfactual thought experiments in world politics: Logical, methodological, and psychological perspectives* (pp. 3–38). Princeton University Press.
Thiel, M. (2019). Theorizing the EU's international promotion of LGBTI rights policies in the global south. In S. Beringer, S. Maier, & M. Thiel (Eds.), *EU development policies. Between norms and geopolitics*. Palgrave Macmillan.
Zartman, I. W. (1989). *Ripe for resolution: Conflict and intervention in Africa*, Updated edn. Oxford University Press.

Part III
The Key Themes

Chapter 7
Between Law and Geopolitics

Contents

7.1 Introduction

This chapter brings together the threads of the geopolitical reality and legal (in)-action of the EU since Lisbon, and makes the case that dissatisfaction with the legal distinctiveness of CFSP that other authors have expressed may be due to the mismatch between geopolitics and law.

The nature of the problem is as follows: geography determines that groups in the area (the EU and its neighbours) interact because there are limited resources. The study of such interaction is best conceptualised in terms derived from rational choice theory and game theory in particular. Equilibrium is the set of decisions for each participant, with the property that no one can improve his situation by deviating from his equilibrium choice as long as the others stick to theirs.[1]

[1] Elster (2015), p. 309.

L. Lonardo, *EU Common Foreign and Security Policy After Lisbon*,
https://doi.org/10.1007/978-3-031-19131-2_7

Crucially, the interaction on shared or limited resources is a game of 'mixed conflict and cooperation', which is the core of game theory: '[o]ne way in which they can arise is if it is better for all if all make the same choice than if they differ, but some individuals prefer that all should do X and others that all should do Y.'[2] Peace in Ukraine is best for both EU and Russia, but for the EU this implies an association agreement with Ukraine, and for Russia the absence of such agreement.

It then becomes necessary to understand what is the EU's equilibrium: the dominant strategy, meaning the one that does not depend on the other participants' decisions, is that of autonomy, in the sense of territorial, material, and technological independence and integrity.

Geopolitics entails that there is a sensitive space in Central and Eastern Europe.[3] It is perhaps not by chance that the EU tried to appropriate that political space, through enlargement and the ENP,[4] and later through sanctions, missions, and association agreements. Only a very small fraction of this was done through the CFSP. CFSP is a sanctuary of Member States' sovereignty that, in its hard core, resists integration into the otherwise unitary EU legal order.[5] Normatively, that is, considering the geopolitical environment in which the EU needs to act, and the heterogeneity brought about by the 2004 enlargement, the legal ambiguity of CFSP is not tenable because it is not functional.

This chapter talks about the EU's need for autonomy (Sect. 7.2.1), which, interacting with the geopolitical need to create a political border where there is no geographical one (Sect. 7.2.2), sheds light on the 2004 enlargement and the re-ordering of the political space in Europe (including the ongoing trends of decline in Atlanticism and in the geopolitical weight of the Mediterranean) (Sect. 7.2.3). CFSP law does not accord well to this geopolitical reality (Sect. 7.2.4). The chapter then puts together three key themes of the book where the mismatch is particularly evident: coherence, accountability, and effectiveness (Sect. 7.3).

7.2 The Geopolitical Reality in Europe

7.2.1 The Need for Autonomy

While there are many uses of the word autonomy in EU jargon ('strategic autonomy' in the context of security and defence, 'open strategic autonomy' for trade, 'digital sovereignty', 'legal autonomy') what they all have in common is that they are meant

---

[2] Elster (1986), p. 8.

[3] This is an important contribution of classic works of geopolitics (Mackinder, 1904; Kaplan, 2013; Spykman, 2007).

[4] This is an important contribution of the literature on EU geopolitics and border studies (Scott, 2011; Bialasiewicz, 2011; Bialasiewicz et al., 2009).

[5] Dashwood (2014); Wessel (2016).

to ensure, at a minimum and as a logical first step, the EU's political survival.[6] In this 'negative' sense, autonomy means achieving a degree of independence. Selected examples of EU action to secure territorial, material, and technological independence follow.

The first form of independence is geographical: the EU needs a territory. This is an existential requirement which—one could argue—is also translated, as a matter of law, into a constitutional objective of 'integrity' (Article 21(2)(a) TEU), namely: '[t]he Union shall define and pursue common policies and actions, and shall work for a high degree of cooperation in all fields of international relations, in order to safeguard its values, fundamental interests, security, independence and integrity'. Yet, that legal obligation of integrity can hardly refer to the EU's territory. The delimitation of the territory of the EU is not a matter of EU law. It is, instead, for Member States to decide what constitutes part of their territory: the EU has a territory only derivatively, in so far as its Member States have one. Thus, in *Slovenia v Croatia*, the Court clarified that it does not have jurisdiction to hear alleged violations of EU law which derive from an unresolved border dispute between those two countries, because that dispute is one regulated by international law and, crucially, it would in any case not fall under EU competence. In *Vies*, the Court recognised that EU law prevails over Spanish law, including when Spain tries to preserve its territorial integrity from secession.[7] Enlargement as a form of territorial protection is discussed below.[8]

Since logistics (still) matter even in the era of globalisation, it is important for the EU to have infrastructures, raw materials, and resources easily available, or, even better, readily available within its territory. For example, the EU has the objective of producing 20% of the semiconductors in the world (so as not to depend on Taiwan). The Russian invasion of Ukraine has made it tragically obvious that the EU needs a degree of autonomy in natural resources such as oil and gas. Security of supply means that reliance on third parties ought to be reduced, and reliance on politically problematic partners is to be eliminated. In this context, it ought to be noted nonetheless that the gas security regulation is not adopted on a CFSP legal basis, but pursuant to a TFEU one (Article 194(2) TFEU).[9] Yet, EU sanctions also have repercussions for EU energy policy, for example in so far as they prohibit the purchase of certain Russian energy. The critical infrastructures directive, adopted in 2008, is also not a CFSP instrument but is based instead on an internal market legal basis.[10]

---

[6] Borrell (2020).

[7] Casolari (2022), p. 587.

[8] Section 7.2.2. The need for a political border where there is no geographical one: enlargement as foreign policy to secure Western Europe.

[9] Regulation (EU) 2017/1938 of the European Parliament and of the Council of 25 October 2017 concerning measures to safeguard the security of gas supply and repealing Regulation (EU) No 994/2010.

[10] Council Directive 2008/114/EC of 8 December 2008 on the identification and designation of European critical infrastructures and the assessment of the need to improve their protection.

Technology has not made geography obsolete either. In the era of cyberoperations, flows of information and people rely, instead, on physical objects. Some of these objects are on the seabed (cables),[11] with landing sites in the in Marseille for the Mediterranean or northern ports for the Atlantic.[12] Some objects of are in outer space.[13] Others, like data centre and internet exchange points, are located in many EU capitals.[14] The EU has in place strategies for the outer space and legal competence to act in the field (and a French-coordinated PeSCo project, DOSA), but a recent report has highlighted worryingly low public awareness in some key Member States when it comes to seabed cable connectivity.[15] At a more abstract level, the battle for 5G technology is a geopolitical one. Thus, the Foreign Direct Investment Screening Regulation[16] foresees coordination between Member States and Commission on critical technology. Again, the Regulation is not a CFSP instrument but a CCP one.

7.2.2 *The Need for a Political Border Where There Is No Geographical One: Enlargement as Foreign Policy to Secure Western Europe*

Remember the mechanism ‘a man-made border that does not match a natural frontier zone is particularly vulnerable’,[17] which operates in parallel with the one positing that a border is ‘perhaps prepared, but never determined, by nature’.[18] In Europe, the lack of natural frontier is in the Eastern flank, in the vast fertile plains from the Elbe to the Volga. Here, the fact that nature has not ‘prepared’ a clear frontier, makes the region ‘particularly vulnerable’. And this has resulted—for reasons of cultural history more than as a geographic necessity—in the EU’s preference for the creation of a clear frontier in what it perceives to be a ‘contested’ space. This reordering of political space is perfectly in line with what scholars of geopolitics have noted in relation to the 2004 enlargement, documenting the acceding members’ will ‘to reposition one's country towards Western Europe, to reposition one's country as Western European and to erode the boundaries between ‘East’ and ‘West’ in Europe’.[19]

---

[11] Guilfoyle et al. (2022).

[12] Bueger et al. (2022), p. 19.

[13] Doboš (2018), p. 161.

[14] Bueger et al. (2022), p. 20.

[15] Bueger et al. (2022), p. 37.

[16] Regulation (EU) 2019/452 of the European Parliament and of the Council of 19 March 2019 establishing a framework for the screening of foreign direct investments into the Union.

[17] Kaplan (2013), p. xix.

[18] Ancel (1938), p. 4.

[19] Mamadouh (2015); Scott (2011).

Spykman, writing in 1942, stated nothing less than 'Maginot and Clemenceau have inherited from Caesar and Louis XIV anxiety over the open German frontier'.[20] This is suggestive, but this geographical determinism cannot be the main factor explaining foreign policy. Nonetheless, that this generates 'anxiety' is also a feeling shared by historians, even those who do not obsess with geography, such as Smith, who writes that 'the Russian anxiety [. . .] is an historic syndrome that alternates between three sets of symptoms: fear of Russia, disregard of Russia and contempt for Russia'.[21] The 'West' is caught by this syndrome, which Smith traces back not so much to geography but to a precise anti-Muscovite sentiment risen in the sixteenth century, when visitors from Western and Central Europe started interacting more frequently with what is today Russia.[22] It is clear that geography is not determinant of the sentiments that someone has toward Russia. Cultural history, interests, personal ties contribute to shaping attitudes:[23] geography is merely the context, but that being said it can contribute to the belief that there is a 'contested' space which ought to belong to either one party or the other (and that this is a zero sum game between two participants).[24]

But while it would be exaggerated to read European history, as Mackinder and other classic authors of geopolitics do, as that of the struggle for the control of the heartland, the analysis of the geographical and geopolitical context of Europe shows a constant and predictable interest for the area going from the Balkans to Russia.

If not necessarily the fruit of grand strategy, the enlargement of the EU eastward with the inclusion of former USSR states in 2004 is an important geopolitical development. It is 'region building'.[25] It is the EU creating political space. In the same light can be read the ENP, and especially the EaP. Further to Sarkozy's proposal for a Union for the Mediterranean, Sweden and Poland proposed an ad hoc framework for the Eastern neighbours, which would become, in 2009, the Eastern Partnership (EaP), comprising the EU Member States and Ukraine, Belarus, Moldova, Georgia, Armenia and Azerbaijan. Its consequence (not necessarily intended in these terms) was to create a political border (and thus a political space) where there is no geographical one. But is this legal/political construct, which goes against the facts of geography (as they exist in the era of writing), durable? Chances are that it is not, in the *longue durée*, because of Kaplan's mechanisms that 'a man-made border that does not match a natural frontier zone is particularly vulnerable'.

---

[20] Spykman (2007), p. 41.

[21] Smith (2019), p. 2.

[22] Smith (2019), p. 12.

[23] Rose (2007), p. 6: 'identity is riddled with - and even formed through - mistakes, mis-recognitions, fantasies, instabilities and contradictions: we never perceive others fully or accurately'.

[24] This interaction between geography and identity is studied by the growing field of psychanalytical geopolitics, which is for now confined mostly to the US (Shaw et al., 2014; Hansson, 2022).

[25] Scott (2016).

The spinal cord of Europe is the heartland: and the EU is firmly rooted there. The richest areas of the EU (in terms of GDP per capita) are in the 'blue banana', and include the regions from Antwerp to Milan (Amsterdam, Luxembourg, Frankfurt, Bavaria—and even Prague) according to 2021 Eurostat sources.[26] This does not include Ireland, where the GDP per capita is 240% of the EU average, but the metrics is skewed by the large tech companies based there (Apple, Google, Airbnb, Uber). The GDP of the six founding Member States is over 64% of the GDP of the EU.[27] The largest economies (total GDP) are the French capital region of Île-de-France, followed by Lombardia in Northern Italy, and Oberbayern in the South of Germany.[28] The contrast with Eastern Europe is stark: GDP per capita falls up to 25% from 'West' to 'East' Germany, and over 50% from 'West' Germany to the 'new' Member States (or Greece and the southern regions of Italy and Spain). It is as if the Berlin wall has not yet fallen.

The means of transport also paint a similar picture. In terms of rail network density, the first four countries are the Czech Republic, Belgium, Germany and Luxembourg; in terms of motorway network density, apart from the great capitals, the highest density is in the Randstad region in the West of the Netherlands, as well as round the major northern ports: Rotterdam, Bremen/Bremerhaven, Hamburg.[29] It is important to recall that the conditions of accessibility of the transport networks are constrained by geographical features, but then they are controlled to a large extent by the geopolitical subject (Member States—through their companies—or private companies): this control being largely a political issue—as opposed to a legal one. It is anyways not through CFSP that the EU exercise its competence in this domain, but rather through its transport policy, or through the regulation of State aid, which, in a nutshell, prevents undue advantage conferred by a Member State to a company.

EU institutions are between Brussels, Luxembourg, Strasbourg and Frankfurt (even though the EU has agencies scattered in all Member States except for Latvia, Romania and Bulgaria). Strasbourg in particular is a symbol of the EU for its geopolitical connotation: in the heartland of Europe, contested between Germany and France, in a region rich with raw materials and a navigable river. It is neither the Nordic Sea nor the Mediterranean, but the vast planes in between where European 'civilisation' now 'flourishes'. One may go as far as to say that the EU has even its own language, the variant of English spoken as a *koiné* in European quarters, and the formal Euro-jargon immediately recognisable by those who are a minimum acquainted with it.

---

[26] EUROSTAT (2020a).

[27] 'Key Figures on Europe -2022 Edition' (n.d.), p. 34.

[28] European Parliament. Directorate General for Parliamentary Research Services (2021), p. 39. Only two regions in the top ten richest ones are not in Europe's heartland: Madrid and Catalonia.

[29] EUROSTAT (2020b).

7.2.3 The Decline of the Sea: The Centre-Periphery Dynamic of Atlanticism and the Mediterranean

It would be exaggerated to contend that the EU has a dominant and a subordinate space (to use classic terms of cultural geography[30]), but it has a centre and a periphery:[31] the former is the (Heart)land, the latter is the sea.

7.2.3.1 Atlanticism Outside the EU

Since WW2, Atlanticism became synonymous of a foreign policy position of alignment with the values and objectives of the Nord Atlantic Alliance.[32] It is here understood more broadly, as the feeling that the two sides of the Atlantic ought to share cultural, economic, and social ties. In this latter sense, even Italy is an Atlantic state. As Lipman said, the Ocean creates an 'Atlantic Community—of the nations that are the bearers of the Western civilization.[33] This belief continues in certain parts of Europe.[34] The UK (and Ireland) and the US have a 'special relationship'. It refers to particularly close political and security ties between those countries. It varied depending on the respective leaders in power (Reagan and Thatcher, for example, had a very strong affinity) and, while the UK was part of the EU, London often felt like a privileged interlocutor of the US, acting as a cross-Atlantic bridge on European Affairs. One of the most evident results of the special relationship is the low profile of the UK in CSDP, and before that, the 'red lines' on unanimity voting in CFSP and the 'non affectation' of NATO commitments in Article 42(2) TEU.[35] With the exception of the St Malo declaration of Tony Blair, 'the UK's traditional diplomatic handling of foreign policy crises [was to] align with Washington and shape the EU response'.[36] This is due to geography, as well as to historical and cultural reasons. The historical legacy (the US being born out of former colonies after all), the shared language, the immigration to the US (from Great Britain first and Ireland later) all contribute to a feeling of proximity.

---

[30] Cosgrove and Jackson (1987), p. 95.

[31] Behr (2007).

[32] See also: Armitage et al (2017).

[33] Lipman (1951).

[34] See also: David Armitage, Alison Bashford and Sujit.

[35] 'The policy of the Union in accordance with this Section shall not prejudice the specific character of the security and defence policy of certain Member States and shall respect the obligations of certain Member States, which see their common defence realised in the North Atlantic Treaty Organisation (NATO), under the North Atlantic Treaty and be compatible with the common security and defence policy established within that framework.'

[36] Whineray (2020).

But the EU is moving in the other direction:[37] away from the Ocean, toward the land. This is not simply due to a Gaullist, anti-American feeling (even though the current has been there throughout post-WW2 history), nor it is exclusively due to a unilateralist (or downright isolationist) US Presidency or Congress (even though there have been outstanding examples of both in this century), but is perhaps another instance of interest for the heartland rather than the sea. One may go as far as to say that in order to be Atlanticist, one has to leave the EU. This is not a provocation. Atlanticism is sometimes defined as 'a wary approach' to European integration.[38] 'Global Britain', the post-Brexit slogan, is, on a plausible reading, a call for a geopolitical tear from Europe's mainland and a turn to Atlanticism: the Ocean and the US.

7.2.3.2 The Shattered Sea

The EU tends toward securing the Eastern border politically, but strikingly does not do so for the South-Eastern one. Compare the reaction to the geopolitical surpries from which this book started. The EU's response to the Arab uprisings, the first geopolitical shock since Lisbon, resulted in a failure (literally, if Libya is considered a failed state). Even though the law has not changed in the intervening ten years, the EU's reaction to the 2022 war of Russia against Ukraine has been, at least initially, more proactive and consistent. This may be evidence of the fact that EU attention tends to the East, rather than the South. The EU cannot meaningfully offer membership as bargaining tool in the Eastern Mediterranean.[39] Greece is one of the few EU countries to have a form of compulsory military service (with Finland and Lithuania), but the EU's CFSP has not been 'there' (whereas Russia and Belarus have been targeted by sanctions on multiple occasions): this is, of course, also due to the fact that Turkey is a NATO member: systems of alliances (in turn a reflection of geography) impact EU foreign policy.

The Mediterranean has three access points in Gibraltar, the Bosphorus, and Suez: only one of them is partially in the EU (the port of Algeciras—which is in fact in constant competition with Tangier). The lack of control over the others only increase the dependence of the EU from its partners Turkey and Egypt (especially relevant because of the crude oil transported from the Gulf). This exacerbates the asymmetries between the two shores of the sea. Another asymmetry—contributing to tearing the Mediterranean into two halves, is that 'North African countries, except Egypt, [. . .] have a very short back economic basin'.[40] This is due to the presence of Sahara desert, which entails that there is little communication, by way of roads or railways, between norther Africa and sub-Saharian Africa, making harbours in the

[37] Heffernan (2005).

[38] Græger and Haugevik (2009), p. 11.

[39] Bastian (2021).

[40] Carrasco and Garate (2010), p. 87.

south of Mediterranean less attractive than those in the north. There is, then, the East-West asymmetry: Eastern Mediterranean had until recently enjoyed closest cultural, economic and linguistic ties with the Western part. The development of strong economies in Western and Central Europe means that Marseille and Genoa are oriented toward the Rhine axis rather than toward Alexandria or Istanbul; a politically complex situation, often marred by conflict, on the Eastern shore has further exacerbated the asymmetry. Quantitative data confirm this: exports of key Mediterranean regions are moving toward the EU, US, and Canada (rather than to South or East Mediterranean).[41] The study of the depths of the sea, and its currents, also confirms the east-west split has geographical roots: the sea east of the Sicily channel is far deeper, current faster and more powerful.[42] Even linguistically, we do not speak Latin (or Greek) nor French, the *lingue franche* of the Mediterranean. Could it be any different? Certainly, and in fact some have proposed to consider the Mediterranean as a (de-centering) corrective to mainstream thinking,[43] to the clash of civilisation heard in extremist circles of the US as among jihadis.[44] A 'renewal' of the importance of the Mediterranean happened before,[45] as if European history swinged between a horizontal and a vertical axis. By the late Middle Ages, the likes of Venice and Genoa controlled prosperous trade routes there, contended with the Ottomans, who also tried to create a new *Mare Nostrum*. Irony has it that it was a Genovese sailor to show Spain the Atlantic way: even more ironically, the nations who most profited from Atlantic trade were Britain, France, and the Netherlands, making the axis swing northwards again.

This decline of the Mediterranean is the result of profound geopolitical transformations. Of the tendency of taking 'Europe' away from the *oikoumene*, the world of Herodotus (extending from Hercules' columns to the Indo valley), and putting it in the heartland. Even though we Europeans are 'the heirs of Antigone and Moses',[46] Europe as we now conceive it was born out of the fracturing of the Ancient World, a world that was centered around the Mediterranean.

Abandoning the Mediterranean is not destiny, but reflects profound trends rooted in the *longue durée*, a 'vocation to the land'. It was possibly accelerated by great fractures in European history. One may count among these the Arab and Ottoman conquest, essentially splitting the Mediterranean in two.[47] Or the Carolingian Empire, which refocused the continent's economy on the Rhine axis,[48] drawing 'a

[41] Carrasco and Garate (2010).

[42] Camprubí (2020).

[43] Cassano (2007).

[44] Nabli (2015).

[45] I owe this observation to Conal O'Gadhra.

[46] Étienne (2002), p. 51.

[47] Whether this fracture happened at the time of the barbaric invasions (Hodges and Whitehouse, 1983), or at the time of the Arab conquest (as Pirenne argued in his seminal (Pirenne, 2005)) was long object of historiographical debate.

[48] It goes without saying that this is also a matter of historiographical debate.

political map that has lasted 900 years', as Victor Hugo says.[49] The Protestant Reformation, further shifting the barycentre of the continent away from Rome.[50] The riches of Atlantic trade favouring Britain, France and the Netherlands rather than Arab-occupied Spain.[51] Then there is Braudel's explanation: Mediterranean countries were (are?) characterised by 'traditionalism and rigidity', making them poorly equipped to reap the economic benefits of new technologies and trade.[52] And then decolonisation.[53] Even France, which has long been a global empire, has paradoxically never really been a maritime country (as opposed to the UK).[54]

In the century-long juxtaposition of land and sea in the history of empires,[55] Carl Schmitt's battle between the land-based Behemoth and the sea-based Leviathan[56] (so dear also to Putin's ideologue, Alexander Dugin[57]), the EU leans toward the former. The EU's vocation is that of a land power, not of a maritime one. The dichotomy 'wherein a wealthy heartland subordinates an inferior periphery being constantly remoulded in the heartland's image, is arguably applicable to the Union'.[58]

7.2.4 The Mismatch Between Geopolitics (2004 Enlargement) and Law (Lisbon)

All of the above contributed to creating a 'new' geopolitical reality—whereby 'new' it means that it differs significantly from the environment in which the law of CFSP was originally designed. The key argument of this book is that the Lisbon Treaty did not reflect the geopolitical reality that had been created by the 2004 enlargement—but a similar point could be made to say that the Maastricht Treaty did not reflect the

---

[49] Hugo (2013), p. 504.

[50] Nietzsche et al. (2017), p. 34: 'Judea triumphed again at once [over Rome], thanks to that basically proletarian (German and English) ressentiment-movement which people called the Reformation, including its inevitable consequence [. . .] the restoration of the ancient, tomb-like silence of classical Rome'.

[51] Camus (1989), p. 87: 'À partir de Colomb, la civilisation horizontale, celle de l'espace et de la quantité, remplace la civilisation verticale de la qualité. Colomb tue la civilisation méditerranéenne.'

[52] Braudel (2017), p. 75.

[53] Bouchard (2012).

[54] Consider also the fact that Rouen, the closest centre to Le Havre (Rouen is to Le Havre what Rome is to Ostia and Athens to Piraeus), is not the capital of France (possibly, too exposed to Viking and English raids to offset the advantages). St Petersburg, instead, was created precisely on the sea.

[55] Armitage (2013), p. 47.

[56] Schmitt and Schmitt (2006).

[57] Dugin (2015), p. 25.

[58] Foster (2013).

geopolitical reality created by the collapse of the Soviet Union. The ultimate reason for this is that CFSP has always (i.e. in the Maastricht Treaty and the in the Lisbon Treaty) retained its legal 'distinctiveness' deriving from the informal developments of the European Political Cooperation in the 70s, despite formal (Maastricht) or structural (Lisbon) adjustment to integrate it into the EU unitary legal order.

This paragraph zooms in on the geopolitical changes created by the 2004 enlargement, and briefly explains the existence of a mismatch with the legal requirements.

The difference between before and after enlargement is obvious to the 'naked eye': the geography of the EU has changed by acquiring new territory—and population—Eastward and in the Mediterranean. Among the consequences of this, there was the fact that the systems of alliances of many new Member States in Central and Eastern Europe had been geared toward the Soviet Union, and the EU also increased its border with Russia. In the Mediterranean, Cyprus membership meant that the EU's border would directly affect Turkey in the occupied territory in the North of the island (over which EU law, in fact, applies). It also meant that patterns of energy dependence were now significantly different[59] (hence, to reduce the divergence, the Polish proposal for a European Energy Security Treaty in 2006, and the adoption in 2010 of the security of gas supply regulation[60]). Patterns in trade also changed,[61] as the EU's diplomacy moved from a strong focus on trade to an interest also in energy, environment, and security. What all of this implies is a greater difficulty in achieving coherence—and unanimity—because the preferences of the 25 MSs in foreign policy were in absolute terms more difficult to arrange than those of the older 15. The heterogeneity brough about by the 2004 enlargement also enables to distinguish it from previous enlargements. They all had geopolitical consequences, but none had so pervasive ones: in the past, only one, two or maximum three Member States joined at a time, whereas between 1995 and 2007, fifteen new Member States joined. Even in relative terms the numbers are clear: in 2004, 10 Member States out of 25 were new. Only the 1973 enlargement to UK, Ireland, and Denmark is somewhat comparable in terms of relative increase (three Member States out of nine were new), and that did in fact result in new forms of foreign policy governance, through the European Political Cooperation.

It goes without saying that the rhetoric during the process of the 2004 enlargement was one of unity (albeit with differences for old and new countries).[62] But the great foreign policy issues of the twenty-first century saw a significant dividing line between the 'old' and the 'new': the 2003 invasion of Iraq (with France and Germany strongly opposing a US operation favoured by UK, Italy, Spain,

[59] Bocquillon and Maltby (2017).

[60] Regulation (EU) 2017/1938 of the European Parliament and of the Council of 25 October 2017 concerning measures to safeguard the security of gas supply and repealing Regulation (EU) No 994/2010.

[61] Elsig (2010).

[62] Zielonka (2010).

Bulgaria, and other future Member States); the 2014 invasion of Crimea (with Hungary's Orban not taking a direct stance on the conflict except within the V4); the 2015 'migration crisis' (with Central Europe's states pursuing anti-immigrants policies—and the UK's referendum one year later, where the 'leave' campaign had similar undertones). The reaction to the 2022 Russian war against Ukraine, instead, showed unprecedented and possibly unforeseeable unity between EU countries, at least in the initial stages of the war.

Another important consequence is that there is much more EU action through CFSP post-Lisbon (admittedly, this is not a consequence of enlargement per se, but it is perhaps a consequence of the post-cold war geopolitical reality more generally). This meant, in turn, that more individuals (natural or legal persons, including third countries) are affected, and so are Member States, EU agencies bodies etc who are more engaged and need to be held accountable.

The reason why there is a mismatch is that the EU requires unanimity for most CFSP decisions, including for the most used and most important tool: restrictive measures. There is also a mismatch because EU diplomatic action is still split between CFSP and other external relations competence, and these shall not affect each other (Article 40 TEU). Finally, there is limited judicial review by EU courts, meaning that accountability and judicial protection are severely curtailed in CFSP as opposed to other areas of EU action.

7.3 The Reaction of CFSP

7.3.1 The Need for a Functional Constitution: Does Law Tend to Catch Up with Geopolitics?

The use of the phrase 'catching up' implies a belief in the fact that law follows geopolitics, that the two are going at different speed but in the same direction: that they will, in sum, inevitably meet at some finishing line. This is, of course, wishful thinking at best. There is nothing inevitable in the process, and nothing linear in it. But it is possible that, if it is to be functional, law will need to adapt to geopolitics (the other way round being much, much more improbable).

Should law be functional and *should* EU lawyers design strategies to reduce the constitutional ambiguity of CFSP? These are entirely different questions. This author's view is that not all doctrinal controversies should be resolved dogmatically, by reference to purely internal criteria of validity or consistency. Legal scholarship should be open to other disciplines (to understand extra-legal factors), because it can: it does not face the same constraints as judges do. Academically, it is possible to argue for a given legal position due to non-legal reasons, but this becomes much more complicated in judicial decision-making.

7.3.2 *Coherence*

Issues of coherence derive from the interaction between geopolitics and law: on the one hand, geopolitics contribute to asymmetry and fragmentation of preferences, on the other hand EU law requires, as a rule, unanimity (rather that qualified majority voting); on the one hand, geopolitics requires a consistent unitary diplomatic response, on the other hand, EU law mandates to distinguish between CFSP and other external action competences. In the light of that, the Lisbon Treaty has sought to enhance the consistency of EU diplomacy by formally abolishing the Maastricht pillar structure, by merging all objectives of the EU's external action, and by introducing a HR/VP with a new role as well as the EEAS—but this proved insufficient.

Diplomacy is one and it is multi-faceted. Distinguishing between CFSP (security and defence) and TFEU (trade, energy, environment, development cooperation etc) competences, as Article 40 TEU does, is a legal technicality that does not reflect political reality, where international agreements encompass themes related to trade, security and defence, energy, human rights, and so on. The agreements between the EU and its neighbours shows this clearly: association agreements include elements of security and defence in a way that it is impossible to disentangle. The 'trade' agreement between the EU and Ukraine, whose negotiations were finalised by 2013, had in fact major geopolitical implications that were not really about trade, and turned out to be an unintended turning document in the history of EU defence, for the consequences that (among other factors) Yanukovych's decision not to ratify it triggered. But the 'bipolarity' of EU external relations means that the law awkwardly forces foreign policy decisions into binary categories. The CFSP vs TFEU also reflects the existence of two parallel institutional apparatuses. It is the 'historical' split between Council and Commission, that is, between CFSP and other external relations competences arose after the failure of the EDC in the 50s, and which was eventually crystallised in Maastricht. This leaves the question open: who is responsible for what? In this respect, Lisbon has not abolished the distinctiveness of CFSP discussed in Chap. 1, and this is the case despite the increasing 'normalisation' of CFSP, that is the use of rules of general application (one principle above all: the rule of law and effective judicial protection, as evidenced by the case law discussed in Chap. 4 and again below in the section on accountability). The (strict) separation between CFSP and other areas of EU external action is not only important because procedural rules differ (unanimity vs qualified majority; limited vs full jurisdiction of the Court), but it has acquired even greater relevance in the light of the fact that CFSP—and the absence of judicial review for some CFSP acts—is a stumbling block to the accession of the EU to the European Convention for Human Rights. Such accession is a constitutional commitment of the EU (it is foreseen in Article 6 TEU), but it was blocked by the Court in Opinion 2/13, among other reasons because it would be contrary to the autonomy of EU law to enable full review of CFSP by the Strasbourg Court (the European Court of Human Rights) whereas there is no such full review for the Court of Justice of the European Union. Yet, the rule of Article 40 TEU is increasingly untenable.

As a result, many interinstitutional disputes between the Commission and the Council, or between the Parliament and the Council, have taken place since before the entry into force of the Lisbon Treaty—and are taking place well after Lisbon, which again bears testament to the fact that CFSP's distinctiveness is all but abolished. The presence of the HR/VP has not ended these disputes either. The mechanics of these disputes underlying procedural or substantive legal bases were discussed in Chap. 4. What disputes on the legal basis in cases such as *Mauritius*, *Tanzania*, *Kazakhstan*, *Armenia*,[63] have in common is that the disagreement between institutions is a matter of form, not of substance. The disagreement, in other words, is not the policy, but on purely procedural requirements. This is evidence of how capricious is the distinction between CFSP decision-making and 'other' foreign policy decision making. The result is not only inconsistent foreign policy choices as a matter of law (why is an operation in the Mediterranean Sea sometimes a CSDP one, sometimes an Area of Freedom Security and Justice one?), but also an irrational use of resources by the legal services of the institutions involved, who are forced to bring cases against each other by a legal-technical 'oddity'. To be sure, CFSP is not the only legal battlefield of interinstitutional disputed in EU foreign policy,[64] but it acquires its significance in the light of the features outlined above.

There is then vertical coherence, that is, consistency between the action by the EU and its Member States. This is a matter of geopolitics, rather than one of law: for there is little than EU law can do to bind Member States to stick to what was established in CFSP decisions. Admittedly, several years into the Lisbon Treaty regime, the theoretical problem of whether Member States can deviate from the obligations contained in a CFSP decision has remained purely hypothetical: in practice, there has never been such derailment. Equally, it has never been the case that Member States were prevented from adopting, for example, unilateral sanctions by virtue of the fact that there is a Union competence in Article 29 TEU: it would be interesting to see what the Court would say if such a case was ever to arise. But the conflation between activities of national authorities and of EU authorities give rise to issues of attribution, whereby it is difficult, for the Court, to disentangle the correct author of a decision.

EEAS, HR, and strategic documents did not manage to help with this split. The very role assigned to the HR/VP in the area of consistency does not cover all the areas that have become relevant to an integrated foreign policy (trade, AFSJ, energy, environment). The European Council merely sets guidelines requiring

[63] C-180/20 - Commission v Council (Agreement with Armenia) ECLI:EU:C:2021:658.

[64] Consider cases on the external representation of the EU (Case C-161/20 Commission v Council (International Maritime Organisation) ECLI:EU:C:2022:260), or on the delimitation of legal bases in other area of external action (C-275/20 - Commission v Council (Agreement with South Korea) ECLI:EU:C:2022:142).

implementations by other institutions. In addition to this, the practice, of entrusting the management of specific aspects of the new common policies to ad hoc agencies—albeit in the name of devolution and administrative specialisation—has contributed to further fragmenting and dispersing the implementation of the political consensus.[65] This administrative response is by no means specific to CFSP, and it is found also in the response to the Economic and Financial Crisis, or to the migration crisis. In some third countries, today, the Union is often present with several assistance or support programmes managed by separate authorities and financed by separate instruments—not counting, of course, the activities carried out by individual member states. It may be noted here that strategy does not really help either in achieving coherence. Either because the documents operate at such a level of abstraction that they cannot be operationalised immediately—that is, they cannot be translated into action without further political consensus on a policy choice—or because they did not work, at least in so far as they did not foresee the geopolitical surprises of the past years.

7.3.3 Accountability

Issues of accountability arise from the application of legal requirements to the geopolitical needs of the EU: it is a central tenet of liberal democracy that power entails accountability[66]—i.e. that public power is established by and limited by law – and this tenet (which is an aspect of the 'rule of law') is also a principle on which the EU is based. Thus, EU law determines that no act or omission attributable to the EU can escape judicial review (except, of course, certain decisions within the CFSP, as discussed in Chap. 4). It follows that those affected by EU action should have the chance to have their rights guaranteed (i.e. to have a remedy in case of breach), including to seek damages. These stem from foreign policy action, i.e. from geopolitical (rather than legal) considerations, but are solved as a matter of law (or, rather, even if they are not solved, the question arises in a court of law).

The starting point of the analysis was the limited jurisdiction of the Court over CFSP. Unlike the general rule of Article 19 TEU (the Court 'shall ensure that in the interpretation and application of the Treaties the law is observed'), Article 24 TEU and 275 TFEU establish that the Court does not have jurisdiction over CFSP, with two exceptions: the Court can review restrictive measures when these are object of an action for annulment; and it can monitor that EU institutions have complied with Article 40 TEU (it can monitor, that is, the respect for the boundaries of CFSP).

It was shown that the European Court of Justice found ways to interpret the exclusion of its jurisdiction narrowly (even though the General Court is still reluctant

[65] Missiroli (2022).

[66] ILA Committee on the Responsibility of International Organisations, 'Final Report' (Berlin 2004) 5.

to do so). First, it considered that international agreements respected procedural requirements, even when the agreements related to CFSP (*Mauritius*, *Tanzania*). Second, it admitted that the validity of restrictive measures may be scrutinised not only in the context of an action for annulment, but also through a preliminary ruling procedure (*Rosneft*). Third, it found jurisdiction to decide on the validity of CFSP acts which were not restrictive measures, when Article 40 TEU was not at stake. Thus is considered the validity of measures related to public procurement (*Elitaliana*) or staff management (*H*, *Satcen*). Fourth, it held it could hear actions for damages stemming from restrictive measures (*Bank Refah*).

This is probably the only area in which the law of CFSP has evolved significantly since Lisbon to reflect the geopolitical reality: EU action in CFSP is not only aimed at Member States, but affects the rights of natural and legal persons even beyond the obvious case of restrictive measures. The decisions by the Court are a step in the right direction for the conclusion they draw: individuals should enjoy judicial protection when their rights are affected, regardless of the legal basis on which EU institutions are acting. In this sense, the Court is enabling the law of CFSP to keep abreast with increased EU action in the field. But the reasoning ought to be undergo further scrutiny, because one could go as far as to state that, by forsaking a literal interpretation, it amounts to an implicit Treaty amendment. Why does the Court reach the conclusions it does?

On the face of it, geopolitics does not influence the Court. Bengoetxea[67] draws a useful distinction between *discovery* ('the actual process or influences producing a judicial decision, which may be a complex of various background political, social and psychological factors never articulated in the judgment itself'[68]) and *justification* ('the reasoning actually provided in the public record of the judgment'[69]). As outsiders, we cannot know about the process of discovery, but the justification is available by definition. The Court's *justifications* have nothing to do with geopolitics and are based instead on legal considerations (the application of general principles of EU law, including effective judicial protection and the rule of law, or the protection of fundamental rights). It would be hard to see how it could be any different, since judicial behaviour is bound by certain professional and legal considerations to present legal arguments as justification.[70]

In many of the landmark decisions on CFSP, the justification is not textual, because, as standard in the Court's reasoning, factors relating to the scheme and overall purpose of EU law prevail.[71] But geopolitical considerations are not part of those extra-textual factors. The effect of the Court's decisions for conduct of the EU's foreign policy is, in a sense, irrelevant for the Court's justification: and arguably this leads to a very positive outcome, because the Court appears to be

[67] Bengoetxea (1993).

[68] Conway (2012), p. 70.

[69] Conway (2012), p. 70.

[70] Beck (2013), p. 6.

[71] Bengoetxea (1993), p. 233.

motivated purely by human-rights based considerations rather than by questions of effectiveness (on which see also section below) or of power.

This can be illustrated by reference to seminal cases on restrictive measures (*Rosneft* and *Venezuela*) or on CSDP missions (concerning EULEX Kosovo) in which questions with geopolitical implications were translated into technical legal question of justiciability (that is, of procedure rather than of substance). In *Rosneft*, the Russian-owned petrol company challenged a 2014 CFSP decisions providing inter alia for the interruption of EU relations with the Russian oil sector after the annexation of Crimea and the downing of a civilian airline in the Donbass. The question has obvious geopolitical implications: how much can the EU be defiant to Russia, in light of the energy dependence on the latter? This is an enduring, extremely complex question, as the difficulty in reaching agreements on sanctions against Russian oil and gas sector even after the 2022 invasion of Ukraine witness. As a matter of law, this was dealt with, first, as a question of jurisdiction (after which there was no need to consider the substance of the question). Were the CFSP decisions in question a 'restrictive measure' for the purposes of Article 275 TFEU or not? The Council contended that Rosneft was trying to challenge a 'decision of principle taken by the Union to effect a partial interruption of its economic and financial relations with Russia'.[72] The Court partially agreed: some sanctions merely established a system of prior authorisation for the sale, supply, transfer or export of certain technologies suited to specific categories of oil exploration and production projects in Russia. These are not open to challenge by individuals. The Court also partially disagreed with the Council, finding that some sanctions against Russian companies were, in fact, restrictive measures: but even then, it was very deferential to that institution, confirming its political choices, as in fact it is established case law.[73] The seminal *Rosneft* decision can be read as indicating that the Court will not be concerned with the geopolitical choices of EU institutions but only with the safeguard of general principles such as effective judicial protection and proportionality: in a word, not with the substance but with the procedure. Even then, some have questioned the appropriateness of the Court's control. In *Venezuela*, the Court was asked to rule on who exactly can challenge restrictive measures. This question is one of *locus standi*, and it is regulated by Article 263 TFEU, which at its fourth paragraph contains the conditions under which 'natural or legal persons' can challenge acts adopted by the EU. The text of the Article in itself is not decisive, as the Court had to hear the question whether Venezuela could be considered a 'natural person' for the purposes of that provision. Should Venezuela (or indeed any other third country) be allowed to challenge restrictive measures the EU adopted against it? It is the case that a legal question in fact underlies (difficult) geopolitical

[72] Rosneft para 94.

[73] Rosneft para 146 'the European Union legislature must be allowed a broad discretion in areas which involve political, economic and social choices on its part, and in which it is called upon to undertake complex assessments. The Court has concluded that the legality of a measure adopted in those areas can be affected only if the measure is manifestly inappropriate having regard to the objective which the competent institution is seeking to pursue'. And again paras 113 and 132.

choices. It shall be recalled from Chap. 4 that the Court found in favour of Venezuela, on this procedural question. During the proceedings, the Council had tried to draw the Court's attention to these practical, functional considerations. Granting standing to Venezuela, the Council contended, would 'unduly restrict the EU in the conduct of its policies and international relations'.[74] The absence of reciprocity means that sovereign decisions of the EU could be challenged by a third State, but not the other way around. This would amount to conceding to third countries a way to solve international disputes which would be precluded to the EU. The Court disagreed, and affirmed instead that the rule of law should prevail over any reciprocity concerns.[75] The most delicate CSDP mission was arguably EULEX Kosovo, whose context was discussed in Chap. 5. Cases related to public procurement and to staff management within that mission have already been heard by the Court, and a potentially significant case is currently pending. In 2021, the General Court was invested with the question whether the EU (that is, the Council, the Commission and the EEAS) could be held liable for the damages allegedly created the EULEX Kosovo CSDP mission. In the currently pending case of *KS and KD v Council, Commission, EEAS*,[76] the applicants claimed that EULEX Kosovo failed in its mission when it insufficiently investigated the disappearance and killing of their family members. The Commission appealed the finding of the GC, which found that it lacked jurisdiction as the mission was a CFSP one. The Commission contends that the General Court essentially ignored the developments of the case law on the Court's jurisdiction (such as *H*, *Elitaliana*, *Satcen*). It argues that jurisdiction must be construed broadly. As a matter of principle, judicial remedies shall be available to the applicants. The ECJ is likely to side with the Commission as a matter of principle, finding that it has jurisdiction to hear the case. The legal issue arising in this kind of cases is also one of attribution: the complex EU decision-making process and institutional machinery make it difficult to locate the ultimate source of authority, the institution (or body, or person) responsible for the adoption of an act. Either way, the geopolitical context is unlikely to be mentioned as a relevant consideration.

The lack of geopolitical influence on the Court's justification is unsurprising because certain factors push judges to argue as a matter of law, not as a matter of geopolitics. It is also neither new, nor unique to CFSP. It is not new because the Court has historically endorsed the Common Agricultural Policy even though scholars have shown how that policy had imperialistic undertones (or effects). Consider, for example, the case law on the management of agricultural quotas and surpluses, possibly the most controversial substantive legal issue in the early stages of EU membership (from which stemmed cases of greatest constitutional importance, such as *Internationale Handelsgesellschaft*[77] in Germany, or *Maher*[78] in

[74] Case C-872/19 P *Venezuela v Council* para. 29.

[75] Para 52.

[76] T-771/20.

[77] C-11/70 *Internationale Handelsgesellschaft* ECLI:EU:C:1970:114.

[78] See the Irish Supreme Court decision in *Maher* v Attorney General [1971. No. 3735 P.].

Ireland). Commenting in 1987 on the *Bela-Muehle*[79] case, in which the Court found that an EU regulation, essentially imposing the burden of the cost of surpluses of milk products on poultry farmers rather than milk producers, was discriminatory and disproportionate, Snyder wrote that the Court 'apparently gave little attention to the possibility that its decision - assuming it had a wider effect - might favour high technology over low technology agriculture, multinational companies over small producers, international trade over local production, import dependency over self-sufficiency, or links with the U.S.A. and Brazil over those with other trading partners'.[80] It is not unique to CFSP because in other cases concerning disputed territories, and involving fisheries or the Common Commercial Policy, the Court did not mention geopolitical tensions as a relevant consideration, and the reasoning was purely justified as a matter of law. But it goes without saying that these were all cases in which EU law did not provide a clear answer, either because EU institutions had not foreseen that they could occur, or because there was some deliberate ambiguity. The Court relied instead on international law, if functionally, in order to justify a certain interpretation of EU law.[81] Thus in the Western Sahara cases, the Court found that international law entailed that an agreement between the EU and Morocco did not automatically extend to Western Sahara.[82] In a case decided before the accession of Cyprus to EU membership, the Court found that the EU-Cyprus agreement did not recognise export certificates issued by the Turkish Republic of Northern Cyprus.[83] In *Brita*,[84] the Court found that EU authorities may question the origin of goods imported from Israel (that is, to check whether they fall within the scope of the EU-Israel association agreement or not), and in *Vignoble Psagot* it held that products coming from the occupied Palestinian territories must bear the label indicating as their origins 'Israeli settlements' and not 'State of Israel'.[85] Additionally, the case law on what constitutes a legal person for the purposes of EU law (who, in other words, has standing before EU courts) also has geopolitical implications: Venezuela was already discussed, but the status was recognised also to other entities (from the Kurdistan Workers' Party to Front Polisario),[86] and not for policy reasons but for procedural legal ones related, once more, to judicial protection.[87]

---

[79] Case 114/76 *Bela-Muehle* ECLI:EU:C:1977:116.

[80] Snyder (1987), p. 177.

[81] For a criticism of the Court's selective reliance on international law, see Kassoti (2017, 2019).

[82] Such as Case C-266/16 Western Sahara Campaign UK ECLI:EU:C:2018:118; Case T-512/12 Front Polisario v Council ECLI:EU:T:2015:953; Joined cases T-344/19 and T-356/19 Front Polisario v Council ECLI:EU:T:2021:640.

[83] Case C-432/92 *The Queen v Minister of Agriculture, Fisheries and Food, ex parte Anastasiou* ECLI:EU:C:1994:277.

[84] C-386/08 *Brita* ECLI:EU:C:2010:91.

[85] C-363/18 - Organisation juive européenne and Vignoble Psagot ECLI:EU:C:2019:954.

[86] Carrozzini (2022), p. 38.

[87] Case T-279/19 Front Polisario v Council para 86, explicitly rejecting policy or expediency reasons.

While one may agree with the conclusion of the Court, the reasoning is far from convincing. The Court is in fact increasingly forced to judicial acrobatics, bending the text of the Treaties in order to reflect the reality of an EU increasingly engaged in CFSP (and thus increasingly affecting the position of natural or legal persons as well as that of its Member States and institutions). This might be due to a general limit of judicial reasoning (which forces judges to keep 'extra-legal' factors outside of the written justification), but it is particularly obvious in the case law on CFSP. One might speculate that occasionally the Court's 'discovery' (the 'actual' reasoning) is motivated by geopolitical considerations (for example, not affecting the delicate balance struck by Member States between defiance and submission to Russia in the adoption of sanctions), or by some other philosophy or vision of EU integration (for example, letting the Court acquire jurisdiction in CFSP for the sake of increasing its presence and visibility in that domain).[88] All of these would be defensible and formally valid, but not legal, arguments for the Court to base its judgments on. They would give the impression that the Court's discretion is boundless, and would severely undermine the image of and confidence in the institutions that many have.[89] By arguing on the grounds of the rule of law and judicial protection, instead, the Court firmly anchor its reasoning in EU law, but makes it unconvincing, because the Court provides no meta-rationale for preferring a systematic interpretation which trumps a literal interpretation of Article 275 TFEU. In the Court's justification, there is no explicit meta-rationale for preferring a systematic interpretation to a literal interpretation.[90] Quite the contrary, the specific nature of CFSP could support the view that close regard should be paid to the wording of CFSP-related provisions.[91] The notion of 'restrictive measure' in Article 275 TFEU is a technical one, for example, whereas cases such as *H, Elitaliana,* or *Satcen* essentially ignore that requirement that jurisdiction in annulment action should be limited to challenges to CFSP acts providing for restrictive measures. It could be respectfully suggested that a way not to incur in this sort of objection—but still reach the same conclusions—would be to establish a meta-rationale for choosing a systematic over literal interpretation: the Court could provide legal reasons in favour of this, and delineate its scope of application (triggering conditions and limits). For example, the Court could make it explicit that certain principles of EU law are hierarchically

[88] That extra-legal factors, to use Beck, 2013 classification of Llewellyn, 1960 factors can affect judicial behaviour is obvious. Given the same law and the same facts, it can happen that different judges write different judgments. Disagreements between GC and ECJ on the jurisdiction in CFSP were mentioned in Chaps. 4 and 5.

[89] This is where 'steadying factors' intervene, as studied by (Llewellyn, 1960; Beck, 2013; Sankari, 2013, p. 10; Cotter, 2022).

[90] As Beck (2013), p. 291 explains, literal, systemic and purposive interpretation are usually combined by the Court, rather than ranked in order of preference.

[91] Beck (2013), p. 311: 'the more detailed and technical the legislation in issue and the more specific its wording the more likely the ECJ is to pay very considerable regard to the wording of a provision'.

superior to the Treaties, and when those principle would be adversely affected by a literal interpretation of the Treaty, a systematic one ought to be preferred instead.

Another criticism one may move to these decisions is principled (it does not concern the reasoning itself): they put too much emphasis on the rule of law. Why fetishize the rule of law when the competitors use tanks instead? What decisions such as *Rosneft* and *Venezuela* means for EU foreign policy is precisely the fact that there are many ways in which companies and third countries against whom the EU adopted sanctions are allowed 'to challenge the fruit of (democratic) enactments of EU institutions'.[92] This does entail a risk that a third country could attempt to tamper with the EU democratic process by initiating proceedings in bad faith, for example to make a point in front of a domestic audience, or to squander resources (time and money) of EU institutions. More broadly, one could state that law is not the right way to conduct foreign policy, especially in an environment in which other powers do not feel they are bound by law (or use it cynically, etc). This author disagrees with these claims, but it may be worth voicing them, if only to disprove them. The great things about having values is that they require no reciprocity. The rule of law is not, in and of itself, an absolute good, but it has proven instrumental to preserving a given organisation of society which responds to certain economic and political demands. If this is considered desirable within the EU, the fact that it is not desirable elsewhere is, strictly speaking, irrelevant. It may be that one day, due to confrontation with external actors, the rule of law will not be functional anymore for the EU (and tanks or weapons will be needed instead): but it is not today. Today, there is in Europe a widespread belief in the desirability of the rule of law and judicial protection, and, if it is truly part of a European 'identity', it should not be discarded quickly.

It is interesting to consider whether the Member States will react to this line of decisions. On one hand of the spectrum, the Member States could decide to put an end to much of the litigation by explicitly endorsing the Court's conclusions and granting it fully-fledged power to decide controversies concerning CFSP. This would be a momentous choice, requiring Treaty amendment. It would cancel the distinctiveness of CFSP to such a great extent that it may well enable the EU to join the ECHR. This is unlikely to happen in the near future. There is no indication of this in the proposals issued from the project on the future of Europe, for example (even though there is appetite for a move to QMV in the area). On the other end of the spectrum, Member States could 'take back control' and design some (more) water-proof way to limit the Court's jurisdiction. For example, as Poli suggests, by introducing specific prohibitions for the Court to hear certain actions,[93] or by amending the text of Article 19 TEU to exclude certain systematic applications. Again, the limited reaction of Member States to the significant decisions handed down by the Court would lead to exclude this option.

---

[92] Lonardo and Ruiz Cairó (2022), p. 131.

[93] Poli (2022), p. 1054.

7.3.4 Effectiveness

Unanimity is the requirement watching over the CFSP as sanctuary of Member States' sovereignty. While a project of federal defence might have been too ambitious in the early 50s (and even then, it did not fail out of States' 'fear' to lose sovereignty, but due to domestic French politics), the political reality is that there are majorities and minorities in CFSP matters. Unanimity is not functional to effective action, considering that in other areas of EU competence, decisions can be taken by a political majority. The consideration that there is a quest for consensus even when QMV is certainly a relevant custom,[94] but does not take away the fact that more forceful and longer bargaining needs to take place to convince more states (i.e. when unanimity is required) than to convince fewer (i.e. when unanimity is only a matter of courtesy, so to say).

Qualified majority voting is often considered an obstacle to smooth decision making in CFSP, and therefore an hindrance to its effectiveness. Some key occurrences of this were discussed in Chap. 6 (on a CSDP mission in Libya in 2011 or Ukraine in 2014). Political splits were also highlighted with regard to other items (in Chap. 2, on the template for the neighbourhood after the 2004 enlargement; in Chap. 6, on the suspension of aid to Gambia over an anti-LGBTI law in 2014). There is no doubt that at least some CFSP decisions deserve a more flexible decision-making procedure—as currently foreseen by the TEU for the amendment of already existing sanctions, or for the adoption of decisions when there was already approval in the European Council, or on procedural matters—but also other declarations (on events or international developments). The objective of QMV is to avoid blackmailing by a minority (or even by one) Member State. This would also prevent obstructionism, which could derive from the pressure exerted by third counties, or be instrumental for a Member State to get concessions in another policy area. An example of obstructionism due to external pressure is hard to pinpoint—no EU country has of yet admitted it openly, but economic dependencies between countries, or even personal friendships between leaders, may give an idea. An example of obstructionism due to political calculations to get concessions in another area is the Cyprus 2020 veto on sanctioning Belarus in the hope to obtain sanctions against Turkey.[95]

QMV is possible when the Council adopts implementing or amending acts (Article 31(2) TEU): in other words, when modifying decisions already adopted previously. This is a very important and broad exception. Sanctions are often adopted by means of update of previous acts, and the rule of Article 31(2) could be construed as implying that no unanimity is required for the imposition of *further* sanctions, when the basic ones were already unanimously agreed. Another alternative is to construe Article 31(1) second paragraph as meaning that constructive abstention applies regardless of whether the objecting country want to abstain or

[94] As the Court explained in *CMR-15*, on which see Chap. 3.

[95] Rankin (2020).

wants to vote against. Granted, this is a very non-literal interpretation of Article 31(1), which clearly states that the Member States 'abstains' (not 'does not vote in favour') and that 'it shall not be obliged to apply the decision' (whereas the point of QMV is to acknowledge that there can be a political minority, that is, a group of Member States who are bound by something they disagree with).

These are all legal options that can be, indeed have been, explored.[96] Hungary (political minority) refused to sanction Russian gas and oil in 2022 and other Member States (political majority) wanted to circumvent it. The choice not to pursue them is political: it would be a sign of weakness to impose sanctions but with one or more Member States against it. It would weaken their weight and legitimacy vis-à-vis a third country, to say nothing of implementation challenges in the absence of clear jurisdiction by the CJEU.

References

Ancel, J. (1938). *Géographie Des Frontières*. Gallimard.
Armitage, D. (2013). *Foundations of modern international thought*. Cambridge University Press).
Armitage, D., Bashford, A., & Sivadundaram, S. (2017). *Oceanic histories*. Cambridge University Press.
Bastian, K. (2021). The EU in the Eastern Mediterranean—a "Geopolitical" actor? *Orbis, 65*(3), 483–489.
Beck, G. (2013). *The legal reasoning of the Court of Justice of the EU, Volume 36 (modern studies in European law)*. Hart Publishing Ltd.
Behr, H. (2007). The European Union in the legacies of imperial rule? EU accession politics viewed from a historical comparative perspective. *European Journal of International Relations, 13*(2), 239–262.
Bengoetxea, J. (1993). *The legal reasoning of the European Court of Justice: Towards a European Jurisprudence*. Clarendon Press; Oxford University Press.
Bialasiewicz, L. (Ed.). (2011). *Europe in the World: EU geopolitics and the making of European space*. Ashgate.
Bialasiewicz, L., Dahlman, C., Apuzzo, G. M., Ciută, F., Jones, A., Rumford, C., Wodak, R., Anderson, J., & Ingram, A. (2009). Interventions in the new political geographies of the European "Neighborhood". *Political Geography, 28*(2), 79–89.
Bocquillon, P., & Maltby, T. (2017). The more the merrier? Assessing the impact of enlargement on EU performance in energy and climate change policies. *East European Politics, 33*(1), 88–105.
Borrell, J. (2020). *Why European strategic autonomy matters*. EEAS website https://www.eeas.europa.eu/eeas/why-european-strategic-autonomy-matters_en
Bouchard, M. (2012). Thalassa, Études Méditerranéennes et L'Arc, Trois Revues Méditerranéennes Dans La France Des Années 1950 et 1960. *Cahiers de la Méditerranée, 85*, 135–146.
Braudel, F. (2017). *La Méditerranée et le monde méditerranéen à l'époque de Philippe II. 1: La part du milieu/Fernand Braudel, Dixième édition*. Armand Colin.
Brzozowski, A. (2022). *EU Approves Russia Coal Embargo, but Already Looks Beyond*, www.euractiv.com. Available at "https://www.euractiv.com/section/europe-s-east/news/eu-approves-russia-coal-embargo-but-already-looks-beyond/"

[96] Brzozowski (2022).

Bueger, C., Liebetrau, T., & Franken, J. (2022) Security threats to Undersea communications cables and infrastructure–Consequences for the EU.

Camprubí, L. (2020). "No Longer an American Lake": Depth and geopolitics in the Mediterranean. *Diplomatic History, 44*(3), 428–446.

Camus, A. (1989). *Carnets. 3: Mars 1951 - décembre 1959.* Gallimard.

Carrasco, P. F., & Garate, J. L. A. (2010). Inter-Mediterranean seaports communications and international trade, globalization, and maritime transport development. *Cahiers de la Méditerranée, 80*, 87–92.

Carrozzini, A. (2022). Working its way back to international law? The general court's judgments in joined cases T-344/19 and T-356/19 and T-279/19 Front Polisario v Council. *European Papers - A Journal on Law and Integration, 7*, 3141.

Casolari, F. (2022). Inter Se agreements between member states, and the outer limits of the Court's Jurisdiction in infringement proceedings: Slovenia v Croatia. In G. Butler & R. A. Wessel (Eds.), *EU external relations law: The cases in context.* Hart Publishing.

Cassano, F. (2007). *Il pensiero meridiano* (2nd ed.). Ed. Laterza.

Conway, G. (2012). *The limits of legal reasoning and the European Court of Justice* (1st ed.). Cambridge University Press.

Cosgrove, D., & Jackson, P. (1987). New directions in cultural geography. *Area, 19*(2), 95–101.

Cotter, J. (2022). *Legal certainty in the preliminary reference procedure: The role of extra-legal steadying factors.* Edward Elgar Publishing.

Dashwood, A. (2014). The continuing bipolarity of EU external action. In I. Govaere, E. Lannon, P. van Elsuwege, & S. Adam (Eds.), *The European Union in the world* (pp. 1–16). Brill | Nijhoff.

Doboš, B. (2018). *Geopolitics of the outer space: A European perspective.* Springer.

Dugin, A. G. (2015). *Last War of the World-Island: The geopolitics of contemporary Russia.* Arktos.

Elsig, M. (2010). European Union trade policy after enlargement: Larger crowds, shifting priorities and informal decision-making. *Journal of European Public Policy, 17*(6), 781–798.

Elster, J. (1986). Introduction. In J. Elster (Ed.), *Rational choice.* New York University Press.

Elster, J. (2015). *Explaining social behavior: More nuts and bolts for the social sciences* (2nd ed.). Cambridge University Press.

Étienne, B. (2002). Fondements Du Politique En Méditerranée. *La pensée de midi, 7*(1), 51–63.

European Parliament. Directorate General for Parliamentary Research Services. (2021). *Demographic Outlook for the European Union 2021.* Publications Office.

EUROSTAT. (2020a). *Regional GDP per Capita Ranged from 32% to 260% of the EU Average in 2019.* Available at https://ec.europa.eu/eurostat/web/products-eurostat-news/-/ddn-20210303-1.

EUROSTAT. (2020b). *The Densest Motorway Networks across EU Regions.* Available at https://ec.europa.eu/eurostat/web/products-eurostat-news/-/ddn-20200528-1.

Foster, R. (2013). *Tabula Imperii Europae* : A cartographic approach to the current debate on the European Union as Empire. *Geopolitics, 18*(2), 371–402.

Græger, N., & Haugevik, K. M. (2009). *Defining Atlanticism.* Norwegian Institute of International Affairs (NUPI).

Guilfoyle, D., Paige, T. P., & McLaughlin, R. (2022). The Final Frontier of Cyberspace: The Seabed Beyond National Jurisdiction and the Protection of Submarine Cables. *International and Comparative Law Quarterly, 71*(3), 657–696.

Hansson, E. (2022). Subjects supposed to know, believe, and enjoy: The geopolitics of ideological transference in the Swedish begging question. *Political Geography, 98*, 102706.

Heffernan, M. (2005). The end of Atlanticism: Habermas, Derrida and the meaning of Europe in the twenty-first century. *Geopolitics, 10*(3), 570–575.

Hodges, R., & Whitehouse, D. (1983). *Mohammed, Charlemagne & the origins of Europe: Archaeology and the Pirenne Thesis.* Cornell University Press.

Hugo, V. (2013). *Oeuvres Complètes de Victor Hugo. En Voyage. Tome 2.* Hachette Livre BNF.

Kaplan, R. D. (2013). *The revenge of geography: What the map tells us about coming conflicts and the battle against fate*. Random House Trade Paperbacks.

Kassoti, E. (2017). The Council v. Front Polisario Case: The Court of Justice's selective reliance on international rules on treaty interpretation (Second Part). *European Papers - A Journal on Law and Integration, 2017*(2), 2342.

Kassoti, E. (2019). The ECJ and the art of treaty interpretation: *Western Sahara Campaign UK. Common Market Law Review, 56*(1).

'Key Figures on Europe - 2022 Edition' (n.d.). p. 78.

Lipman, W. (1951). Lessons for survival. The Atlantic.

Llewellyn, K. (1960). *The Common Law Tradition: Deciding Appeals.* Quid Pro, LLC.

Lonardo, L., & Ruiz Cairó, E. (2022). The European Court of Justice allows third countries to challenge EU restrictive measures: Case C-872/19 P, *Venezuela* v *Council. European Constitutional Law Review, 18*(1), 114–131.

Mackinder, H. (1904). The geographical pivot of history. *Royal Geographical Society, IV*, 298–321.

Mamadouh, V. (2015) The geopolitics of EU external relations'. In *The SAGE Handbook of European Foreign Policy: Two Volume Set* (1 Oliver's Yard, 55 City Road London EC1Y 1SP, Sage Publications Ltd), pp. 53–72.

Missiroli, A. (2022). *L'Europa Come Potenza. Diplomazia, Sicurezza, Difesa.* Il Mulino.

Nabli, B. (2015). *Géopolitique de La Méditerranée*. Armand Colin.

Nietzsche, F. W., Ansell-Pearson, K., & Diethe, C. (2017). *'On the Genealogy of Morality' and other writings*. Cambridge University Press.

Pirenne, H. (2005). *Mahomet et Charlemagne* (2nd ed.). PUF.

Poli, S. (2022). The right to effective judicial protection with respect to acts imposing restrictive measures and its ransformative force for the common foreign and security policy. *Common Market Law Review*, 1045–1080.

Rankin, J. (2020) EU fails to agree on Belarus sanctions after Cyprus blocks plan. *The Guardian* (21 September 2020).

Rose, G. (2007). *Feminism and geography: The limits of geographical knowledge.*, Reprint. Polity Press.

Sankari, S. (2013). *European Court of Justice legal reasoning in context*. Europa Law Publishing.

Schmitt, C., & Schmitt, C. (2006). *The nomos of the earth in the international law of the jus publicum Europaeum.*, First paperback edn. Telos Press.

Scott, J. W. (2011). Reflections on EU geopolitics: Consolidation, neighbourhood and civil society in the reordering of European space. *Geopolitics, 16*(1), 146–175.

Scott, J. W. (2016). *EU enlargement, region building and shifting borders of inclusion and exclusion*. Routledge.

Shaw, G. R., Powell, J., & De La Ossa, J. (2014). Towards a psychoanalytic geopolitics: The militarization of public schooling in the USA. In P. Kingsbury & S. Pile (Eds.), *Psychoanalytic geographies*. Ashgate Pub.

Smith, M. B. (2019). *The Russia anxiety: And how history can resolve it*. Allen Lane.

Snyder, F. (1987). New directions in European community law. *Journal of Law and Society, 14*(1), 167.

Spykman, N. J. (2007). *America's strategy in world politics: The United States and the balance of power*. Transaction Publishers.

Wessel, R. A. (2016). Lex Imperfecta: Law and integration in European foreign and security policy. *European Papers - A Journal on Law and Integration, 1*, 439468.

Whineray, D. (2020). *How Britain Can Shape Europe's Foreign Policy After Brexit*, Carnegie Endowment for International Peace. Available at https://carnegieendowment.org/2020/02/01/how-britain-can-shape-europe-s-foreign-policy-after-brexit-pub-80961.

Zielonka, J. (2010). *Europe as empire: The nature of the enlarged European Union.*, Reprint. Oxford University Press.

Chapter 8
Conclusions

The main theme of this book is how law and geopolitics interact to influence EU foreign policy. The 2004 enlargement is a watershed moment in EU foreign policy and for Europe's geopolitics—and from which the need for Treaty reforms, achieved eventually in Lisbon three years later, ultimately rose. In turn, EU law—and CFSP in particular—has not yet caught up with that enlargement. If history 'moves' through contradictions, then the EU legal system, with its multi-layered, cumbersome, exasperatingly technical mechanisms remindful of a Medieval empire,[1] will need to draw level with the geopolitical reality that the enlargement created, and that the 2022 Russian invasion of Ukraine shattered again—and it is possible to speculate that once it will have done so, geopolitical equilibria in Europe may move again (or, more likely, that they will have moved by the time EU law has 'caught up' with the current ones).

The issues that this book arise 'between law and geopolitics' because geopolitics makes the continent fragmented due to great asymmetries in size, demographics, location and thus political priorities of Member States, whereas the legal CFSP still crystallises a Cold War state of being by imposing unanimity between Member States and excluding, by and large, judicial review and enforcement capabilities: the law of CFSP has not caught up with the geopolitical realities of Europe. The 2004 enlargement meant new patterns of dependence on Russia for energy, and on China for other raw materials; it also meant social and demographic transformations, all to be managed through standards of governance conceived for, and somewhat functioning, in Western Europe; crucially for EU foreign policy, it meant that the EU acquired a whole new neighbourhood (at the same time close and exotic), at the fringes of 'Europe'. The book showed that geopolitics influences the preferences of Member States and the decision-making in CFSP according to some patterns, the

[1] Zielonka (2010), p. 9.

L. Lonardo, *EU Common Foreign and Security Policy After Lisbon*,
https://doi.org/10.1007/978-3-031-19131-2_8

most important one of which appears to be that 'a man-made border that does not match a natural frontier zone is particularly vulnerable'.[2]

Three great challenges are to be met if the law of CFSP is to enable the EU to act 'geopolitically.

The challenge of coherence has not been fully met. Article 40 TEU establishes a split in the law of EU foreign policy, imposing a separation between the CFSP and other external policies. But geopolitical considerations are addressed through a foreign policy carried partly through the CCP (trade), the AFSJ (migration), State aid control, energy policy, etc. This is hardly a fit for purpose system, and it was inherited from the Cold War in Maastricht. The 'double-hat' of the HR/VP helped achieved some coherence, but it has not prevented the parallel (and often uncoordinated) growth of strategies, instruments and policies: some under the supervision of the Commission and the control of the Parliament, others under the authority of the Council and financed off-budget by the Member States. In addition, coherence is no longer to be sought and pursued only for external action but for the Union's entire range of common policies, as the Ukraine crisis has also shown: sanctions against Russia also pursue trade and energy policy; measures to assist with the management of immigrant flows is used as a foreign policy tool to support Ukraine; financial assistance to Ukraine (and Moldova) is not done (exclusively) through CFSP instruments. The EEAS was set up to fulfil precisely this key function: that is, to promote and facilitate a comprehensive or integrated approach. But, as Missiroli writes, 'a little bit of old and new bureaucratic-administrative rivalries in Brussels and a little bit of mistrust on the part of many national diplomacies - combined with a lack of their own resources and decision-making expertise - have so far limited its impact'. The Union still cannot count on a clearly identifiable authority who ensures their consistent implementation. The solution, going forward, is not another institutional reform: it is the abolition of the rigid separation between CFSP and other external competences. This cannot be done without Treaty amendment. But it could be facilitated if QMV in CFSP became the normality. This would enable, for example, the conclusion of international agreement with a dual (CFSP and TFEU) substantive and procedural legal basis.

Judicial review is the only area in which the law of CFSP is evolving significantly and is keeping abreast with the political reality. Judicial review is an important aspect of any EU policy, and it is increasingly so in CFSP, even though the Court is still to pronounce itself on the precise boundaries and intensity of this control. Significantly, for the moment there are no explicit geopolitical considerations in the reasoning of the Court. While geopolitics does influence law-making, its role is not explicit in the Court's case law: the judicial creativity, which moves decisions beyond the text of the Treaties, in squarely couched in the language of integration and of protection of fundamental rights. While the method may be questioned as a matter of principle, the result of the Court's case law moves in the right direction: it pushes the CFSP from the outer boundaries of the European integration project

[2] Kaplan (2013), p. xix.

under the structures of EU law, from which the politicised CFSP could be brought into the legal arena. This is not to say that EU "law" is the only possible solution: but a unified legal system is more coherent, more accountable, and possible more effective than a fragmented one with many authorities jumping on each other's feet. "EU foreign policy through law allows the Union to better exert itself through a variety of ways"[3] is thus true only in so far as that law is better than a system in which there are many competing "laws" (CFSP vs non-CFSP competence, EU law vs national law, EU law vs international law etc). It is not law for the sake of it. Otherwise, one could argue, others will invade with tanks while we discuss legal technicalities. The Court is forced to legal acrobatics to deliver a fair judgment. How much this can happen before the Treaties 'break', meaning how much the literal interpretation can yield to other (systematic or teleological) considerations is not obvious: in whatever direction it may go, it is clear that CFSP is an excellent laboratory for European integration, from which important lessons may be drawn in the future. By this it is meant that either the Member States will rewrite Treaty provisions to limit more precisely the Court's intervention by codifying the case law or by pushing back against it; or, in the opposite direction, they could expressly extend the Court's jurisdiction. There seems to be political appetite for neither.

The unanimity rule is also outdated, because it has been overtaken by political reality. Some CFSP decisions (declarations on international events, certain sanctions) deserve QMV. This would avoid and prevent unjustified or instrumental obstruction. The idea that there should not be a political minority in CFSP—something that the unanimity rule seeks to create—is simply not reflective of political realities and it is, one could say, a relic of the Cold War. Major Treaty reform would not be necessary. The Lisbon Treaty's architects have equipped the EU Treaties with 'passerelle clauses'—provisions usually aimed at modifying the decision-making of the Council of the EU. The passerelle clause for CFSP is Article 31(3) of the Treaty on European Union, which empowers the European Council to, by unanimous agreement, allow the Council of the EU to take decisions by QMV in some areas of the CFSP. Another option is an emergency brake—cancelling a vote for vital reasons of national policy—while constructive abstention is an option which allows a Member State to abstain from a unanimous vote without blocking it.

The book testifies that the EU takes its legal structures very seriously. This insistence on the rule of law may be commendable for some, naïve for others in a context in which competitors do not respect the same standards. But the rule of law it is deeply—indeed constitutionally—ingrained in the EU legal system. One should be aware of its limitations, without for this reason discarding it as dysfunctional when there is no reciprocity.

In sum, politically, the EU cannot do away with geopolitics and (some) law. A deliberate geopolitical vision, a doctrine, should feature more in EU strategic documents (if not necessarily explicitly in the decision-making), which are meant

---

[3] Butler (2019), p. 71.

to provide a long-term view that is not bound by the volatility of political developments.

References

Butler, G. (2019). *Constitutional law of the EU's common foreign and security policy: Competence and institutions in external relations*. Hart Publishing.

Kaplan, R. D. (2013). *The revenge of geography: What the map tells us about coming conflicts and the battle against fate*. Random House Trade Paperbacks.

Zielonka, J. (2010). *Europe as empire: The nature of the enlarged European Union*, Reprint. Oxford University Press.

GPSR Compliance

The European Union's (EU) General Product Safety Regulation (GPSR) is a set of rules that requires consumer products to be safe and our obligations to ensure this.

If you have any concerns about our products, you can contact us on ProductSafety@springernature.com

In case Publisher is established outside the EU, the EU authorized representative is:

Springer Nature Customer Service Center GmbH
Europaplatz 3
69115 Heidelberg, Germany

Batch number: 10732044

Printed by Printforce, the Netherlands